FEMINISM, CAPITALISM, AND ECOLOGY

T0308764

FEMINISM, CAPITALISM, AND ECOLOGY

Johanna Oksala

Northwestern University Press
Evanston, Illinois

Northwestern University Press
www.nupress.northwestern.edu

Printed in the United States of America

10 9 8 7 6 5 4 3 2 1
Library of Congress Cataloging-in-Publication Data

Names: Oksala, Johanna, 1966– author.
Title: Feminism, capitalism, and ecology / Johanna Oksala.
Description: Evanston, Illinois : Northwestern University Press, 2023. | Includes
    bibliographical references and index.
Identifiers: LCCN 2023000544 | ISBN 9780810146105 (paperback) | ISBN
    9780810146112 (cloth) | ISBN 9780810146129 (ebook)
Subjects: LCSH: Ecofeminism. | Philosophy, Marxist. | BISAC:
    PHILOSOPHY / Political | PHILOSOPHY / Movements / Phenomenology
Classification: LCC HQ1194 .O373 2023 | DDC 305.4201—dc23/eng/20230110
LC record available at https://lccn.loc.gov/2023000544

For the memory of my mother, Kirsti Oksala

Contents

Rags and Bones

For almost as long as I can remember, I have been afraid that humanity was heading full throttle towards an environmental catastrophe. Such fears, both of mine and others, evidence-based or not, were mostly dismissed as irrational fearmongering and green millenarianism. Nevertheless, most people have always understood that the changes in the planet's biosphere are deterministic biochemical and geophysical processes, and that with our current level of scientific knowledge, their outcome can be predicted with reasonable certainty. The *Titanic* became a popular metaphor for our predicament: just like its passengers and crew, most people seemed willfully ignorant of the gravity of our situation, and harrowingly clueless about the effective measures needed to avert the impending catastrophe.

Now it seems that we can at last see the proverbial iceberg. Climate change, in particular, is recognized as an "existential threat" and the defining question of our time.[1] While scientists have been warning us about its consequences for decades already, ordinary people, even in the Global North, are now starting to experience its consequences firsthand: intense heat waves, raging wildfires, stronger storms, and unprecedented floods. Significantly, they have also started to connect the dots between climate change and capitalism. After Naomi Klein's best-selling book *This Changes Everything* (2016), which argued that climate change was unsolvable unless we addressed the economic system fueling it, ecological critiques of capitalism have moved from the margins to the mainstream.[2] Even if Fredric Jameson's famous quip that it is easier to imagine the end of the world than it is to imagine the end of capitalism remains true for many people, for a rapidly increasing number of us, imagining the end of capitalism is starting to seem like the only realistic option we have left if we want our civilization to survive. The end of capitalism has become something that is not just desirable for various ideological reasons, but *necessary* because the climate emergency demands it.

My wager is that a viable feminist critique for our time must seize this moment and confront the environmental crisis head-on. If feminist theory does not seriously engage with ecological problems and think through its relationship to environmentalism, it is going to be difficult to recognize it as a relevant political force shaping our future in a meaningful way. Conversely, environmentalism needs feminism. Understanding environmental problems requires understanding their gendered dimensions and effects. Environmental protection cannot take place at the cost of worsening gender inequality, but must be tied to an acute understanding of the current and historical connections between environmental destruction and gender subordination. Not only do our fundamental metaphysical views about nature continue to be deeply interwoven with derogatory views about women and the feminine, but the connection between environmentalism and feminism is also salient in very concrete, material terms: women, in particular, are directly and negatively impacted by environmental harms, risks, and challenges.[3] Feminist environmental analysis is therefore vital for an adequate understanding of the key issues in environmental theory and politics, but it can also bring more diverse knowledges and more effective political responses to the fore.[4]

Our theoretical and political attempts to bring together feminism and environmentalism must, furthermore, connect them systematically to critiques of capitalism. In the twenty-first century, feminists no longer have the option of merely supporting forms of environmental politics that attempt to preserve an external nature somewhere outside of capitalist markets. Rather, the goal must be more radical: feminists must critically and fundamentally question the capitalist economy itself, which is the immediate cause of environmental devastation and anthropogenic climate change. In other words, feminists and environmentalists must share the common struggle of creatively pushing back against capitalism. This struggle is going to be vital for not only solving acute environmental problems such as climate change, but also for addressing the deeper problems of global social and environmental justice to which they are inevitably tied.

The aim of this book is to lay down the philosophical groundwork for such political projects. I will reconstruct the theoretical grounds on which an effective contemporary political alliance between feminist and ecological struggles against capitalism can be built today by exposing the systemic logic on which the destruction of the environment and gender oppression rely in capitalism. I will take the existing traditions of materialist ecofeminism and Marxist feminism as my starting points, but I will argue that many of their central claims need to be both updated and revised.

The term "ecofeminism" was coined in the 1970s when the emerging large-scale environmental movement intersected with various social justice movements such as feminism. Ecofeminism continued to develop as a theoretical and political platform throughout the 1980s and produced groundbreaking analyses on the intersecting oppressions of women and nature.[5] However, by the 1990s, it began to be strongly criticized for essentialism, ethnocentrism, and anti-intellectualism. Instead of becoming an integral aspect of feminist theory complementing and correcting its anthropocentric critiques with ecological perspectives, "ecofeminism" became almost a label of derision. As the American ecofeminist Greta Gaard provocatively writes, ecofeminists came to be viewed as "anti-intellectual goddess-worshippers who mistakenly portray the Earth as female and issue totalizing and ahistorical mandates for worldwide veganism" (Gaard 2011, 32). My contention is that a radical reevaluation and recuperation of ecological feminism is vital today, for both political and theoretical reasons.

Throughout the 1970s and 1980s, Marxist feminism too developed as a diverse, but distinct political and theoretical project united by its commitment to understanding women's oppression as grounded in socio-material relations intrinsic to capitalism.[6] Similar to ecofeminism however, by the 1990s Marxist feminism seemed to have lost its direction: the attempts to either fuse patriarchy and capitalism into a unified system or to construct some form of dual or triple systems theory had already gone through various cycles of criticism.[7] Today, many of the premises on which Marxist-feminist theory was built in the 1970s appear highly problematic. Theoretically, fields such as post-structuralism, queer theory, environmental theory, and critical race theory have become vital areas of study. Capitalism itself has also morphed into new shapes: we have arguably entered a distinct moment in the history of capitalism marked not only by unprecedented environmental destruction, but also by digitalization, rising precarity, and soaring surplus populations, for example. We have been forced to develop new concepts such as "information economy," "biocapitalism," "financialization," "surveillance capitalism," and "precarization" in our attempts to respond to the conflicted and troubled present.[8]

This book will attempt to study some of these distinctive contours and challenges of today's highly versatile form of capitalism, as well as chart the opportunities for ecofeminist resistance to them. My focus will be on transformations that could be loosely called *biocapitalism*. In theoretical analyses of the distinctive features of contemporary capitalism, a great deal of emphasis has been placed on information capitalism and immaterial forms of labor. The oft-repeated claim is that in today's post-Fordist economies we no longer work physically to make things; instead, we produce immaterial ideas and innovations and exchange information. This is a very selective story of contemporary capitalism, however, usually told from the perspective of the Global North. I will emphasize throughout my critical analysis of capitalism here that the living bodies of certain groups of people, animals, and whole ecosystems form the very material basis on which supposedly immaterial or cognitive capitalism rests.[9] I will also investigate how the latest developments in biocapitalism in the narrower sense of biotechnological capitalism—capitalism that profits from commercialized biotechnology—target precisely the materiality and vitality of living bodies themselves: new kinds of biological substances and processes are produced through biotechnology and brought into the capitalist circuits of valorization.[10] The huge growth potential of the "bioeconomy" is emphasized by political institutions throughout the world, and bioscience and biotechnology are understood as one of the chief means of reconciling environmental sustainability with economic growth in contemporary capitalism.[11] The rejoinder is that the most significant transformation that we are currently witnessing is a shift from industrial capitalism to biocapitalism.[12]

Another distinctive dimension of my analysis of capitalism is my foregrounding the relevance of post-structuralist theories to contemporary critiques of capitalism. I will attempt to weave some of these theories' key concepts and insights, such as biopolitics and subjectivation, together with Marxist theory. One of my key philosophical claims, developed in chapter 2, is that ecofeminist critiques of capitalism cannot be built on reductive forms of materialism—dialectical or scientific—but should instead adopt post-structuralist critiques of naturalism as their philosophical starting point. I will also argue, mainly in chapter 5, that we crucially need to combine Marxist theory with post-structuralist insights on subjectivation—understood broadly as the social formation of the subject—to develop throughgoing feminist critiques of commodification. Once we recognize critiques of commodification as central to feminist anticapitalist struggles, the upshot is that not only political economy and political institutions need to change radically, but also the political subjects themselves.

In sum, the terrain in which feminist critiques of capitalism must be constructed has fundamentally changed in crucial respects. As Salar Mohandesi and Emma Teitelman (2017, 38) assert, feminist debates on the nature of contemporary capitalism are never purely academic but have important political implications. If the present resembles the past in crucial ways, then we can be certain that the inherited strategies, organizations, and forms of political struggle are still appropriate. "But if capitalist accumulation, the composition of the working classes, and the role of the state have completely changed, then strategies must be rethought" (38). Hence, I insist that it is not enough to find new answers to the old questions about the connections between patriarchy, capitalism, and nature. Instead, we must pose new kinds of questions and develop new kinds of theoretical and political approaches. This is what my book attempts to do.

Capitalism: Should We Still Talk about It?

Even capitalism's ardent advocates admit that a host of serious problems currently plague capitalist economies. The era of cheap energy is coming to an end: capitalist economies are for the first time in their history having to shift to energy sources that are less efficient, while the costs for emission sinks are growing.[13] Although most advanced economies appear to have stabilized since the 2008 financial crisis, many economists warn that we are far from having solved it.[14] Debt levels are still rising across the globe, and previous economic growth levels have not recovered, particularly in Europe. As the economist Mariana Mazzucato (2018, 270) writes, the repercussions of the financial crisis will not only continue to echo around the world for years to come, but the crisis has also shaken our confidence in capitalism and triggered myriad criticisms of the contemporary capitalist system itself: it is too speculative, rewards "rent-seekers" over true "wealth creators," and has permitted the rampant growth of finance, for example. Income inequality also continues to rise in most advanced economies, as well as globally at alarming rates. Every January, to coincide with the World Economic Forum in Davos, Oxfam reports how much richer the world's richest people have become. In 2018, its report showed that 82 percent of the increased wealth generated the previous year went to the richest one percent of the global population, while the 3.7 billion people who made up the poorest half of humanity saw no increase in their wealth. The following year, billionaire fortunes increased again by 12 percent—or $2.5 billion a day—while the 3.8 billion people who made up the poorest half saw their wealth decline by 11 percent.[15]

In other words, economic globalization has not turned out to be the win-win game that its supporters claimed it would be. While it has undoubtedly lifted millions of people out of poverty and facilitated the rise of a middle class in many emerging economies, the large-scale offshoring of manufacturing jobs has meant that employment opportunities have dried up elsewhere, such as in the infamous Rust Belt in the United States. Job and social insecurity have also spiked. Moreover, the effects of mass migration have increased competition for the remaining low-skilled jobs and put downward pressure on their compensation globally. The promise that capitalist development would inevitably deliver wealth, equality, and democracy across the globe sounds less assured than ever. Rather than ecologically sustainable and equitably shared prosperity, capitalism has arguably produced increasing inequality, poverty, banking crises, convulsions of populism, and an impending climate catastrophe.[16] It has brought us to the point where its destructive effects seem to be unequivocally outstripping its material gains.

Issues such as these make it readily understandable why social and political theorists are increasingly turning to critical analyses of capitalism in their attempts to map out more equal and sustainable futures for societies. As Nancy Fraser (2014, 1) writes, after decades in which the term "capitalism" could scarcely be found outside the writings of Marxist thinkers, commentators from various theoretical backgrounds now worry openly about capitalism's sustainability, and activists throughout the world are mobilizing in opposition to its practices. However, it is not always clear what is meant by "capitalism" in the critical assessments of it. While many theorists simply dismiss "capitalism" as a totalizing and empty notion better suited to political rhetoric than academic research, the left-wing tendency to blame every conceivable social problem on some omnipotent but under-specified thing labeled "capitalism" is equally counterproductive.

When the term "capitalism" is used in theoretical discussions, it is commonly, and fairly uncontestably, defined as an economic system identifiable by distinct features such as the private ownership of the means of production, the dominance of wage labor, and open, decentralized markets.[17] What gives this concept explanatory rather than merely descriptive power, however, are the features that identify its inherent logic, laws of motion, or systemic imperatives. The groundbreaking importance of Marx's *Capital*, and the developments in Marxist theory thereafter, were primarily due to the rigorous attempt to identify these laws or imperatives and to show their problematic consequences for social reality.[18]

In her now classic study on the history of capitalism, *The Origin of Capitalism* ([1999] 2017), Ellen Meiksins Wood effectively refutes all ahistorical understandings of capitalism which view it as essentially synonymous with any form of trade or market activity. Many advocates of capitalism essentially equate capitalism with these activities or forms of sociality, which humans have practiced since time immemorial, and which supposedly correspond to natural human inclinations to "truck and barter" and to seek to maximize profits. Meiksins Wood shows how such question-begging explanations of the development of capitalism originate from classical political economy and Enlightenment conceptions of progress, but are also operative in many explanations of Marxist historians. Meiksins Wood emphasizes the need to understand the specificity of capitalism and its radically distinct features in comparison to earlier economic formations such as feudalism. While markets have indisputably existed in human societies for millennia, Meiksins Wood's key point is that in capitalist societies, material life and social reproduction are *universally* mediated by the market. This means that all individuals must, in one way or another, enter into market relations in order to gain access to the means of life. In other words, "until the *production* of the means of survival and self-reproduction is market-dependent, there is no capitalist mode of production" (Meiksins Wood [1999] 2017, 141).

This unique system of market-dependence generates specific systemic requirements and compulsions shared by no other mode of production—the imperatives of competition, accumulation, profit-maximization, and increasing labor productivity—which regulate not only all economic transactions but social relations more generally (Meiksins Wood [1999] 2017, 7). Meiksins Wood shows, for example, how in feudalism there was no compulsion to increase labor productivity because there was no imperative of market competition. The aristocracy would try to acquire more arable land, landed estates, and noble titles, and they could simply use more coercive force to extract more surplus labor from the peasants or direct producers. What is distinctive about capitalist societies, in contrast, is that the appropriation of wealth does not depend primarily on extra-economic powers and privileges, but on the relentless drive to maximize profit by developing the forces of production.

It is important to emphasize that these drives, compulsions, or systemic imperatives that characterize capitalist economies should not be understood as deterministic, transhistorical iron laws; rather, all economic imperatives must always be understood as being embedded in varying, historically specific social relations and political practices, which are ultimately constituted by human agency. This implies that they are subject to change: they can be refashioned and will inevitably take radically different forms depending on the societal contexts in which they operate. I suggest that we also accept the truism that all theoretical attempts to understand social reality are already discursively framed and therefore politically contestable. For my argument, it is nevertheless important to acknowledge that such imperatives and compulsions place distinct constraints on the economic and political activity in societies in which capitalist modes of production prevail. That is why they have such significant explanatory power. To pick out some easy examples, the compulsion to increase profits by lowering wages explains why much of the world's labor-intensive production has moved to the Global South in recent decades, and the imperative to cut raw material costs explains why capitalist development has usually gone hand-in-hand with environmental destruction. Hence, identifying the economic logic of capitalism—its systemic imperatives—remains the key to unlocking the theoretical usefulness and the explanatory force of this concept.

The ability to identify systemic and functional features of capitalism is also of crucial importance for our critiques of it, as well as for our advocacy and imagination of different kinds of alternatives to it. It is highly significant for any political analysis to recognize that some constraints are inherent to the logic of specific economic mechanisms. This does not imply that they cannot be politically altered, but if we recognize that certain things must occur in order for the capitalist economy to work satisfactorily on its own terms, then this has direct implications for viable attempts to alter them politically. In other words, if the harms and injustices of capitalism that we are concerned about were merely accidental, we could try to correct them by pursuing reforms that do not alter the basic logic or framework of capitalist economies. If, on the hand, we must conclude that these harms and injustices are systemic and fundamental for the functioning of capitalism, then deeper structural changes are needed. We cannot be concerned merely with the question of how wealth should be distributed more equitably, for example; rather, we must expose and investigate the systemic economic mechanisms, functional requirements, and political arrangements that generate these distributive inequalities in the first place. My aim is to show that for feminist theory, it is particularly important to analyze the systemic features of capitalism that create and maintain gender subordination in order to make sense of a number of contentious contemporary political issues, such as the global reproductive market. To put the point bluntly, commercial surrogacy clinics are not booming in India because of the sunny weather there.

Eco-Functionalist Critiques of Capitalism

One of my central aims in this book is to redevelop functionalist critiques of capitalism in response to the ecological crisis and gender inequality. By "functionalist critique," I mean critiques of capitalism that attempt to identify precisely its systemic features—what must occur systematically in conjunction with it in order for it to function satisfactorily. To be clear, by functionalism I do not mean determinism: I am going to argue, for example, that the heteropatriarchal nuclear family and the gendered division of labor within it have an important function in capitalism, but this does not mean that capitalism would have created the heteropatriarchal nuclear family or could not operate without it. As I already noted, all economic imperatives characterizing capitalism must be understood as embedded in historically specific social relations and political practices and can therefore take a variety of forms.

Rahel Jaeggi (Fraser and Jaeggi 2018, 116) notes that there is a long Marxist tradition of functionalist critiques of capitalism, from pauperization theory to the theorem of the tendential fall of the rate of profit.[19]

Such functionalist critiques have attempted to show that capitalism undermines its own capacity to function on the basis of the grounds it lays for itself, and hence it ultimately refutes itself. However, as the communist countries reverted one by one to capitalism in the 1990s, functionalist critiques of capitalism retreated. Measured purely in terms of productivity, capitalism seemed to have won the competition for the best economic system hands down. It also seemed increasingly evident that even if capitalism was inherently crisis-prone, it was also exceptionally resilient, managing to resurrect itself after multiple crises and continuing to expand its productivity dramatically over time. And once the political Left lost the functionalist argument and had only moral ones, its defeat seemed sealed. The demands for social justice and economic equity were dismissed as misplaced compassion in the face of hard economic realities, and the calls of conscience regarding child labor or the plight of animals were reframed as individual moral problems that could be best remedied by modifying individual consumer preferences—one could always turn vegan and buy fair-trade coffee.

My contention is that we are at a new theoretical and political juncture now in terms of the viability of functionalist critiques of capitalism. Ecological critiques of capitalism are a form of functionalist critique insofar as they are demonstrating the unsustainability of capitalist economies, but the current environmental crisis we are facing is qualitatively different from previous capitalist crises. It is systemic, objective, and deeply structural. It is caused by the imperative for endless accumulation, which is essentially destabilizing for the system. But what is at stake is not merely the continuity of our economic system or even our particular way of life, but ultimately all life on earth.

Ecological critiques of capitalism have stirred public debate since at least 1972 when the first report of the Club of Rome, *The Limits to Growth*, was published. Using computer simulations, the report demonstrated that economic growth could not continue indefinitely because of resource depletion. The report sold 30 million copies in more than 30 languages, making it the best-selling environmental book in history.[20] Yet in the following decades, the report was repeatedly attacked for operating with unduly pessimistic assumptions, and its influence waned. Today, climate change has given ecological critiques of capitalism a new form and urgency. The regrettable truth is that the limits-of-growth debate of the 1970s has not been exceeded; rather, the most acute environmental problem of the twenty-first century may not be the end of cheap resources but the end of cheap waste. With climate change, we have reached a point at which environmental degradation can no longer be treated as a regrettable side effect of an otherwise functioning and desirable economic system threatening us sometime far in the future. Rather, climate change demonstrates, in a graphic form, how environmental destruction already undermines the functioning of the capitalist economy itself. Eco-functionalist arguments can thus provide us with renewed, strong grounds on which robust anticapitalist critiques should be erected.

The key systemic claim common to all eco-functionalist critiques of capitalism is that there is an inherent contradiction between the logic of ecology and the growth logic driving capitalist economies. There are different ways of formulating this contradiction. On the most general level, it can be recognized as a version of Marx's fundamental insight that capitalism's major contradiction resides in its orientation toward production for private profit rather than for human needs, and the devastation of the environment is just one of the many forms that this contradiction takes. [21] The systemic feature of capitalism that is especially pernicious in terms of environmental devastation, however, is its need for constant economic growth.

The most important of the prevailing laws or imperatives of capitalist economies that Marx identified was the imperative of "capitalist accumulation"—what we today would more commonly call the imperative of economic growth. A stable capitalist economic order is structurally reliant on economic growth, and GDP growth is the single most important goal of governments across the world today. The necessity of growth in a stable capitalist economy can be explained in slightly different terms on the levels of micro- and macro-economics.

On the microeconomic level, it manifests as the imperative of individual enterprises to accumulate profits that they can spend on expansion and innovation in order to survive in the competition against other firms in open markets. In other words, to stay ahead in the game, they must be able to design new, exciting products and adopt new technologies that improve their efficiency and labor productivity, otherwise they will perish in the competition. The imperative to accumulate profits thus further explains the goals of cheapening labor and expanding markets, the constant push for improvements in the productivity of labor, innovations in product design, and so on. On the level of macroeconomics, economic growth is necessary for balancing the effects of constantly growing labor productivity. As long as the economy is growing, it is able to soak up all the workers who have become unemployed because of the gains in the productivity of labor. When the economy is not growing, we have rising unemployment and diminishing spending power with all of their attendant social and economic problems. In short, enterprises in capitalist economies must assume that their profits will grow, consumers believe that their purchasing power and living standards will go up, governments

expect that their tax revenues will rise, and lenders and investors antici-
pate that borrowers will repay their debts and that businesses will pay
dividends.[22]

When the economic growth imperative is combined with the ecological truism that infinite growth on a finite planet is impossible, a
contradiction emerges. As the eco-Marxist theorist John Bellamy Foster
(2002, 18–19) writes, the principle characteristic of capitalism is that "it
is a system of self-expanding value in which accumulation of economic
surplus—rooted in exploitation and given the force of law by competition—must occur on an ever-larger scale," and this implies that there
will inevitably be "an inherent conflict between the maintenance of ecosystems and the biosphere and the kind of rapid, unbounded economic
growth that capitalism represents." Economic growth almost unavoidably
means the increasing extraction and absorption of energy and materials, and the dumping of an ever-growing amount of waste into the
environment.

In terms of climate change, for example, the contradiction means
that as economic growth occurs in carbon-based capitalist economies, the
demand for fossil fuels rises and with it, emissions as well. It is important
to recognize that even if we managed to rapidly and completely accom-
plish the necessary shift to fossil-free, renewable energy, economic growth
would still present a significant problem for environmental sustainability,
even in terms of climate change. A significant amount of greenhouse
gases results from non-fossil fuel sources such as deforestation, soil erosion, and landfill. That amount is not static but grows with the economy,
adding more greenhouse gases (GHGs) to the atmosphere each year.

The conventional response to this contradiction of infinite economic
growth on a finite planet has been to insist on "green growth" or "sustainable growth," which would mean successfully *decoupling* economic growth
from the increasing use of natural resources and/or harmful environmental impacts such as greenhouse gases.[23] Decoupling thus refers to
the end of the necessary correlation between increased economic production and decreased environmental quality. Through investments in
clean energy, recycling of materials, and the adoption of more efficient
technologies, for example, economic growth would no longer remain
correlated with the growth of the material flows underpinning transgres-
sions of the critical planetary boundaries. The future green capitalist
economy would be built on much greater resource efficiency and would
operate with more "immaterial" economic activities. This would lead to
a reduction of the environmental impact of each additional monetary
increment of GDP.

Such "green growth" is advocated by politicians from both the Left and Right with the promise that it would not require any significant economic sacrifices but would instead create millions of new high-paying jobs.[24] Decoupling would thus mean that we could enjoy the benefits of continuing economic growth—we could have high-paying jobs as well as new electric cars—in an economy that was functioning with continually declining material throughput. Since capitalist economies have shown themselves to be unrivaled when measured in terms of efficiency, the economic logic of capitalism seems to support the possibility of decoupling. It appears as the perfect solution to the problem of continuous yet sustainable growth.

Unfortunately, decoupling has not proven to be a credible solution, whether we study the existing empirical evidence or the basic arithmetic of growth. In 2009, the Sustainable Development Commission in the United Kingdom released a landmark report in which the economist Tim Jackson assessed the possibilities of decoupling (updated in 2016).[25] The report makes an important distinction between relative and absolute decoupling. Relative decoupling refers to any decline in the emission intensity of a given unit of economic output. In other words, it signals a decline in emission intensity relative to the GDP (which could still be rising), but it does not necessarily mean that we are using fewer materials or emitting fewer pollutants overall. Absolute decoupling refers to a situation in which material resource use or harmful environmental impacts such as emissions decline in absolute terms, even as economic output continues to rise (Jackson [2009] 2016, 84). It is possible to find empirical evidence for relative decoupling—declining resource intensities relative to the GDP, for example—particularly in post-industrial Western economies, which have outsourced a large portion of extraction, manufacturing, and distribution outside of their territories. Accounting models based on a nation's emissions and material use are highly misleading, however: it is like assessing someone's attempts at weight loss based on the food they prepared themselves at home when most of their diet was fast food. When it comes to GHG emissions, what matters most are the cumulative global emissions, not the regional progress made in some countries.

Evidence for overall reductions in emissions and resource throughput—absolute decoupling—is much harder to find. The declines in energy and carbon intensity have generally been offset by increases in the scale of economic activity over the same period. Globally, the use of natural resources, for example, has expanded more than tenfold in the last hundred years, and its speed has only accelerated in the last couple of decades. In 1900 it was 7Gt (gigatons), in 2010 it was 70Gt, and currently it is over 88Gt (Vaden et al. 2019, 5). The efficiency gains in the greening of the production process have generally been dwarfed by growing consumption. Thus far, the only significant emission reductions globally have occurred in the context of economic recessions.[26] It is of course possible to imagine that some unprecedented technological breakthrough is just around the corner that will give us boundless cheap and clean energy, as well as creating the possibility to endlessly recycle materials, and that the critical assessments of decoupling based on our current empirical evidence cannot predict such a situation. But even in such highly optimistic circumstances, there are some immovable limits to what can be achieved through decoupling because the laws of physics unequivocally state that we cannot produce something out of nothing.

It is helpful here to briefly consider the example of my native country, Finland, a relatively small and technologically advanced country. Tere Vaden et al. (2019) calculate the timeline and size for what "successful decoupling" for Finland would mean: they project a 2 percent annual GDP growth rate combined with a decline in global resource use by 2050 to a level that would be environmentally sustainable, as well as compatible with a maximum 2 degrees of global warming. To achieve this, resource decoupling in Finland would have to result in 6.6 times more economic output out of every ton of material used, while the use of materials would have to decrease 70 percent. They conclude that such a scenario is scarcely intelligible, let alone realistic. Globally, the challenges are obviously even greater. The speeds at which resource and emission efficiencies have to improve if we are to meet our carbon targets and stay within safe planetary boundaries are simply mind-boggling. The environmental economist Tim Jackson concludes: "The truth is that there is as yet no credible, socially just, ecologically sustainable scenario of continually growing incomes for upwards of nine billion people" (Jackson [2009] 2016, 102). In other words, our only realistic option at the moment for tackling the environmental crisis and for sharply reducing GHG emissions is to challenge the imperative of continuous economic growth and hence the core functional logic of the capitalist economy itself.

Environmental critiques of capitalism thus represent an important and timely form of functionalist critique that demonstrates how the capitalist system is undermining itself by crossing the planetary boundaries that mark a safe operating space for humanity. This does not mean that capitalism will automatically collapse, however, or even that economic growth will inevitably stop or slow down soon. As Jason Hickel (2020, 124) writes, we are already sliding into dangerous tipping points, and growth shows no signs of ending. Instead, capital can move into new growth sectors such as sea walls, border militarization, arctic mining, and desalinization plants. In other words, it is relatively easy to imagine scenarios where GDP keeps growing even as social and ecological systems are collapsing around us. Ultimately such scenarios will be short-lived, however. If we cross crucial planetary boundaries for long enough, unstoppable feedback processes will accelerate the destruction of the planet so quickly that it will become impossible to control them. Droughts, crop failures, floods, fires, storms, rising seas, fatal heat waves, and ecosystem collapse would then rapidly start to overwhelm the capacity of states to meet the needs of their citizens, leading to the collapse of their infrastructures and to civil unrest, unprecedented migration, and countless deaths. Hence, it is important to acknowledge that we cannot simply wait for capitalism to collapse of its own accord by crashing into external planetary limits. When that happens, it will already be too late to build viable alternatives to it. It seems clear that the political consequences we draw from our eco-functionalist critique must spur us to immediate action now.

Hence, environmental problems can no longer be treated as a subcategory somewhere low on the list of harms attributable to capitalism. Rather, they must be recognized as the central, even vital issue. This contention has direct implications for the kinds of alternatives to capitalism we can imagine and advocate: they cannot be backwards-looking and nostalgic. We obviously cannot turn back to some form of left-wing authoritarianism such as the kind found in the Soviet Union, which was still built on the idea that economic activity should be based on growth and top-down management. But it is equally important to accept that neither can we magically go back to some green version of an out-of-date postwar social democracy, which was built on the economic boom of the post-World War II decades.

The period between the late 1940s and the early 1970s is often nostalgically referred to as the "golden age" of capitalism in western Europe and the United States because it was marked by unprecedented economic growth, high levels of employment, and a dramatic rise in living standards. In the same time period, these countries also became significantly more egalitarian in economic terms and built extensive welfare states. Many socialist and feminist thinkers therefore see a causal relationship between the various socialist policy measures in these countries during this time and their economic and social success. Their contention is that a social democratic welfare state is not only compatible with strong economic performance, but in fact makes it possible. The task ahead now is to replicate this success—that "golden age"—through increased social spending, gender-sensitive budgeting, and other socialist and feminist measures of economic redistribution.[27]

Once we bring the environment to the center of our analysis, however, the economic history of this period looks notably different. The "golden age" was not the result of exceptionally successful socialist economic policies; it was economically possible because of the availability of cheap, non-renewable energy and a complete lack of regard for the limits of planetary resources and sinks. A major source of the economic boom after World War II was the widespread use of cheap oil. A whole new way of life was built on it: an enormous automobile industry, a highly productive agriculture, which depended on petroleum-based artificial fertilizers and pesticides, and the use of plastics in every aspect of our housing, clothing, and medical care.[28] Whatever we may think of globalization and its adjacent harms, it should also be kept in mind that the postwar economic boom was geographically very limited. It was built on extremely restrictive and unfair global trade arrangements, amounting to the brutal exploitation of what was then known as the Third World. The countries at the "core" of global capitalism might have become internally more egalitarian and wealthier during this time, but this came at the expense of the countries in the "periphery." In short, intense global exploitation as well as the expropriation of natural resources were the "hidden abodes" behind these "golden years." By the late 1970s, this unprecedented economic growth had ground to a halt in western Europe and the United States, resulting in periods of severe stagflation and mass unemployment, which in turn spurred the shift to neoliberal economic policies in the 1980s.

In short, the welfare states of the postwar period became possible because millions of people mobilized and demanded change. But the long postwar boom also meant, crucially, that political concessions could be funded out of growth, not from the radical restructuring of the economy, or even from any particularly significant redistribution of profits. Today, we are facing a very different situation in terms of economic growth and cheap energy: both have become much harder to come by. As a result, a fundamentally different kind of political mobilization is necessary, one that is not based merely on class antagonism over profits. Contemporary ecofeminist and ecosocialist demands will have to cut into growth itself rather than merely count on getting a bigger slice of a constantly growing pie.

The Limits of Functionalist Critiques

There are important theoretical advantages as well as political consequences to functionalist critiques of capitalism. The aim of functionalist critiques is not to condemn capitalism on the basis of moral outrage, but to show that it does not work satisfactorily, even in its own terms. As

Rahel Jaeggi notes, functionalist critiques seem to be free from a number of moral and political entanglements: they do not have to rely on either freestanding moral justification or a consensus regarding thorny moral and political issues which, in secular, liberal, and pluralistic societies, are beyond our reach (Fraser and Jaeggi 2018, 117). In other words, we can merely perform a series of calculations that combine facts about our current rates of GDP growth, demographic statistics and predictions about population growth globally, ecological facts about available resources and sustainable carbon dioxide levels, and then just crunch the numbers. The balance sheet demonstrates unequivocally that our current forms of economic activity are unsustainable.

However, there are also important limitations to functionalist critiques. Fraser and Jaeggi (2018, 117) also point out that the functionalist mode of critique is never as normatively neutral and freestanding as it seems. In a social and historical world, the functional is always already interwoven with power relations and normative assumptions, and ethical questions are therefore invariably interwoven with economic ones. This means that we must step out of the narrow "economism" that characterizes some Marxist analyses and recognize the normative "impurity" of our eco-functionalist critiques. Our critique must be explicitly historicized and politicized by asking what kind of political and moral assumptions underlie the judgment that something is not functioning properly and whose perspective such a judgment expresses. Even if we understand capitalism strictly as an economic system, its social meanings and problems are never strictly economic. My contention is that the aim of effective feminist critiques of capitalism should be to show how the supposedly "purely" economic issues transmute into political and moral ones.

Hence, while emphasizing the importance of developing strong eco-functionalist critiques of capitalism, I also recognize and want to make visible their limits. Functionalist critiques are built on the necessary constraints of the economic logic of capitalism—what the system either allows or disallows when it functions well—and they must therefore operate on the basis of a narrow, economic understanding of capitalism and its functional requisites. The fact that moral and ethical considerations are bracketed out means that many of the most serious problems of contemporary capitalism fall out of sight too. In a functionalist framework, politically contested activities such as commercial gestational surrogacy and sex work, for example, are reduced to questions of adequate compensation, safe working environments, and the optimal balancing of supply and demand. I will show that functionalist critiques are unable to grapple with these and many other tenacious ethical problems riddling contemporary capitalist societies and that we therefore also need normative critiques. This is particularly pressing in connection with societies' increasing *commodification*.

The attempt to commodify—to turn activities, events, products, and materials into sellable commodities, and thus to extend the realm of the markets—can be viewed as one of capitalism's key drives or imperatives. This drive has particularly characterized the neoliberal form of capitalism, which has dominated global economic development in the past decades. With purely economic or functionalist arguments, it is difficult—if not impossible—to show faults in this development. Commodification is an important means of producing economic growth given that GDP is measured in terms of market transactions. If previously noncommercial or public services, cultural products, life forms, physical spaces, and social relations are privatized and redefined as commodities, it clearly follows that more market transactions will be generated. And formally, this translates into further economic growth measured in terms of GDP.

The essentially metaphysical and moral argument I want to defend, however, states that markets change the internal character and the moral meaning of what is traded on them, as well as the surrounding form of life in which they are embedded.[29] When more and more things and activities become purchasable commodities, this will inevitably affect the way that people view them, relate to themselves, and to each other. In her seminal book *Contested Commodities*, Margaret Radin (1996) shows how capitalist liberal societies are always defined by socially, politically, and legally established boundaries between what we believe can be treated as a commodity, given monetary value, separated from a person, transferred, and sold in the markets (e.g., labor, cars, animals, sex); what can be alienated and transferred, but not sold (e.g., adopted children); and what cannot be alienated and transferred at all (e.g., political rights such as voting). It is important to recognize that the way we draw the lines between such categories is the result of contested political processes and moral debates.

I contend that feminist critiques of capitalism should form a vocal strand in the debate on the appropriate limits of commodification and create a radical arena for its thoroughgoing political contestation. Although critiques of commodification have suffered serious setbacks in feminist theory since the early 1970s, I want to emphasize their relevance for the feminist resistance against current forms of neoliberal capitalism. I will show that the recent intertwinement of advanced biotechnology with global capitalist markets, in particular, mandates new kinds of political responses and interventions because it forces us to confront thorny and profound ethical problems concerning embodiment, sexuality, kinship, autonomy, and dignity. Our sole aim should not be to make markets fairer or less discriminatory; rather, and more fundamentally, our critique should seek to curtail the space in which markets operate. Such a critique would have to be based on a radically different conception of emancipation than the liberal one that equates freedom with undistorted competition and equal access to free markets, as well as on a different set of core values.

As many critics of capitalism have argued, the alternative moral framework on which our critiques of capitalism should be built constitutes a much more difficult problem than what is often recognized in the critical analyses that focus merely on capitalism's crisis tendencies or its unfair distribution of wealth. They point out that the overcoming of capitalism ultimately requires a complete reappraisal of values and must center on the question of what we, collectively, value more than material wealth (and economic growth and corporate profits as the means of achieving it). A frequent suggestion on how to bypass the problem of normative grounding in critiques of capitalism has been to limit them to immanent critique and appeal to the liberal political principles and values which the opponents, supposedly, already share.[30] Socialists have traditionally borrowed a myriad of values, ideals, and principles from liberalism, such as equality, democracy, individual freedom, and self-realization, and then tried merely to show that such values can be better realized in socialist rather than in capitalist societies (Gilabert and O'Neill 2019). In other words, the assumption is that our opponents will also immediately recognize child labor or debilitating poverty as moral ills to be avoided.

I intend to show that engaging in an immanent critique of capitalism in this sense is not enough, however. The ecofeminist critiques of capitalism that I want to develop here cannot be understood as immanent critiques of liberalism that rely merely on the already internalized normative commitments of liberal subjects. I will draw on the Marxist-feminist tradition of social reproduction theory in particular in order to show that feminists must also fight for values, ideals, and principles that liberalism has traditionally disavowed and devalued, such as care, intimacy, interdependence, empathy, and sustainability.

In Marxist-feminist theory, *social reproduction* is traditionally understood to encompass the activities required to create, maintain, and restore the commodity called "labor power." In other words, it includes the activities necessary for sustaining workers, who are not machines but embodied social beings who must eat and sleep, as well as raise their children, care for their families, and maintain their communities. Marxist feminists working in the tradition of social reproduction theory have criticized capitalism for systematically undervaluing such activities and for depleting the collective and individual capacities necessary for regenerating human beings and sustaining social bonds.[31] Cinzia Arruzza, Tithi Bhattacharya, and Nancy Fraser (2019, 73), for example, argue in their book *Feminism for the 99%: A Manifesto* that social reproduction struggles not only remain pertinent, but have become especially explosive today because neoliberalism demands more hours of waged work per household and provides less state support for social welfare.[32]

My contention is that social reproduction theory can provide a rich resource for developing not only functionalist but also normative critiques of capitalism. In her now classic book *Women's Consciousness, Man's World*, Sheila Rowbotham writes: "The family under capitalism carries an intolerable weight: all the rags and bones and bits of old iron the commodity system can't use. Within the family women are carrying the preposterous contradiction of love in a loveless world" (Rowbotham 1973, 77). I am suggesting that the overlooked and undervalued "rags and bones" of capitalism, such as meaningful relationships with other humans and with nonhuman animals, non-monetizable affects such as love, empathy, and compassion, and the experiences of care and nurture could form a basis for alternative and more ecological feminist theory and politics. This does not mean that ecofeminist critiques can be built on abstract and freestanding moral frameworks, however. We cannot appeal to women's "nature" or their closer proximity to all things "natural," nor can we assume that the class subject "working-class women" brought along its own normative justification because its emancipation was inevitable in the unfolding of historical materialism. Rather, we need to foreground the important role that the daily practices of social reproduction—for which women are chiefly but not exclusively responsible—have played in the history of capitalism. In sum, despite my focus on developing an eco-functionalist critique here, I want to insist that feminist environmental theory and politics cannot avoid getting entangled in historical contingencies, moral ambiguities, and thorny philosophical dilemmas in their contestations of capitalism.

Intersecting Oppressions

The morally open-ended nature of anticapitalist political struggles is a further reason why I believe that feminists should be particularly wary of static and totalizing conceptions of capitalism. Our underlying theoretical analysis of capitalism must be complex and differentiated enough to be able to distinguish among its variegated, sometimes contradictory

mechanisms and effects that are nevertheless compatible with the underlying logic of capitalist accumulation.

Seminal Marxist-feminist thinkers such as Nancy Fraser (2014) have
argued that capitalism must denote something broader than a distinctive
economic system: it must be understood as a comprehensive social formation, "an institutionalized social order" that also includes the noneco-
nomic realms, the background conditions, or "hidden abodes" that enable the economy to function—social reproduction, the earth's ecology,
and political power.[33] Theoretically, such an expanded view of capitalism
as an institutionalized social order keeps us from missing the true depth
and breadth of capitalism. It allows us to see that "the heterogenous
ills—financial, economic, ecological, political, social—that surround us
can be traced to a common root" (Fraser 2014, 55). Politically, it then
enables strategic anticapitalist organizing in a wide variety of social, cultural, and political sites: it can clarify the relations among the disparate
social struggles of our time and "foster the close cooperation, if not full
unification, of their most advanced, progressive currents in a counter-
systemic block" (55).

Such a broad understanding of capitalism seems particularly important for feminist theory and politics because it also brings into view those
aspects of gender oppression that are not strictly economic. It recognizes
the importance of social reproduction—the gendered labor that forms
capitalism's human subjects and their communities—as an indispensable
background condition for the possibility of capitalist production. When
capitalism is recognized as an extensive and pervasive social order linked
not only to gender oppression but also to race, sexuality, ethnicity, colo-
niality, imperialism, heteropatriarchy, and ableism, it becomes apparent
that it clearly outstrips the economic realm. Such a broad conception of
capitalism thus also appears to solve the problem of how to understand
and theorize the intersecting forms of oppression connected with gender,
race, and class as different dimensions of capitalism.

My critical concern with Fraser's conceptualization of capitalism
as an institutionalized social order is twofold. First, theoretically, an
expanded conception of capitalism implies the danger of treating capitalism as a monolithic, all-encompassing entity, which fails to account
for its historical and geographic variations and internal contradictions.
While such a conception succeeds in forging connections between seemingly fragmented and isolated phenomena, it does so at the cost of hiding
contradictory mechanisms, historical contingencies, and unprecedented
singularities under a totality. Not only varied forms of gender oppression
have historically contingent relationships to the distinct and contradictory economic mechanisms and compulsions characterizing contempo-

rary capitalism—feminist political struggles do too. In chapter 4, I will develop this line of critique through the question of whether capitalism is emancipatory or oppressive for women. I will show that sometimes we must identify opposing ways to relate capitalist economic logic and gender oppression—capitalism wants women to both work and to stay at home, for example, and we can find both incentives today. Women are increasingly torn between the conflicting demands of femininity in neoliberal capitalist societies.[34]

My second concern is that despite the appearance of being politically inclusive, on closer scrutiny, the expanded theory of capitalism becomes internally contradictory because it makes us lose sight of the distinction between capitalist economy and capitalist society. A broad understanding of capitalism effectively conveys the idea that *capitalist societies*, and our daily lives in them, are organized through various competing and divergent forms of oppression and sets of norms, embedded in a heterogenous network of social practices and power relations which are in constant struggle and tension with one another. As Fraser, in my view correctly, writes, "capitalist society is normatively differentiated, encompassing a determinate plurality of interrelated social ontologies" (Fraser 2014, 67). The "non-commodified zones" of capitalist societies do not, crucially, simply mirror commodity logic but embody distinctive normative and ontological grammars of their own: social practices oriented to reproduction tend to engender ideals of care, mutual responsibility, and solidarity, for example, while ecological practices foster such values as stewardship, non-domination of nature, and intergenerational justice. Politically, this normative heterogeneity of capitalist societies implies that political struggles against capitalism, and its narrow economic normativity, do not have to emerge from some pure outside. These struggles can draw from and build on the existing, alternative sets of norms embedded in the myriad social practices around us, such as practices of social reproduction. They can "draw on capitalism's own complex normativity to criticize it, mobilizing against the grain the multiplicity of ideals that coexist, at times uneasily" (69).

However, in order to meaningfully mobilize the political potential of these diverse political struggles against capitalism, they must draw their political strength from the fact that they challenge the narrow logic of *capitalist economy* operating with strictly monetizable and commensurable values. In other words, these struggles must pit the values of care, solidarity, and intergenerational justice, for example, against the values which define and drive capitalism as an economic system—economic growth, profit-making, equal exchange, and consumer choice, for example. Hence, my point is that a politically effective and theoretically intelligible resistance against capitalism in fact requires and presupposes a narrow understanding of capitalism as an economic system, as its opposite pole. Fraser's defense of an expanded conception of capitalism as an institutionalized social order must thus *both* implicitly presuppose a narrow economic conception of capitalism as a clearly specified foil that can form the focus of a politically sustained critique, *and* explicitly disavow such a narrow conception as mistaken and reductive, in order to reach the political and theoretical conclusions that Fraser aims for.

I will therefore adopt and maintain here a distinction between *capitalist societies* and *capitalist economies*. By capitalist economy I refer to a historically specific economic system of production, distribution, and exchange characterized by a particular economic logic or laws of motion and a corresponding restrictive normativity. Capitalist societies, and our daily lives in them, on the other hand, are organized through various competing and divergent normativities, embedded in a heterogenous network of social practices and power relations, which are in constant struggle and tension with one another.[35] While the normativity specific to capitalist economic production promotes objectives and ideals such as economic growth, efficiency, free competition, and negative liberty, for example, we are also engaged daily in social practices, human relationships, and activities that are based on very different set of norms and which would make no sense if assessed by strictly economic criteria.

This also implies that while the different axes of oppression in capitalist societies, such as gender oppression, sexual oppression, and racial oppression, are clearly intersecting and mutually enforcing, they nevertheless require their own specific theoretical analyses because they have their own historically and culturally specific grammars and distinctive features. In other words, sexism, racism, and homophobia cannot just be merged together and lumped under the general harms caused by capitalism. We must recognize that they have systemic, and not just historically contingent or opportunistic, links to the functioning of the capitalist economy, and these links are formed in distinct ways. As Asad Haider (2018, 13) argues, race, gender, and class name entirely different social relations, and they themselves are abstractions that must be explained in terms of specific material histories. Furthermore, there is an important distinction between an analytical understanding of the relationships between capitalism and multiple oppressions and what appears experientially salient about them to the exploited and oppressed people themselves. In other words, experiential salience does not necessarily equate with theoretical importance.[36]

While gender forms the primary axis of my functionalist critique of capitalism here, critiques along the axes of race and sexuality are equally pertinent and cannot be reduced to the axis of gender or treated as subsidiary questions in relation to it.[37] Just as Marxist feminists have brought to light the problems of class reductionism and the omission of gender in Marxist theory, Black Marxist theorists have similarly pointed out that "Marx and Engel's colorless, raceless workers are actually *white*" (Mills 1990, 138).[38] They have demonstrated that racial capitalism does not operate on the basis of a purely color-blind market logic, but through the ideology of white supremacy. In his seminal work, Charles Mills contends that in Marxist theory, typically, racism has been recognized merely as a set of ideas and values imposed on the working class by the bourgeoisie, and not as a fundamental structure of domination or as the social ontology of capitalism (Mills 1999, 139). Mills shows how the ascriptive hierarchy and caste distinctions characterizing feudalism were abolished only for white male workers with the emergence of capitalism; for nonwhite people around the world a new system of ascriptive hierarchy was established instead—European expansionism, white settlement, slavery, and colonialism. This was "the other face of modernity" and it established "the material basis for European superiority to the rest of the world" (Mills 1999, 137).[39] There is also a growing literature on environmental racism that draws important links between environmental and racial critiques of capitalism and shows that racial oppression and segregation have produced a dramatically imbalanced vulnerability to environmental harms.[40]

I will discuss racial capitalism and the legacy of colonialism in connection with several specific issues such as ongoing primitive accumulation, gestational surrogacy, and domestic labor. I will attempt to show how race and racism have in these instances important and systemic connections with both capitalism and gender subordination, but I make no claim to offer a comprehensive analysis of the connections between capitalism and racial oppression here.[41] To do so would require another research project.

Similarly, an extensive analysis of the specific connection between capitalism and settler colonialism must fall outside the purview of this project. Indigenous studies scholars have effectively questioned the traditional Marxist idea that the colonization process was driven by the general capitalist objective of turning the native inhabitants into proletarianized laborers, and they have emphasized instead the centrality of *dispossession*: the theft of land and the way it was transformed into private property and an exchangeable commodity. Robert Nichols (2020), for example, contends that Marxist theory displays a persistent tendency to reduce processes of colonial dispossession to processes of capitalist commodification and enclosure, thereby obviating the need for a robust examination of the specificity of settler expansion and Indigenous resistance on and through land.[42] As he points out, the problem is not merely that "the earth has been commodified, privatized, and 'enclosed' but that colonization generates a form of commodification so as to divest Indigenous peoples *in a distinct and particular way* of their ancestral homes" (2020, 97).[43] In other words, the colonization process cannot be adequately theorized through the capitalist logic of proletarianization, market formation, and the extraction of raw materials, but requires understanding the complex historical intertwinement of capitalist economic objectives with state demands for territorial sovereignty.

Overview of the Chapters

The individual chapters of this book support the broad, overall contentions delineated above, as well as putting forward more specific arguments. The starting point of my inquiry is the existing tradition of materialist and Marxist ecofeminism. In the first chapter, "The Futures of Marxist Ecofeminism," I outline two different ways that the connections between capitalism, the subordination of women, and the destruction of the environment have been made in ecofeminist literature. I distinguish between materialist ecofeminism, which is empirically grounded, and Marxist ecofeminism, which puts forward a functionalist argument about the connections between capitalism, gender oppression, and environmental destruction. These two theoretical positions are necessarily simplifications of much more complex and varied discussions, and their role is merely to expose to critical scrutiny the different philosophical grounds for developing ecofeminist critiques of capitalism. I will defend the Marxist ecofeminist position but contend that it needs to be both updated and revised to account for the different, sometimes contradictory mechanisms for the capitalization of nature that have become prominent today. I will underscore two developments in particular: the dominance of neoliberalism and the development of biotechnology.

The key theoretical finding in chapter 1 is the systemic link between gender oppression and ecological devastation: they occupy analogous positions in the logic of capitalist accumulation, in which the mechanisms of exploitation are dependent on an invisible base of expropriation. The political upshot is that an alliance between feminism and environmentalism should not be understood as an instance of affinity politics in which separate political goals might, on occasion, be shared. Rather, feminists and environmentalists share a common political goal in their resistance against capitalism because they both have an interest in challenging an economic system that is incapable of recognizing the value of "externalities." Despite the important development of feminist and environmental economics, these fields of inquiry make apparent their own limits: the environment and women's reproductive labor are attributed values that are incommensurable with money and therefore cannot be fully monetized and internalized into the circuits of a capitalist market economy. This means that they continue to be undervalued and depredated in the capitalist system of commodity exchange. Feminist ecopolitics must thus begin from the fundamental recognition that we need an economic system in which values other than profit, consumer preferences, and economic growth have a chance of coming to the fore.

Chapter 2, "Ecofeminism at the End of Nature," challenges the common reasoning in feminist and environmental theory according to which the eradication of the nature/human dualism would lead to environmentally more progressive, non-anthropocentric ethics and politics. I begin with a critical discussion of two seminal attempts in socialist environmental theory to argue for the end of nature: the eco-Marxists theorist Jason Moore's influential book *Capitalism in the Web of Life* and Steven Vogel's book *Thinking like a Mall: Environmental Philosophy after the End of Nature*. Through a critical analysis of Moore's and Vogel's positions, I will tease out the problematic political consequences that the theoretical erasure of the nature/human distinction has for environmental theory, and more specifically, for ecofeminist critiques of capitalism.

I will then develop an alternative ontological framework that builds on Michel Foucault's and Giorgio Agamben's critiques of biopolitics. I take Foucault's and Agamben's key insight for my argument against post-natural environmental philosophy to be that in order to advocate for radically new, non-anthropocentric forms of politics, we have to be able to understand and identify the forms of exclusion on which our current conception of politics is built. This requires politicizing our understanding of nature as that which is excluded from the political sphere, as well as recognizing that the way we draw the ontological boundary between nature and politics is itself a political act. Hence, I will explicate the politicized ontological framework that effective feminist and environmental critiques of capitalism, in my view, must presuppose. I will also ask what such a politicization of ontology might mean in practice. My argument is that the politicization of the boundary between the natural and the human realms must inevitably not only lead us to critical questions about the naturalization and animalization of women and racialized people, but extend to our treatment of nonhuman animals.

In the third chapter, "The Nature of Gestational Surrogacy," I develop a functionalist analysis of commercial gestational surrogacy. I question the common idea in contemporary socialist and Marxist-feminist theory that commercial gestational surrogacy should be treated as a new form of transnational labor because of the politically emancipatory potential that such a conception holds. I begin by assessing Melinda Cooper and Catherine Waldby's version of the idea that surrogates are laborers in their influential book *Clinical Labor*. Their argument for understanding gestational surrogacy as labor draws on Marx and can be interpreted as continuing the tradition of Marxist feminism that demands recognition and adequate compensation for women's socially reproductive labor. My key aim is to show that once we submit commercial gestational surrogacy to a rigorous Marxist-feminist analysis, however, it becomes difficult to understand it as a form of labor. While I acknowledge some of the political advantages of the labor paradigm, I develop a sustained critique of it by focusing on its theoretical and political shortcomings. I analyze the functional role that commercial gestational surrogacy occupies in the dynamics of global capitalism and identify the aspects that distinguish it from other forms of waged care work. Rather than being an instance of gendered exploitation, it should be viewed as gendered and racialized expropriation. Functionally, surrogates occupy the position of raw material or a biological resource in the value circuits of biocapitalism.

My main concern is not the correct application of Marxist theory, however, but rather the feminist political and ethical consequences that follow from the theoretical question of how we conceive of gestational surrogacy and how we theorize the processes of value production on which biocapitalism relies. The analysis shows how different theoretical understandings of gestational surrogacy have radically different political consequences for the feminist debates surrounding it. My contention is that we should recognize and take seriously the new forms of kinship that surrogacy creates. Such a recognition would then result in very different kinds of political demands than merely the traditional socialist demands for fairer compensation and more extensive labor rights. It might translate into feminist support for global surrogacy modeled on the one on international adoption, for example.

Chapter 4, "Can Gender Subordination Be Eliminated in Capitalism?" analyzes the functional role of generational reproduction in capitalism. I start from the provocative claim put forward by some feminist thinkers that the global rise of neoliberalism as the leading political and economic paradigm has spelled the end of Marxist feminism.[44] I will respond by insisting that feminists still need to pose the definitive Marxist-feminist question on the necessary connection between capitalism and gender subordination. While neoliberalism and the rapid development of biotechnology have reconfigured the context for investigating this question, its centrality for feminist theory has not been eradicated. On the contrary, it is vital that we pose it in renewed forms today.

The argument moves from empirical facts to theoretical thought experiments. I begin by explicating the liberal position that, rather than being oppressive, capitalism is in fact emancipatory for women. I will outline the theoretical underpinnings of the liberal position through Ann. E. Cudd's work before subjecting it to a Marxist-feminist critique. I then make the argument that the question of whether capitalism is emancipatory for women can ultimately only be answered negatively if it is argued for theoretically. I will follow those Marxist feminists, such as Lise Vogel, who have attempted to show that gender oppression stems necessarily from the economic logic of the capitalist mode of production due to the indispensability of women's reproductive labor for capitalist accumulation. Hence, while challenging the post-structuralist feminist claim that traditional Marxist-feminist analyses of social reproduction have become outdated, I also question the historicist strategy that some Marxist feminists have adopted in their response to such accusations. I insist that Marxist feminists have to engage in theoretical, functionalist analyses— what some critics have pejoratively called "ideal theory." In order to show that the economic logic of capitalism can explain something significant about gender oppression in capitalist societies, the question about the relationship between capitalism and gender oppression has to be posed as a theoretical or philosophical question, and not merely as an empirical question. I will show, with the help of such a philosophical investigation, that the entwinement of capitalism and gender oppression is structurally indispensable for capitalism for reasons related specifically to generational reproduction.

Whereas chapter 4 considered critically the post-structuralist claim that neoliberalism has spelled the end of Marxist feminism, chapter 5, "The Commodification of Affects," responds to the opposing Marxist-feminist claim that neoliberalism forces feminists to turn away from post-structuralism and the identity politics it allegedly promotes, and return to forms of resistance that build on the significance of class. Hester Eisenstein (2009, 212–13), for example, argues that the so-called postmodern turn in women's studies scholarship in the 1980s, with its emphasis on discourse and its distrust of grand narratives, undermined a systematic analysis of the capitalist system. The neoliberal turn requires that feminism must now turn away from post-structuralist analyses that focus on individual acts of resistance and back toward a structural analysis of global capitalism and forms of political resistance building on the significance of class.[45] Against such critics, I contend that we have to refuse the stalwart binary between Marxism and post-structuralism, and instead try to bring them together in a way that is theoretically rigorous and sophisticated, as well as politically effective and enabling. I will contend that instead of returning to the traditional model of a class subject, we need to update Marxist theories of resistance with post-structuralist insights on subjectivation. I will outline some of the difficulties as well as ways forward for such projects in chapters 5 and 6.

In chapter 5, I investigate the seminal attempt by Michael Hardt and Antonio Negri to bring together Marxist and post-structuralist frameworks in their trilogy *Empire*, *Multitude*, and *Commonwealth*. I focus on their influential notion of affective labor and its significance for feminist theory and politics by discussing Kathi Weeks's interesting appropriation of it. I contend that in order to imagine effective political responses to the problems currently facing us, feminist politics needs theoretical distinctions within the category of affective labor that allow us to advance a political and ethical problematization of our current forms of work, as well as to engage in deep critiques of the commodification of emotions. I argue, against Weeks, that such political projects do not have to rely on the ideas of a "true self" or "true love" propping up naturalized and idealized forms of the family. Rather, anticapitalist feminism could be viewed as a political project, which demands restrictions on the commodification of our everyday life in order to challenge the dominant modes of subjectivation and to create new or different forms of the subject, family, and forms of love and kinship.

Hence, feminist critiques of capitalism should not simply condemn capitalist markets in toto, but rather, form a bold and vocal strand in the public, political, and moral debate on the desirable limits and rules of the markets. Most proponents of socialism acknowledge that there must be some role for markets in a well-functioning economic order. Markets are not only an efficient way of gathering information about people's preferences and for balancing supply and demand, but are also a necessary component of those socialist visions that focus on decentralizing and democratizing the economy by promoting workers' cooperatives and small, self-owned businesses, for example. The political debates among socialists thus generally concern the limits of the markets, as well as the rules regulating the exchanges in them. Feminist and environmental concerns should form a loud voice in this debate on the future and the extent of the markets.

In the last chapter, "Is It Wrong for Feminists to Pay for Housework?"

I provide a functionalist, politico-economic analysis of paid housework. Many philosophers have suggested that sometimes asking the right questions can be more important than providing the right answers. According to such an understanding of philosophy, the aim of imaginative philosophical inquiry would be to show that certain kinds of questions are meaningless or irrational, are based on false assumptions, or become senseless when posed in the wrong context. The title of the sixth chapter appears to be a good candidate for this type of philosophical inquiry, and I will try to show why. However, I will also attempt to show why posing this question is nevertheless important, perhaps not for moral philosophy, but for feminist politics.

I begin by discussing Gabrielle Meagher's article 'Is It Wrong to Pay for Housework?' and contend that rather than posing this question as an abstract moral question, it is crucial to place it in the specific historical and socioeconomic context in which we encounter it today. A functionalist, politico-economic analysis of paid housework should then open our eyes to the fact that feminists need to make demands that are not merely ameliorative but embody a radically emancipatory future for all women. I critically assess one such demand, the idea of universal basic income (UBI)—a monthly income paid by the government to each member of society regardless of income from other sources and with no conditions attached. A feminist demand for UBI could contribute to attempts to tackle the deep causes of the growing socioeconomic disparities between women—long-term unemployment, precariousness, and marginalization generated by globalization, slow growth, and automation. My principal reason for defending UBI as an important ecofeminist tool, however, is the fact that feminist political opposition to capitalism can no longer be grounded merely on the problems of income inequality or lack of worker autonomy, as serious as these problems are. The feminist demand for UBI must be incorporated into a broader vision of eco-social transformation that includes an acute awareness of the ecological limits to growth. In the Global North, we desperately need to transition to economies that are not based on the imperative of ceaseless growth, and this, perhaps most profoundly, will require feminists to rethink the role of work.

In sum, this book attempts to retrieve and restore Marxist-feminist and ecofeminist theory by questioning and updating some of their central ideas, premises, and arguments. I try to push against the tide, not in order to be contrarian, but in an effort to get a firm grasp of the complex—and in many ways unprecedented—political situation in which we find ourselves. This will require moving beyond the traditional confines of Marxist-feminist theory and engaging with contemporary debates on such contested issues as the commercialization of biotechnology, affective labor, and universal basic income. The aim of this inquiry is thus not just to knock down taken-for-granted assumptions, but, more importantly, to see what kind of political possibilities come into view once the field of anticapitalist theorizing is realigned in new ways. My hope is to contribute to a new feminist ecopolitics built with the rags and bones left behind by capitalism's breakdown.

1

The Futures of Marxist Ecofeminism

When ecofeminism became the target of intense feminist criticism in the 1990s, it was chiefly targeted for its alleged ontological and methodological essentialism. Whether the connection between women and nature was understood as biological or as socially and historically constructed, it had traditionally operated as a key instrument of women's oppression. Feminism had fought hard against the idea that women were somehow closer to nature than men, and were therefore less rational, cultured, and capable of moral and political deliberation. Ecofeminism seemed to reverse these arguments by emphasizing the inescapable link between women and nature and thereby merely reinforcing forms of patriarchal domination. A further problem concerned the methodological essentialism inherent in much of the early ecofeminist theorizing of that time. It appeared unaware of the ways that its own claims and theories were socially constructed and embedded in particular, often specifically Western social and political contexts. The common charge was that it promoted an idealist and uncritical understanding of Third World women's purported "embeddedness" in nature and their supposedly more holistic understanding of it.[1] Hence, ecofeminism was deemed, at best, an irrelevant distraction from feminism's real work of addressing social injustices, or was, at worst, a form of oppression itself.

Materialist ecofeminists were able to subvert these pitfalls by making a more limited, empirical argument. They avoided the charges of essentialism by rejecting all spiritual, abstract, and totalizing connections between women and nature, and emphasized instead the actual material conditions of women in specific geographic and cultural contexts. Based on such an emphasis, it was possible to argue that women in many parts of the Global South, for example, were "closer to nature" only in the very concrete and material sense that they typically had to fetch water and firewood, as well as being responsible for the small-scale subsistence farming that ensured the survival of their families. This meant that they were often the first victims of environmental destruction.

In their defense of materialist ecofeminism, Greta Gaard and Lori Gruen, for example, acknowledge that environmental degradation affects all people and is not exclusively a women's issue. Their argument is that it is nevertheless a feminist issue because women and children are the first to suffer its consequences. They note that women are responsible for up to 80 percent of food production in developing countries, and for this reason women are most severely affected by food and fuel shortages and the pollution of water resources (Gaard and Gruen [1993] 2005, 163). According to them, it is thus not necessary to evoke metaphorical or essentialist ideas about women's greater propensity for protecting nature because for women living under harsh material conditions, environmental activism is simply a form of self-defense.[2] Similar ideas are put forward in the United Nations Population Fund's study of the consequences of climate change: "Women—particularly those in poor countries—will be affected differently than men. They are among the most vulnerable to climate change, partly because in many countries they make up the larger share of the agricultural work force and partly because they tend to have access to fewer income-earning opportunities . . . Drought and erratic rainfall force women to work harder to secure food, water, and energy for their homes" (UNFPA 2009, 4). In other words, materialist ecofeminism can be understood to build on the acknowledgment that specific groups of women have a distinct connection to the environment through their daily interactions with it. In these specific instances at least, there is a clear strategic incentive for feminism and environmentalism to join forces: protecting the environment also directly improves the lives of poor women.

Although such contextual and empirically grounded arguments are politically and strategically important, they provide insufficient theoretical grounds for ecofeminism. Instead of exposing a systemic or structural connection between gender oppression and environmental destruction, they merely describe a trend characterized by their current intertwinement. Environmental problems tend to exacerbate already existing social problems because the weakest and most vulnerable groups have the fewest resources for mitigating them. When more systemic explanations of the link are provided, they are often formulated in frustratingly vague terms and are based on the idea of the twin dominations of women and nature. The historical and conceptual association between women and nature is understood to be politically significant because it has formed an important justification for patriarchal domination: *the feminization of nature* and *the naturalization of women* are two aspects of a single historical process that has functioned as an ideological requisite for women's and nature's ensuing subordination.

Gwyn Kirk, for example, argues that "in the service of capital accumulation, white-dominated, capitalist patriarchy . . . creates 'otherness'"; it oppresses both women and nature, but also "people of color and poor people worldwide. . . . This continual process of objectification is the central mechanism underlying systems of oppression based on class, race, gender, and nation" (Kirk 1997, 349). Mary Mellor states that "industrialism, capitalism, colonialism, racism, and patriarchy are the different manifestations of a many-headed Hydra that has its fingers around the throat of women, poor people, and the planet" (Mellor 1992, 155). Gaard and Gruen write similarly that "the current global environmental crisis is the result of the mutually reinforcing ideologies of racism, sexism, classism, imperialism, speciesism, and naturism." These ideologies are best understood as "*force fields* that intersect with one another . . . to create complex interrelated and mutually reinforcing systems of oppression" (Gaard and Gruen [1993] 2005, 170).

Listing oppressive ideologies and noting that they are intersecting or connected to one another is obviously valid in the sense that they must occur in some kind of social totality. Such explanations help feminists to describe experiences or instances in which different axes of domination intersect, but they are less helpful in explaining how and why they occur together in specific forms.[3] If ecological feminism seems to cover all forms of oppression and injustice, it further risks losing a clear theoretical focus and political aim. Materialist ecofeminism would, at best, amount to an instance of "affinity politics," a flexible formation that is able to accommodate many different theoretical and political positions behind the twin goals of "planetary survival and an egalitarian future" (Carlassare 2000, 101).

I contend that the major contribution of Marxist feminist thinkers to the project of ecofeminism has therefore been the insight that we can identify distinct mechanisms specific to the systemic logic of capitalism that tie together gender oppression and environmental destruction. In other words, Marxist ecofeminism not only repudiates gender essentialism by insisting that the connection between gender oppression and environmental devastation is historically and culturally specific, but through its critical analysis of capitalism, it can provide a rigorous argument for why this connection is nevertheless systemic and not merely historically contingent or accidental. The feminization of nature and the naturalization of women do not function merely as ideological justifications for an abstract and general logic of domination, but concretely structure capitalist society through gendered social and economic practices and divisions of labor. The systemic character of the connection between gender oppression and environmental devastation becomes discernible once we recognize the indispensable function that the naturalization of women's reproductive labor plays in contemporary capitalism.

The majority of the Marxist-feminist theorists writing in the 1970s and 1980s on women's reproductive and caring work theorized it as a form of labor and appropriated the Marxist framework intent on exposing the mechanisms of exploitation. The domestic labor debates, for example, were essentially concerned with the question of whether women's domestic or reproductive labor was productive labor and thereby produced surplus value.[4] A distinct strand in this scholarship, however, focused on the critique of *primitive accumulation* instead. The critique of primitive accumulation lent itself more readily to ecofeminist theorizing because it was not concerned with the productivity of human labor but focused instead on its necessary preconditions. It was able to bring into Marxist-feminist analyses activities and resources, such as women's reproductive labor, that were productive of important use-values, but not of exchange value, and were therefore structurally excluded from commodity markets.

Primitive Accumulation and Women's Reproductive Labor

In the accounts of classical political economists, "primitive accumulation" referred to the idea that an accumulation of a sufficient mass of wealth was necessary before properly capitalist economic forms could develop. In the thought of early economists such as Adam Smith, this wealth was supposedly amassed by means of the merchant class's commercial acumen and frugality, and eventually reached a point at which it was sufficient to permit substantial reinvestment and start capitalist forms of production.[5] Marx's critique of "so-called primitive accumulation" broke sharply with this account. Marx insisted that the accumulation of wealth by itself was not a sufficient condition of capitalism; what was decisive was the transformation of social property relations. But he also demonstrated that the accumulation of wealth necessary for the birth of capitalism was not the result of some people's acumen and frugality but relied heavily on outright plunder and theft. As he famously formulated the idea in the first volume of *Capital*, capital comes into the world "dripping from head to foot, from every pore, with blood and dirt" (Marx [1867] 1990, 435). Primitive accumulation was essentially a violent process of expropriation: extracting resources and appropriating them for free or without adequate compensation. Examples include the enclosure of the commons, forced migration, and the slave trade. Colonialism historically functioned as an extremely effective political strategy for this kind of expropriation: resources such as gold, ivory, and rubber were extracted from the Global South to enrich the Global North.

There is an ongoing debate on whether primitive accumulation was a historical process that preceded the establishment of properly capitalist forms of production, or whether it is best understood as an ongoing process. While the historical process of wealth transfer from capitalism's periphery to the center was crucial for enabling the emergence of capitalist economies in Europe, many Marxist thinkers emphasize the continuing importance of expropriation and its necessary, structural links with capitalism.[6] Cedric Robinson ([1983] 2020, 4), for example, argues in his now classic book *Black Marxism* that assigning slave labor to some "precapitalist" stage of history would be a grave error. "For more than 300 years slave labor persisted beyond the beginnings of modern capitalism, complementing wage labor, peonage, selfdom, and other methods of labor coercion." Slavery in the Americas played a significant role in the development of capitalist economies in Europe and resulted in capital accumulation for the advance of productive forces there (Robinson [1983] 2020, 120). In other words, slavery was critical not just for the emergence of capitalism, but for its expansion and preservation for centuries.[7]

Similarly, when primitive accumulation is theorized in the context of settler colonialism, and understood not just in terms of appropriating the means of production, but more specifically as land grabbing or the dispossession of land, it becomes clear that the land-based struggles of Indigenous peoples cannot be located in some colonial past. Despite the settler colonial states' repeated assertions otherwise, primitive accumulation or dispossession continues to define the relations between modern states, Indigenous communities, and First Nations.[8]

The idea of "ongoing primitive accumulation" is also central for Marxist-feminist theorists such as Maria Mies, who argues in her seminal work that both nature and women's reproductive labor are expropriated as a "free resource" under capitalism (Mies [1986] 1998). [9] The domination of nature and the extraction of natural resources can be viewed as examples of primitive accumulation. Naturally produced use-values are plundered for productive consumption as raw materials and treated as commodities in capitalist circuits of valorization. Similarly, capitalism depends on the reproductive labor of women to renew and maintain the workforce and extracts this labor from them mostly without compensation. Mies forges a historical and structural link between the birth of capitalism, colonization, the subordination of nature through industrialization, and the simultaneous destruction of women's autonomy over their bodies that characterized the witch hunts in Europe. Colonies, nature, and women were dominated, controlled, and violently expropriated by white capitalist men in a structurally similar way and as part of the same historical process driven by the goal of capitalist accumulation.

> The violent subordination of women under men and the process of capital accumulation was first acted out on a mass scale during the witch-hunts in Europe. But ever since, it has constituted the infrastructure upon which so-called capitalist production relations could be established, namely the contractual relationship between the owners of labor power and the owners of the means of production. Without this infrastructure of non-free, coerced female or colonial labor in the broadest sense, the non-coerced, contractual labor relations of free proletarians would not be possible. Women and colonial peoples were defined as property, as nature, not as free subjects who could enter a contract. Both had to be subordinated by force and direct violence. (Mies [1986] 1998, 170)

Mies uses the metaphor of an iceberg to illustrate the way that capitalist exploitation of wage labor relies on violent processes of expropriation: capitalism is an iceberg economy where capital and waged labor form the visible economy counted in GDP and where women's reproductive work, work in the colonies, and nature's production are externalized from the official economy and form the large underwater part (Mies [1986] 1998, xi). Ideologically, the essential processes of externalization were justified by the "naturalization" of women and the colonies: they were defined as uncontrolled, dangerous, savage nature to be subdued by force (90). "In the course of the last four or five centuries, women, nature, and colonies were externalized, declared to be outside of civilized society, pushed down, and thus made invisible as the under-water part of an iceberg is invisible, yet constitutes the base of the whole" (77). The rationale for this process of externalization was simple: it allowed capitalists to forego costs that they otherwise would have had to cover. When the labor of women and colonial subjects was considered a natural resource, it was freely available like air and water (110).

According to Mies, the same process of expropriation that characterized early capitalism is still ongoing because it is a structurally necessary aspect of capitalism. The prevalence of both direct and structural violence against women, particularly in the Global South, should be understood against the logic of ongoing primitive accumulation, which constitutes the precondition for capitalist exploitation. Mies's examples range from such overt instances as slavery and sex trafficking to more complex phenomena such as mail-order brides, sweatshop labor, and sex tourism. Hence, although some subjects have access to labor markets—they possess the right to sell their labor and have the ability to compete within markets—others are simply expropriated of their bodies, land, and even life, and treated as disposable. Intersecting with gender, racialization has functioned and continues to function as the key instrument for drawing the boundary between these two groups (Dawson 2016, 147; Fraser 2016, 166).[10]

To sum up this section, the Marxist-feminist argument contends that, in addition to the appropriation of surplus value produced by wage labor, capitalism relies on the ongoing and violent expropriation of women's bodies and labor, nonhuman animals, and the biosphere. The expropriation of women's reproductive labor is functionally analogous to and historically contemporaneous with the extraction of natural resources. At various points in history and to varying degrees today, women have been violently forced to give up autonomy over their bodies and reproductive capacities, and these capacities and the labor connected with them have been extracted from them for free and put to the service of capital accumulation. This process is masked and legitimized by an essentially ideological process that "naturalizes" women—understands them as being less civilized, less rational, and closer to nature. The theoretical or systemic grounds for linking the oppression of women to ecological devastation are not primarily ideological, however, but functional. Both "women" and "nature" have a similar, indispensable function in the mechanisms of expropriation: they occupy analogous positions in the logic of capitalist accumulation in which the mechanisms of exploitation are dependent on the invisible base of expropriation. In other words, women and the colonies are not only conceived of as "nature," they are expropriated as "nature."

The Commodification of Nature

Marxist-feminist thinkers such as Mies provide a powerful account of the extent of capitalist expropriation by forging a systemic link between capitalism, gender oppression, racial oppression, and ecological devastation. Such an account makes it possible to draw together witch hunts, colonialism, open-pit mines, and sex tourism under the same systemic logic, but the drawback is that we end up with very abstract theorizing about an extremely broad and heterogeneous set of phenomena—geographically, culturally, historically, and theoretically. I contend that this framework therefore requires some revision and updating to make it more precise.

In addition to identifying and analyzing capitalism's drive to expropriate, cut costs, and "free-ride," discussed so far, in my view it is also necessary to identify at least two other inherent tendencies that characterize the ways in which capitalism today absorbs both natural resources and women's reproductive labor into its value circuits: *the commodification of nature as nature* and *the real subsumption of nature.* At times these mechanisms strengthen and reinforce each other, but at times they work at cross-purposes.

My contention is that identifying these additional mechanisms should be seen as a response to the shifts that have taken place in capitalism in recent decades. As many theorists argue, capitalism today is more fluid and flexible than the Eurocentric capitalism that led to the colonialism of the eighteenth and nineteenth centuries (Nanda 1997, 366). I want to underscore two developments in particular: the rise of neoliberalism as the dominant economic paradigm, and the spectacular development of biotechnology and its extensive commercialization.

The Commodification of Nature as Nature

According to eco-Marxist thinkers such as Mies, the key problem with capitalism's expropriation of nature (including women's reproductive capacities) is free-riding: its failure to pay its bills. Nature is externalized as a costless resource that is implicitly assumed to be infinite and can therefore be expropriated without compensation. As Jason Moore writes, the "free gifts" of nature are not "low-hanging fruit" that can simply be picked, however. The idea of primitive accumulation effectively conveys how "cheap natures" are in fact produced: they are expropriated through violent and destructive processes such as slavery or open-pit mines (Moore 2015, 64).[11]

However, a particularly significant trend characterizing contemporary neoliberal capitalism is the opposite tendency: the attempt to internalize more and more activities and assets into capitalist markets. According to neoliberal economic theory, marketization is a particularly effective means of speeding up economic growth, given that GDP is measured in terms of market transactions. Hence, although we can certainly still identify significant processes of externalization operating today—the polluting of the atmosphere with excessive greenhouse gases being perhaps the most acute—we must also identify mechanisms that seek to internalize the environment more fully into capitalist markets. Whereas in the early phases of capitalism, "virgin territories" still existed for venture capitalists to discover and expropriate, such new frontiers from which to extract uncompensated value are much harder to find today. Venture capitalism has been forced to take new, more imaginative forms.

Neil Smith has put forward the powerful argument that we are currently living through a period in which our socioeconomic relationship with nature has been dramatically transformed: nature has become capitalized to an unprecedented extent. Capitalist nature has always been commodified in the sense that naturally provided use-values have been plundered for productive consumption. However, today a whole new range of "ecological commodities" has been produced. Smith writes: "Whereas the traditional commodification of nature generally involved harvesting use values as raw materials for capitalist production—wood for tables, oil for energy, iron ore for steel, various corns for bread—this new generation of commodities is different" (Smith 2007, 2). The new ecological commodities, such as carbon or pollution credits, paradoxically commodify nature as nature, as something that is produced as external to capitalist expropriation, but then internalized into the capitalist economy by giving it exchange value. The value of the commodity produced—for example, an area of rainforest that offsets a certain amount of carbon produced by air travel—rests precisely on the fact that it cannot be productively consumed. "Landowners possessing tracts of forest land (generally in poorer tropical countries) are paid not to cut their forests, while major polluters in more industrial parts of the world can purchase these credits as a means to allow them to continue to pollute" (19).

Hence, we can identify a twin movement: capital externalizes costs—for example, by emitting pollution—which provides opportunities for capital accumulation through mechanisms of internalization by other firms (or sometimes even the same firms) in the form of pollution trading, for example. Capitalism's appropriation of the environment thus uses mechanisms of both internalization and externalization relatively flexibly—depending on the social and political context—in order to maximize profits and to fuel economic growth. Neither set of mechanisms is unproblematic from an ecological perspective. Capitalism's free-riding on nature is obviously problematic, but the attempt to protect the environment by turning it into an internal part of capitalist markets has serious problems too.

First, from the perspective of economics, it is difficult to fully internalize the externalities produced by the environment within a self-regulating market system. The environment is not produced like other commodities; it is a complex, integrated whole which ultimately includes the whole biosphere. As John Bellamy Foster explains, in order to internalize the environment within the market system, complex ecosystems have to first be broken up into distinct goods and services, such as air quality, a specific species of plant or animal, or the maintenance of global temperature, for example. These specific parts are then imputed prices through the construction of supply and demand curves. The process of pricing is also fraught with difficulty, however. In hedonic pricing, consumer preferences are established through the demand for goods and services that are closely associated with a given environmental product. In the contingent valuation method, hypothetical markets are constructed, and consumers are asked to indicate their preferences through surveys. Using these survey responses, economists then aggregate the results across the entire population in order to construct demand curves for the hypothetical environmental commodities. Finally, market mechanisms and policy instruments are created in order to either change prices in existing markets or to create new markets. Due to the difficulties in all these stages, markets in environmental protection have not functioned very well, even in their own terms, as markets (Foster 2002, 27–28).

From a philosophical perspective, the problems with the mechanisms of internalization are perhaps even more serious. As the philosopher Michael Sandel argues, markets do more than allocate goods and services; they also importantly express and promote meanings, values, and attitudes toward the goods and services that are exchanged. Through mechanisms of internalization, the environment becomes a set of distinct, market-based utilities, the value of which is determined by the egoistic consumer preferences of human individuals. Hence, the philosophical problem is not just that it is technically difficult to establish correct prices through survey methods, for example, and consequently to protect aspects of the environment that have not been assigned proper economic value. The problem is more fundamentally that such methods cannot compute values that are incommensurable with money (Sandel 2012).

I will give an example from my native country, Finland, where the government intends to meet the EU's energy and climate targets with significant investments in bioenergy. Critics of this strategy have pointed out that because the strategy relies on extensive logging, it will in fact end up making climate change worse by diminishing the capacity of the existing forests to act as carbon sinks. In the ensuing debate, a recurring argument in favor of the government's strategy has been that it is possible to increase logging without diminishing carbon sinks by cutting old-growth forests and then replacing them with younger, faster-growing forests, which are managed through intensive cultivation systems, and which will function more effectively as carbon sinks. Irrespective of whether this claim is true or not, what the example should make clear is that such a framework focusing solely on carbon trading cannot recognize any value in the fact that forests are old and ecologically diverse. Their destruction is not caused by their exclusion from the market mechanisms intended to protect the environment, but rather by their inclusion in them.[12]

When we recognize that the environment and women's reproductive labor have functionally analogous positions in the logic of capitalist accumulation, we can identify a parallel shift in neoliberal capitalism's relationship to women's reproductive labor. It corresponds to the recent attempts to commodify the private realm and to turn women into wage laborers. The rapid neoliberalization of our economies in recent decades has resulted in significant changes in women's traditional role as care providers in the home. We have seen the increasing transformation of the affective and care activities that women used to perform at home into paid services, whether in child care, domestic help, or health services. In other words, today the reproductive labor of women is not so much externalized from the commodity markets into the private realm and then expropriated for free; it is increasingly internalized into the capitalist markets and exploited as wage labor. This has resulted in new forms of gender oppression, as it is often poor, immigrant women from ethnic minorities who now end up providing the commodified care services. The so-called "global care chains" and the growth in the trafficking of women have become some of the gendered effects of this development.[13]

The emergence of this feminized service economy is also inherently connected to the current "crisis of care": the lack of sufficient numbers of qualified care-workers who actually care. Feminist economists in particular have shown how, similar to the case of the environment, care work creates important positive externalities that cannot be fully captured in market transactions. It therefore exposes some of the limits of commodification from an economic perspective. As economists such as Nancy Folbre and Julie A. Nelson explain, many people share in the benefits when children are brought up to be responsible, skilled, and loving adults. Employers benefit from skilled and cooperative workers, the elderly benefit if a skilled younger generation of workers generates high taxes and cares for them, and so on (Folbre and Nelson 2000). The problem is that these gains cannot be captured fully by those who created them. Parents, for example, cannot demand a fee from the employers who hire their adult children. This means that, similar to other externalities, those created by care produce an incentive to free-ride, to let others pay the costs. Folbre and Nelson conclude that markets alone cannot solve the current crisis of care: "in the absence of collective coordination less than optimal amounts of care will be provided, because the care providers are not fully compensated for the social value of their services . . . There are limits to the substitutability between family and market provision, limits that our society needs to discuss, define and enforce" (137).

In sum, we can identify two opposing ways to connect capitalist economic logic to the gender division of labor—capitalism wants women to both work and to stay at home—and we can find examples of both incentives today. Capitalism externalizes the costs of reproductive labor by expecting women to take care of their homes for free, as well as internalizing them by creating new markets for care work. Again, similar to the environment, neither option is unproblematic. When reproductive work is not commodified, we have the free-riding problem; when it is turned into paid services, we face the crisis of care. As I will argue in the conclusion, this suggests that merely attacking neoliberalism in favor of more social democratic forms of capitalism is not going to solve the problems of gender oppression or environmental devastation in capitalism. The political and economic transformations required must be more radical and contest the core logic of capitalism itself.

The Real Subsumption of Nature

In addition to the mechanisms of internalization prominent in neoliberal capitalism, I contend that the mechanisms of expropriation—the free-riding on nature—have to be complemented with another distinct set of mechanisms for the capitalization of nature. These mechanisms aim to manipulate and intensify biological productivity itself by rendering (biologically based) natural assets more profitable or malleable for commercial exploitation. Such mechanisms are theorized in an illuminating way as *the real subsumption of nature* in an influential article by William Boyd, Scott Prudham, and Rachel Schurman (2001). Inspired by Marx's notions of formal and real subsumption of labor, Boyd and his colleagues formulate the concepts of the *formal and real subsumption of nature* in order to distinguish between two different ways in which capitalism appropriates nature.[14]

The formal subsumption of nature corresponds roughly to the mechanisms of expropriation or primitive accumulation discussed above in connection with Mies's work. Under the formal subsumption of nature, capitalist enterprises attempt to gain access to or control over natural resources, but they are "unable to control, intensify, manipulate, or otherwise 'improve' upon nature to suit their purposes" (Boyd, Prudham, and Schurman 2001, 562). Capital operates with a logic of extraction and confronts the natural world as a given set of biophysical processes and material characteristics: examples include the logging of forests, the mining of ore, the trolling of fish and so on. Despite its obvious benefits, such an approach to appropriating natural resources also generally implies obstacles to accumulation, because companies must adjust their production strategies to address the exigencies of nature. The dependence on natural production schedules, for example, can pose serious challenges to the continuous deployment of labor and machinery. This is why developing mechanisms for the real subsumption of nature becomes essential.

The real subsumption of nature refers to strategies by which capital seeks to intentionally alter biophysical processes in order to overcome obstacles in production, gain competitive advantage, and increase profitability. The logic of extraction is replaced by a logic that seeks to enhance biological productivity itself. "The desired result . . . is higher yields, shorter turnover times, improved disease resistance, etc. Nature, in short, is (re)made to work harder, faster, and better" (Boyd, Prudham, and Schurman 2001, 564).

A helpful illustration of the difference between the formal and real subsumption of nature can be found again in the forestry industry. Whereas early capitalism was characterized by the extensive logging of old-growth forests and the ensuing deforestation, as the example of Finland shows, today firms and state agencies aim to intervene in the biological basis of forest growth. "Instead of confronting trees as 'ready-made' objects, the logic of plantation forestry involves ongoing intervention in and alteration of tree growth processes" (Boyd, Prudham, and Schurman 2001, 566). The forestry industry involves no longer just felling trees and extracting the timber, but the use of chemical fertilizers and pesticides, intensive nursery operations for seedling cultivation, and the manual and mechanical planting of trees, as well as attempts to directly manipulate genetic material (566).

Although the real subsumption of nature by capital is nothing new, the rapid development of biotechnology has provided unparalleled means for its expansion and intensification. In today's biocapitalism, biotechnology is understood to be the key for solving the challenges obstructing capitalist accumulation, such as climate change, the end of cheap energy supplies, and an aging population. Whereas in the case of formal subsumption, profitability could be enhanced simply by establishing property rights over natural resources, the real subsumption of nature necessitates the privatization and commodification of biotechnological knowledge rather than of nature itself (Boyd, Prudham, and Schurman 2001, 564). Complex bioscientific knowledge and technological expertise are required today for the intensification of natural resource productivity.[15]

If we again turn to investigate the parallel developments in the capitalization of women's reproductive labor, what does the real subsumption of nature correspond with there? I want to suggest that the emergence of assisted reproductive technologies (ARTs) has transformed the opportunities for the exploitation of women's reproductive labor due to the ability of these technologies to radically alter the biological processes of human reproduction. Women's biologically reproductive labor has of course never taken place completely outside of capitalist circuits of valorization. The practice of slave-breeding, for example, was employed explicitly as a means of expanding the slave-owners' wealth and labor force.[16] However, today with ARTs, the biophysical processes of human reproduction can be altered in ways that have made possible the creation of a new kind of global fertility market. It is difficult to provide accurate accounts of its size, but even by careful estimates it is significant. Some estimates put the size of the global market for commercial transnational surrogacy alone at six billion dollars annually worldwide (Smerdon 2008, quoted in Mohapatra 2014, 147).

ARTs have radically altered the process of human reproduction by completely disengaging reproduction from sex and genetic motherhood from pregnancy. Heterosexual intercourse is no longer necessary for biological reproduction because in-vitro fertilization and intrauterine insemination can lead to conception. The commercialization of these technologies means that if the intended parents are unable to conceive on their own, they can purchase sperm and eggs through intermediaries who control market access to these gametes. Either the intended mother's or donor eggs are fertilized with either the intended father's sperm or donor sperm. If the genetic mother is unable to carry a fetus to full term, it is possible to implant the embryo into the womb of a surrogate mother who will then gestate the fetus to full term. This process is again biotechnologically mediated and increasingly organized through market intermediaries. Commercial clinics will screen and hire the surrogates and prepare their uterine lining for the embryo transfer. This preparation involves lengthy medical procedures and complex drug regimes.[17]

The bodies and reproductive capacities of the women acting as surrogates are thus capitalistically appropriated, but not simply as external natural resources. Rather, gestational surrogacy can be viewed analogously to the real subsumption of nature by capital: capital is able to take hold of and transform biological reproduction and use it as a source for the creation of new markets and of new forms of capital accumulation. The bodies of the surrogates are effectively utilized as exploitable nature and turned into essential components in a sophisticated biotechnological process, as well as integrated into capitalist circuits of valorization. Unlike the reproductive labor of most women, the surrogates' reproductive labor is completely commodified. I will discuss commercial gestational surrogacy and its feminist critiques in more detail in chapter 3. I will also return to the question of racialized expropriation and its intertwinement with gender there.

Feminism and Environmental Politics

Feminism can develop its critical perspective today only in the context of global capitalism. The new contours of the relationship between life and politics are intimately tied to the expansion of capitalist accumulation: it is impossible to understand the root causes of the environmental crisis today without a critical analysis of global capitalism, just as it is impossible to understand the rapid development of the life sciences and their application in biotechnologies outside the framework of biocapitalism. Feminist theory cannot operate with static or totalizing notions of capitalism, however. The analysis of capitalism has to be complex enough to be able to distinguish among different, sometimes contradictory mechanisms that are nevertheless compatible with the underlying logic of capitalist accumulation. By distinguishing between the mechanism of externalization and internalization as well as the formal and real subsumption of nature, my aim is to provide a theoretically more nuanced account on the functional analogues between capitalism's appropriation of women's reproductive labor and the productions of nature. My main motive here is essentially political, not theoretical, however. Recognizing the dynamic and contradictory nature of capitalism is politically important because it implies that although some of these mechanisms might appear, in the short term, to be undeniably good for women, the environment, and developing countries, this does not invalidate the fundamental importance of a feminist critique of capitalism.

It should also be evident now why a political alliance between feminism and environmentalism is not just an instance of affinity politics in which separate political goals might, on occasion, be shared. Rather, my key claim is that feminists and environmentalists share a common political goal in their resistance against capitalism. First, they both share the urgent project of questioning how the line between the processes of market internalization and externalization that I have described above is politically negotiated. As the example of commercial surrogacy makes clear, a key political issue today is whether different processes of biological life or "nature" are brought within the domain of the markets or whether their appropriate place is considered to be outside of that domain. This has direct consequences for pressing political questions concerning equal access and democratic political control over such processes, but it is also fundamental for the assignment of their moral meaning and value. Just because something can be bio-technically produced, for example, does not mean that it should be sold. Negotiating the limits of commodification is essentially a political project that requires placing limits on the markets on ethical and philosophical grounds.

Second, the real subsumption of nature introduces thorny political questions about risks, rights, and responsibilities. The problem embedded in the real subsumption of nature, including the application of the new biotechnologies, is that such technologies contain unprecedented risks as well as unpredictable environmental and medical outcomes.

These risks may include the potential escape and proliferation of novel life forms such as superweeds and virulent strains of viruses and bacteria, or they may materialize as the medical complications resulting from the hyperstimulation of ovaries with hormone shots or the mandatory caesarean delivery of babies. Such serious, life-threatening risks must inevitably raise vexing political questions over who should shoulder these risks and provide compensation when things go wrong. Again, this issue implies a pressing need for political struggles that bring together feminism and environmentalism against biocapitalism.

Third, these two issues—the limits of commodification and the risks in the biophysical manipulation of nature—must open into a still broader and deeper political question. If my analysis is correct, then both feminism and environmentalism should have an interest in challenging the whole economic system that is incapable of recognizing the value of "externalities." Despite the important development of feminist and environmental economics, these fields of inquiry make apparent their own limits: the environment and women's reproductive labor are attributed values that are incommensurable with money and therefore cannot be fully monetized and internalized in the circuits of a capitalist market economy.[18] This means that they continue to be undervalued and depredated in the capitalist system of commodity exchange. The absurdity of trying to monetize the unmeasurable becomes obvious once we ask ourselves questions such as what the economic value of the planet is or what you would be prepared to pay for the life of your child. Feminist ecopolitics must thus begin from the recognition that we need an economic system in which values other than profit, consumer preferences, and economic growth have a chance to come to the fore.

2

Ecofeminism at the End of Nature

While a revival of ecofeminism seems politically highly relevant, or even urgent, it could be objected that theoretically it is outdated. If ecofeminism is understood as an attempt to critically assess the connections between the oppression of women and the expropriation of nature, then it seems that neither one of the categories, women or nature, exists any longer. With the rise of post-structuralist modes of thinking in the 1990s, the category of "women" came under heightened critique. Gender turned out to be a historically contingent and resignifiable fiction arduously maintained by an ongoing performance. And now it seems that nature has come to an end too: several "post-naturalist" environmental thinkers have recently argued that the distinction between the human and the natural realms has either collapsed or become meaningless. Jedediah Purdy, for example, argues in his book *After Nature* that we live in a new era, the Anthropocene, which "finds its most radical expression in our acknowledgement that the familiar divide between people and the natural world is no longer useful or accurate" (2015, 2).[1] Similarly, the environmental philosopher Tim Morton (2010, 55) exhorts us to "give up Nature," and Steven Vogel announces that we now live in a "post-natural" world (2015, 26).

By proclaiming the end of nature, these thinkers are making an ontological claim (either descriptive or prescriptive), yet the concern that usually animates such pronouncements is not ontology as such, but rather the political and ethical consequences that are understood to follow from it. The core idea of "post-natural" environmental theory is that faulty metaphysical reasoning is at the root of our ethical and political complacency, which enables humans to remake and destroy the nonhuman world. Simon P. James sums up this form of reasoning in environmental philosophy in the following way:

> The misguided metaphysical notion that human beings and their works
> are separated by an ontological gulf from natural things encourages
> the misguided thought that the former are in some sense superior to the

latter, which, in turn, lends support to the notion that we human beings are morally entitled to use "merely" natural things in any way we see fit . . . There is, in short, a clear line of implication leading from (a) the seemingly innocuous contrast between nature and human to (b) metaphysical dualism to (c) anthropocentric ethics to (d) the real-world devastation of the earth. (James 2015, 114)

My aim in this chapter is to challenge such reasoning. Although the idea that humans are part of nature seems obvious, and is intuitively appealing for ecofeminist critiques, I will question the ontological premises of post-natural environmental theory as a viable foundation for feminist critiques of capitalism. I will also repudiate their assumed political and ethical consequences, namely the idea that eradicating the nature/human dualism would necessarily lead to environmentally more progressive, non-anthropocentric ethics and politics.

The overcoming of the nature/human dualism seems fundamentally compatible with the different forms of materialism that Marxist theory either implicitly or explicitly expounds. Marxist thinkers have understood and theorized the metaphysical underpinnings of the theory in different ways—dialectical materialism, scientific materialism, historical materialism. Marxism, as a philosophical position, is nevertheless unequivocally understood to be a form of naturalism: humans are natural beings in an evolving, organic relationship with the rest of nature, which is knowable according to natural laws. I will therefore begin with a critical discussion of two recent and seminal attempts in socialist environmental theory to argue for the end of nature from a naturalist metaphysical framework: Jason Moore's influential book *Capitalism in the Web of Life* and Steven Vogel's book *Thinking like a Mall: Environmental Philosophy after the End of Nature*. Through a critical analysis of Moore's and Vogel's positions in the first section, my aim is to tease out the problematic political consequences that the theoretical erasure of the nature/human distinction has for environmental theory, and more specifically, for ecofeminist critiques of capitalism.

In the second section, I will advocate what I call ecopolitical, as opposed to biopolitical, feminist theory, which attempts to *politicize*, rather than eradicate, the boundary between the natural and the human realms. My account builds theoretically on Michel Foucault's and Giorgio Agamben's critiques of biopolitics. The term "biopolitical" has become ubiquitous in academic discussions and is often used very loosely to refer to any political issue that is somehow connected with biological processes or life sciences. I use it here in a specific philosophical sense, however, to refer to explicit attempts to eradicate the traditional ontological boundary between politics and biological life. Foucault and Agamben have, in different ways, argued that the defining feature of the Western tradition of political thought since antiquity has been the separation of a political way of life from mere biological life. What characterizes modernity, however, is the rise of biopolitics: the biological processes characterizing human life as a species have become the key issues for politics.[2]

I will also ask what the politicization of the boundary between the natural and the human realms might mean in practice. My contention is that it must inevitably lead us not only to critical questions about the naturalization and animalization of women and racialized people, but extend to our treatment of nonhuman animals and the environment. In sum, my aim in this chapter is to explicate the politicized ontological framework, derived from post-structuralist philosophy, that effective feminist and environmental critiques of capitalism should adopt and build on.

Post-Natural Environmental Theory: Capitalist Natures

Jason Moore argues for the eradication of the nature/human distinction in his influential book *Capitalism in the Web of Life*. His key contention is that any truly critical investigation of capitalism today must be conducted in a post-Cartesian ontological framework that shuns such dualisms as mind and body, human and animal, and nature and culture. Only such a philosophical framework enables us to recognize that capital's appropriation of unpaid work "transcends the Cartesian divide, encompassing both human and extra-human work outside, but necessary to the circuit of capital and the production of value" (Moore 2015, 55).

Moore uses the expression "work/energy" to denote the ontological inseparability of human labor and nonhuman energy in the processes of capitalist accumulation. His key claim is that capitalism depends on a repertoire of strategies for appropriating this unpaid work/energy of humans and the rest of nature outside the commodity system (Moore 2015, 54). Without these massive streams of unpaid work/energy the cost of production would rise, and capitalist accumulation would slow down considerably. In other words, the massive contributions of unpaid work necessary for the capitalist mode of production are required from certain groups of humans, particularly women, but also from nonhuman animals and the biosphere more generally.

Even though Moore does not explicitly identify himself as an ecofeminist, his book is clearly indebted to the work of Marxist ecofeminists such as Maria Mies discussed in the previous chapter. Like Mies, Moore too foregrounds the idea of ongoing primitive accumulation, understood as a continuous process of expropriation, and emphasizes that "the logic of capital owes its success as much to the extension of appropriation as it does to the capitalization of production . . . the dialectic of productivity and plunder" (Moore 2015, 292). However, instead of identifying two functionally analogous sources of wealth additional to the mechanisms of exploitation—nature and women's reproductive labor—Moore argues for these two sources' ontological inseparability from each other. For him, the connection between human labor power and extra-human work is not just functionally analogous, but "intimate, dialectical, immediate" (230). In other words, in contrast to the ecofeminist position outlined in the previous chapter, Moore's philosophical argument about the systemic link between gender oppression and environmental devastation in capitalism is not functional, but ontological. Moore uses human reproduction as a paradigmatic illustration of their necessary entanglement:

> Where does the social moment of raising children end, and the biological moment begin? Clearly, we are dealing with a zone of reproduction that transcends any neat and tidy separation of sociality and biology, which are better viewed as internal to each other. Neither is this zone of reproduction—the domain where unpaid work is produced for Capital— a narrowly human affair . . . it also involves the unpaid work of extra-human natures. (Moore 2015, 17)

Hence, when capitalism is viewed through Moore's post-Cartesian materialist metaphysical framework, it should become evident that social processes are inseparable from biological ones and vice versa. Capitalism channels the unpaid work of various extra-economic processes, both human and nonhuman, from outside the commodity system into the circuits of capital.

The novelty of Moore's project lies in the attempt to radically question the ontological categories on the basis of which capitalism operates rather than to accept them simply as given. However, the theoretical move of erasing the boundary between the natural and the human realms effectively also erases the question of how this boundary has been constituted and, crucially, what political functions it serves in contemporary capitalism. While Marxist-feminist analyses such as that of Mies supported a critique of the ideological naturalization of women, which has operated as an effective strategy for the legitimization of their oppression, Moore's ontological argument ends up merely reaffirming such naturalization. In Moore's framework, women, or their reproductive labor at least, is understood as inseparable from other biological or natural processes. The contribution such labor makes to capitalist valorization is naturalized and conflated with the inputs of the rest of nonhuman nature. When women's reproductive work and the work of nonhuman nature are superimposed in this way, we not only risk obfuscating the differences between them, but also—and more seriously—depoliticizing the ways in which such obfuscation has historically operated to legitimize oppressive practices.

To sum up the problem of Moore's post-natural theory from a feminist perspective: by adopting a post-Cartesian, naturalist metaphysical framework that conflates women's reproductive labor and the energy outputs of nature, Moore ends up ontologizing the historically and politically contingent subject-position of women in capitalism that feminists have attempted so radically to contest and transform. This theoretical move risks depoliticizing feminist and environmental critiques of capitalism in precisely the same way that the goddess-worshipping ecofeminists of the 1980s were accused of doing—by naturalizing women's bodies and reproductive labor.

Similar to Moore, Steven Vogel too attempts to eradicate the ontological distinction between the human and the natural realms, but the starting point of his post-natural environmental theory is the empirical fact of climate change. He contends that as a result of large-scale changes to the climate, the oceans, and the whole biosphere caused by human activity, we have now entered a new historical period in which every single region of the Earth is different than what it would "naturally" be. Human intervention has directly or indirectly affected everything in the world—from the upper atmosphere to the deep seas—so there is no longer any nature that would stand apart from the human (Vogel 2015, 2). We have literally come to the end of nature.[3]

For Vogel, this empirical fact has far-reaching metaphysical consequences—consequences that so far we have failed to adequately recognize. The end of nature should not be a cause for lament, but should help us accept that there never was a nature apart from us because humans too are part of nature. Humans are themselves natural in the trivial sense that they are "simply another organism in the world" (Vogel 2015, 65). But Vogel makes the further claim that they are also part of nature in the sense that they themselves produce "nature," "or more precisely produce their own environment" (44). Vogel turns to Marx to argue for the constitutive importance of human practices, but he reads Marx through a reductively naturalist framework: "The environment comes to be what it is through our practices, just as it comes to be what it is through the actions of beavers, honeybees, earthworms, trees and all the other organisms that make up the world" (65). Hence, the constructed environment that the human animal produces is no less "natural" than the dams that beavers build. That constructed environment is our "nature," and we are essentially just technologically advanced beavers.

In questioning the ontological distinction between the natural environment of animals and the socially constructed environment of humans, Vogel takes up the provocative example of a shopping mall and asks why the destruction of a mall should be any less objectionable than the destruction of a natural environment, such as a forest. According to him, it is impossible to ontologically define the criteria that would set a mall apart from a natural ecosystem. He goes to great lengths to show how a mall possesses "a similar sort of complexity and teleology as a butterfly" and "might be said to possess something like interests and a good" (Vogel 2015, 158). While this counterintuitive argument is a logical consequence of his ontological position, which refuses to distinguish human products from the products of nature, it leads him to a problematic naturalization of capitalism. Vogel is now in fact asking us to view a mall—a specific instantiation of capitalism—as the natural ecosystem of humans.[4] When historically contingent economic and political organizations like malls are subsumed under the same ontological categories as biological ecosystems of nonhuman animals such as beavers, we seem to lose the theoretical footing from which to pursue political critiques of capitalism. Such critiques must necessarily build on the ontological denaturalization of the status quo, and on the assumption of the radical contingency of the human social realm, in order to show that alternatives to capitalism are not only desirable, but also possible.

Arguing that humans are just another type of organism in the world and that only natural as opposed to supernatural laws and forces operate in it is not a new or radical "post-natural" metaphysical view—it is an old philosophical view commonly called metaphysical naturalism. When naturalism is understood as a rejection of supernatural explanations, we are hard-pressed to find philosophers in the contemporary world who would reject it. Instead, contemporary philosophical debates in moral philosophy and phenomenology, for example, center on the questions of how to account for things such as moral values and duties, normative orders, and ultimately human consciousness itself in a naturalistic framework.[5] For my argument here, however, a key issue is our understanding of politics. Most of us, including Vogel, believe politics to be a realm in which we do not make decisions based on biological instincts but, ideally, on values and moral arguments; a realm where human life has no predetermined aims, but humans are able to choose their goals and give different meanings to their lives; and where numerous alternative social norms, political practices, and creative experiments are possible. These are essentially metaphysical beliefs about politics, however, and not empirical facts.

Despite all the criticism of human exceptionalism and the faulty dualistic metaphysics on which it relies, when it comes to formulating the political consequences of his "post-natural environmental theory," Vogel, tellingly, starts to backpedal. In the last chapters of his book, which deal explicitly with politics, he no longer shies away from identifying specific characteristics that distinguish humans from the rest of the species and which, importantly, justify the exclusion of nonhuman animals from the political realm. Vogel's position is strikingly Aristotelian when he writes: "Among these characteristics is language use, first of all, as well as what might be called the realm of politics" (Vogel 2015, 170).[6] For Vogel, defending such human exceptionalism is not a contradiction in his avowed non-anthropocentric theory because his claims about human beings are, supposedly, not metaphysical, but empirical: they are "contingent facts of the world" which could, in principle, change (195). He thus excuses himself from the charge of contradicting himself with the caveat that he is not guilty of "metaphysically based anthropocentrism" (195).

While we could perhaps charitably accept that Vogel's understanding of human beings is empirically derived from observing adult, able-bodied humans, his understanding of politics is clearly not so derived; it is metaphysical, idealistic, and/or definitional. He defines politics as a realm of discursive deliberation, where "individuals who know themselves to be members of a community decide together, in language, what behaviors they wish to engage in as a community" (Vogel 2015, 225). The argument for excluding nonhuman animals from the political realm rests on the assumption that politics is, by definition, a realm of discursive deliberation, and therefore only beings capable of such behavior are included. The political outcome of Vogel's "non-anthropocentric" theory is, ironically, that nonhuman animals are simply and arbitrarily excluded from the political realm.

To sum up this section: when "post-naturalists" such as Moore and Vogel argue that it is impossible to distinguish between the natural and the human realms, they are treating these categories as if they were faulty idealizations, and the task of the true philosopher is to reveal the real, monist and materialist ontology hidden beneath them. This means that they fail to recognize the basic post-structuralist insight that all ontologies are the historical and political consequences of a specific way of life—in our case, a specifically capitalist way of life. I suggest that we therefore turn the questioning around. Instead of taking the "real" post-natural ontology as our starting point and then attempting to derive non-anthropocentric political consequences from it, we follow Foucault and Agamben in asking how the boundaries between the ontological categories themselves, such as the human and the natural world, are drawn in political, social, and economic practices in particular historical circumstances. This makes it possible to pose the question that must follow, namely, how feminist and environmental politics might be able to contribute to the task of redrawing those boundaries in a different way.

Feminist Ecopolitics

Feminism's relationship to the naturalist claim that humans are just another animal species is much more complicated than that of environmentalism because traditionally feminists have had to fight hard against the naturalization and animalization of women. Feminist thinkers have contended that anthropocentrism should perhaps more properly be termed "androcentrism," since women and racialized people have been historically excluded from the human side of the distinction and firmly associated with nature.[7] This historical and cultural association between women and nature is politically significant because it has provided an important justification for patriarchal domination: the naturalization and animalization of a group effectively functions as an ideological requisite for its ensuing oppression. Such an association is not merely historical and conceptual, but also continues to structure and reinforce a range of oppressive behaviors, policies, and institutions. As I argued in the previous chapter, Marxist-feminist work on social reproduction effectively shows how such an association organizes capitalist societies, their institutions, social practices, and divisions of labor. While capitalism fundamentally relies on women's reproductive labor to reproduce a stable workforce, this labor has been, for the most part, naturalized and allocated to the private sector. *Homo economicus*, the economic man of capitalist societies, is traditionally understood as a rational, self-interested utility maximizer, whose bodily needs and vulnerabilities are confined and cared for in the feminized and naturalized private sphere.

The distinction between nature and human, or biological and political, also importantly defines our understanding of the political sphere and its exclusions and practices of violence in modern liberal democracies. Michel Foucault significantly introduces biopolitics in the first volume of *The History of Sexuality* as the overturning of the ancient categories of biological and political existence that have fundamentally organized Western political thought: "For millennia, man remained what he was for Aristotle: a living animal with the additional capacity for a political existence;

modern man is an animal whose politics places his existence as a living being into question" (Foucault [1976] 1978, 143). In other words, the defining feature of the Western tradition of political thought since antiquity has been the ontological separation of the political from the biological. What characterizes modernity, in contrast, is the erosion of the boundary that separates a political community from its biological existence. "What might be called a society's 'threshold of modernity' has been reached when the life of the species is wagered on its own political existence" (143).

Hence, Foucault's key idea is that our society crossed a historical threshold when the biological processes characterizing the life of human beings as a species became a crucial issue for political decision-making. We are no longer governed only as political subjects of law but as living beings who form a population with its specific natality rate, mortality rate, average life expectancy, and so on. The protection and enhancement of human life have become the overriding aims of modern politics.[8] Modern capitalist societies are thus essentially biopolitical in terms of their political organization and rationality: the injustices, violences, and environmental emergencies that fundamentally structure them are legitimized as the price we must pay for the health, longevity, and material well-being of the human population.

Giorgio Agamben's analysis of the relationship between political power and biological life in his influential book *Homo Sacer: Sovereign Power and Bare Life* ([1995] 1998) builds on the key ideas of Foucault, but the way he appropriates them for his own theory is highly original and challenging. Agamben too emphasizes that the defining feature of the Western tradition of political thought has been the separation of a political way of life from mere biological survival, but his focus is on the ways that this distinction has historically enabled and legitimized forms of violence and exclusion. Agamben acknowledges that politics has been, since the time of Aristotle, explicitly separated from natural life. The ancient distinction between *zoe* and *bios*, natural life and political life, grounded the idea that politics was concerned with something more than just the perpetuation of biological life. Politics was fundamentally defined by such specifically human characteristics as justice, morality, language, and self-reflexivity. According to Agamben, the distinction between natural life and political life was always an unstable distinction, however, because of the exclusion of what he terms "bare life"—the forms of life that in one way or another fail to measure up to what is understood as truly human life. For Agamben, this exclusion of bare life from the political sphere must be understood as the very act that establishes a community as political (Agamben [1995] 1998, 8).

Hence, instead of defining the political with the idea of a good life—

the form of life proper to human community—Agamben focuses on the other side of this fundamental dichotomy: on exemplary sites in which human life is in different ways reduced to bare life, to the simple fact of living common to all living beings, such as the detainees of refugee camps, brain-dead patients in hospital wards, and inmates on death row. He wants to show that our conception of the political is not fundamentally constituted by the idea of a community inclusive of beings capable of morality, self-reflexivity, and speech, but by the exclusion of life that is deemed unworthy of politics.

My aim here is not a comprehensive analysis of Foucault's or Agamben's critiques of biopolitics. I merely want to appropriate their key insights for my argument against post-natural environmental philosophy. To be clear, Foucault and Agamben are not defending any essential ontological differences between nature and politics, human and nonhuman animals, good life and biological life. Rather, their historical ontologies are attempts to show how these categories are historically constituted but have nevertheless fundamentally organized our thought, way of life, and practices of politics. I take their key contribution for my questioning to be that in order to advocate for radically new, non-anthropocentric forms of politics, we have to be able to understand the force and history of our foundational ontological categories: how they have emerged as a result of specific historical practices of power/knowledge and how they continue to be instrumental in establishing the forms of exclusion on which our current conception of politics is built. This insight will then entail the need to politicize our understanding of nature as that which is excluded from the political sphere, as well as to recognize that the way we draw the ontological boundary between nature and politics, and human and animal, is itself a political act burdened with a violent history.

As Agamben's work persuasively shows, whatever is associated with nature or mere biological life is understood not only as socially inferior, but as incapable of proper political behavior and therefore as not belonging to the realm of politics with its concomitant rights and representation. It is important to recognize that the naturalization of women and racialized people, for example, has not only historically justified their social inferiority and a specific division of labor, but has also been an effective means for their political exclusion. As I showed with the example of Moore's theory, from the perspective of ecofeminist philosophy, the post-naturalist eradication of the nature-human distinction thus appears as an inadvertent disavowal of such exclusion because it makes it impossible to expose and critically contest the political effects of the naturalization and animalization of women.

At one time, those excluded from the political sphere included groups such as women, slaves, and colonized peoples, and the idea that they should be granted any kinds of political rights sounded ridiculous to many. Today, the categories of exclusion have shifted and consist of people such as undocumented refugees and immigrants, for example. A large category of exclusion that persists is nonhuman animals. The fact that most people consider the notion that nonhuman animals should be included in the political community to be completely outlandish, only further demonstrates how deep the ontological division between nature and politics runs in our thinking. However, instead of simply accepting the idea underlying most democratic theory—propounded above by Vogel, for example—that modern democracies are essentially discursive communities, I suggest that we pose searching questions about their current boundaries and the practices of violence that are used to police them. As Ned Hettinger points out, modern democracy is

> a political procedure that arrogates all power, authority, and legitimacy to one out of millions of species. It is a system that legitimizes decision-making authority by reference to a set of abilities—namely consent, voting, delegation—that non-humans are constitutionally unable to manifest. The vast majority of the interests, goods, and values that should count according to non-anthropocentric moral theory have no guaranteed standing in democratic procedure. Democracy allows individual humans to set aside their own interests and cast their votes for non-human interests and values. But this merely highlights the injustice of a system that prohibits non-humans from counting politically in their own right. (Hettinger 2001, 505)

Some environmental political theorists have made important suggestions on how we could rethink democracy in order to incorporate nonhuman nature in it. These include suggestions to appoint legal guardians who would carry out fiduciary responsibilities toward nonhuman beneficiaries and vote on their behalf, as well as establishing the legally enforceable rights of nonhuman nature. The environmental political theorist Robyn Eckersley, for example, asks if it is possible, in principle, to incorporate the interests of the nonhuman community into the ground rules of democracy and suggests that this could be done through the discourse on rights. She notes that the language of rights has traditionally been used as a means of translating complex moral ideas about intrinsic value into ordinary political language and legislation. "Political struggles for further 'democratisation' and liberation have often involved struggles for political recognition and *inclusion* through the extension of rights" (Eckersley 1995, 177).

Eckersley discusses the seminal work of Christopher Stone, who had already argued in 1974 that extending legal rights to natural entities was not unthinkable when legal rights were already conferred on non-speaking persons such as infants and fetuses, legal fictions such as corporations, municipalities, and trusts, and entities such as churches and nation-states. Given that there was no common thread or principle running through these right holders, Stone contended that there was no good reason for not extending legal rights to natural entities as well. Arguing explicitly against the Aristotelian view propounded by Vogel, for example, that democracies are inherently discursive communities, he writes: "It is no answer to say that streams and forests cannot have standing because streams and forests cannot speak. Corporations cannot speak, either; nor can states, estates, infants, incompetents, municipalities, or universities. Lawyers speak for them, as they customarily do for the ordinary citizen with legal problems" (Stone [1974] 2010, 8).

Stone was clearly ahead of his time; nearly fifty years after his book was published, several countries such as Ecuador, Bolivia, India, and New Zealand have now introduced the rights of nature in their constitutions or secondary legislation. As Stefan Knauss (2018, 713) writes, the idea of the rights of nature, once considered utopian, has now become reality in the sense that rights of nature are de facto accepted by ordinary institutions of modern nation-states. Ecuador was the first modern nation-state to adopt nature as a subject of rights in its new constitution of 2008, a constitution that is often singled out as the most progressive constitution in the world, not only for its recognition of the rights of nature, but also for the substantial rights it grants to Indigenous peoples.[9] According to most commentators, however, the actual transformations effected by these legal reforms have so far been partial and uneven. In Ecuador, for example, significant tensions and contradictions exist between ethno-environmental concerns and progressive welfare politics. In 2008, when the new constitution was instituted, oil and mining comprised the largest sector (26.8 percent) of Ecuador's GDP, while almost half of its population lived below the poverty line. In other words, any critical assessment of the actual efficacy of Ecuador's new constitution needs to underscore the fact that there is a fundamental conflict between the powerful economic constraints characterizing capitalism and any legal protections granted to the environment. As Mary Elizabeth Whittenmore (2011, 663) writes, this basic conflict "begs the question of whether nature can truly have rights in a country whose economy survives on nature's exploitation."

In traditional Marxist analyses, legal reforms are often dismissed as "superstructural" for this very reason, and they are therefore treated as secondary to the restructuring of the economic relations of production.

In terms of solving the environmental crisis, however, it seems clear that both legal and economic restructuring are required, and furthermore, they must presuppose one another. Legal reform is, and has been, an important means of economic restructuring, particularly in historical situations such as the one we face today, in which questions about the private ownership of natural assets have become critical. It is also important to recognize that the legal reforms in Ecuador have not been purely symbolic either. Although it might still be too early to draw final conclusions, after a decade, individuals, organizations, and state institutions have successfully applied Ecuador's new constitution, and Ecuadorian courts have produced actual jurisprudence demonstrating that natural rights are of practical application.[10]

I am also aware that the rights discourse has been subjected to extensive philosophical critique from feminist, Indigenous, and ecological perspectives. Critics have pointed out, for example, that the rights discourse buries the important insight that the well-being of individuals is always ineradicably linked with the well-being of the broader social and ecological communities of which they are a part. Rights discourse risks reifying a land formation such as a space, river, mountain, or other topographical feature as a static object that can be protected and preserved rather than treating it as a dynamic set of living relations that exceed any particular legal codification. Indigenous studies scholars have further pointed out that the rendering of nature as an abstract legal entity means that the legal language of the settler colonial state becomes the dominant mode of political expression, and this makes it difficult to voice opposition to it in alternative conceptual and normative frameworks. Furthermore, political projects for defending the rights of nature must appeal for legal protection to the very states that have historically dominated and dispossessed Indigenous peoples of their land.[11]

Hence, my aim is not to argue here that legal rights would provide a catch-all solution to our environmental problems. We should experiment with the extension of the rights of nature not just for economic, political, and moral reasons, but in an attempt to transform our deeply held metaphysical beliefs about humans, animals, politics, and nature. Political struggles over the rights of nature are not just about the protection of a specific natural space or entity, but should be recognized as one concrete means of politicizing the boundary between human and nature: they are struggles over the very meaning of the relationship between human societies and the broader ecological worlds they are part of. Understanding nature as a rights-bearing entity that holds value, apart from its human use, fundamentally challenges our traditional way of understanding nature as property in the capitalist vocabulary of possession.

It is important to stress here that rather than simply advocating for animal rights or rights of nature, my argument in this chapter essentially concerns metaphysics. My contention is that it is through non-anthropocentric, experimental politics—of which the attempt to extend political rights to nonhuman species, natural spaces, and ultimately the earth itself could serve as an example—that our deeply ingrained and oppressive ontological categories can be transformed.[12] For me, it is significant that Stone, for example, understands legal reform not only as a concrete means for protecting natural entities because it effectively denies landowners' right to damage or destroy ecosystems on their land with impunity, but also as a means for facilitating a general change of consciousness. Stone notes how throughout legal history each successive extension of rights to some new entity has initially been understood as unthinkable: "there will be resistance to giving the thing 'rights' until it can be seen and valued for itself; yet it is hard to see it and value it for itself until we can bring ourselves to give it 'rights'—which is almost inevitably going to sound inconceivable to a large group of people" (Stone [1974] 2010, 3). Robert Nichols (2020, 151–52) similarly contends that the Indigenous movements to (re)animate the earth with forms of personhood and subjectivity should be recognized as attempts to "decolonize the mind." The full political implications of such a move might not be visible to us yet, because these movements are essentially engaging in avant-garde practices and experimenting with something truly radical.

> It may be that the radical potential of such movements does not reside exclusively in their achieving a narrow objective (e.g., the protection of this or that mountain) but in the manner in which they challenge the broader vocabularies at work . . . These are imperfect, incomplete, and aspirational projects of collective resignification of the basic terms of political order. (Nichols 2020, 158)

Nichols also reminds us, importantly, that any politics aiming at collective resignification is going to be an open-ended, long-term project which must be firmly anchored in real-life political institutions and material, economic practices (Nichols 2020, 158). In other words, my metaphysical argument in this chapter should be read in the context of my overriding ecological critique of capitalism in this book. Its political implications should nevertheless be clear: the new ways of understanding our relationship to nature that we desperately need today must emerge from radical political practices and experiments—the hard labor of collective struggles—not from the vapid pronouncements of philosophers. The premise that ecological challenges today are so enormous that we cannot solve them without inventing a new metaphysics seems to me both triumphalist and defeatist at the same time. This idea gives philosophy too great of a standing while politics is given too little. I believe that we don't need to invent a new "post-natural" or "post-human" metaphysics; rather, what we need is a new politics.

To conclude, the environmental crisis has pushed us into a situation that is both philosophically and politically unprecedented: the relatively firm ontological boundary between the natural and the human realms definitive of modernity has become drastically unstable due to the extreme capitalist appropriation of what we are used to understanding as nature. This places ecofeminism squarely in front of new challenges. We need to problematize the nature/human distinction and recognize its instability, but this does not mean collapsing the distinction. Merging human societies into the ecosystems they are a part of does not automatically lead to any kind of emancipatory politics in terms of human beings' relations to one another or to the environment. Rather, we need to politicize, in a theoretically sophisticated way, our understanding of nature as that which is excluded from the political sphere by questioning the idea of a stable ontological boundary between them and by acknowledging that the way we draw this boundary is itself a political act. Ecopolitical feminism does not need to invent a new metaphysics to provide a better understanding of environmental problems, nature, humans, or their relationships. There is a more fundamental need to understand how all ontology—our understanding of reality—is achieved in social and political practices and networks of power rather than being simply given. Only such a politicized ontology can make it possible for us to show how naturalization and animalization have functioned, and continue to function, as effective political strategies of exclusion, and how feminist and environmental politics are imperative in countering them.

3

The Nature of Gestational Surrogacy

The pressing political problem with the rise of biocapitalism and the unprecedented growth of biotechnological industries and markets is that they have intensified the demand for new kinds of contested biological services and substances such as surrogacy, the provision and sale of body tissues, and participation in clinical trials. The providers of these services and substances are often unemployed or underemployed people drawn from the Global South.[1] This situation introduces new kinds of pressing political and ethical challenges for feminist critiques of capitalism and anticapitalist politics and requires imagining new kinds of transnational feminist projects and alliances.

In the theoretical literature on biocapitalism, commercial gestational surrogacy is often treated as a paradigm of the new forms of labor that have emerged with it.[2] I will begin by critically assessing Melinda Cooper and Catherine Waldby's version of this idea in their seminal book *Clinical Labor* (2014). This book stands out from the recent science and technology studies literature on biocapitalism in that it explicitly examines the "extensive yet unacknowledged labor force whose service consists in the visceral experience of experimental drug consumption, hormonal transformation, more or less invasive biomedical procedures, ejaculation, tissue extraction, and gestation" (Cooper and Waldby 2014, 7). According to these authors, there is now an extensive body of literature that focuses on the expert cognitive labor of scientists and the centrality of that labor to the bioeconomy. But the labor of those who provide the in vivo platform for clinical experimentation and tissue provision rarely figures in these accounts as labor. The authors' key argument is that these services should be understood and analyzed as forms of labor rather than being conceptualized and regulated within the institutionalized framework of bioethics.[3]

Cooper and Waldby's insistence that gestational surrogacy should be theorized as labor can be interpreted as continuing the tradition of Marxist feminism that demands recognition and adequate compensation for women's socially reproductive labor. Their focus on the new forms of biotechnologically assisted reproductive labor can be seen as merely an extreme case of a more general Marxist-feminist argument that women's reproductive labor has been naturalized in capitalism and therefore not recognized as value-producing labor indispensable for capitalist accumulation. The failure to recognize these reproductive practices as labor has resulted in inadequate compensation and has hidden forms of exploitation specific to women.[4]

My aim in this chapter is to show that once we submit gestational surrogacy to a rigorous Marxist-feminist analysis, it becomes difficult to understand it as a form of labor. While I acknowledge some of the political advantages in applying the labor paradigm to gestational surrogacy, in the sections below I develop a sustained critique of this paradigm by focusing on its theoretical and political shortcomings. I analyze the functional role that gestational surrogacy occupies in the dynamics of global capitalism and identify the aspects that distinguish it from other forms of waged care work.

My main concern is not the correct application of Marx or his labor theory of value, however, but rather the feminist political and ethical consequences that follow from the theoretical question of how we conceive of gestational surrogacy and how we theorize the processes of value production on which biocapitalism relies. Hence, my methodological choice of functionalist analysis does not imply that the argument amounts to abstract and politically sterile speculation with no practical consequences for feminist politics. On the contrary, my key aim is to show how different theoretical understandings of gestational surrogacy have radically different political consequences for the feminist debates surrounding it. Feminist theory does not only reflect economic or social arrangements; it also produces political reality by defining the terms available for feminist politics and activism.

My brief discussion of gestational surrogacy in India should be read against this set of methodological choices and commitments. I recognize that my information and understanding of gestational surrogacy in India is necessarily selective and limited, as well as filtered through my own culturally specific assumptions, yet I nevertheless believe that turning to a concrete case study represents my best hope for combating overtly abstract reasoning and what Chandra Talpade Mohanty (1988, 62) has called "discursive colonialism"—the idea that Western feminist analyses may have distorting and harmful effects on the lives of women in the Global South whom they are meant to represent. The aim here is not to provide a comprehensive study of gestational surrogacy in India. I draw my examples from India because it was the first country in the Global South to develop a flourishing industry in transnational commercial surrogacy. There is therefore an extensive body of important feminist research on it available.[5] Although there are always regional variations in terms of how we might understand gestational surrogacy, the particular global marketplace for gestational surrogacy in India illustrates a dense node of biocapitalism.[6]

Gestational Surrogacy as Clinical Labor

Assisted reproduction technologies have developed in tandem with globalization and have led to new global "fertility flows"—the movement of eggs, sperms, and donors between different countries. Despite the prohibitions or restrictions in many countries on surrogacy arrangements, today transnational commercial gestational surrogacy is a fast-growing aspect of "medical tourism." Infertile American and European couples wishing to have a child are increasingly traveling to countries where commercial surrogacy is legal, yet virtually unregulated and readily available for a fraction of what it costs in the United States, for example. Countries in the Global South such as India have become transnational hubs for such reproductive tourism.[7] There are varying accounts of the size of the global market for transnational surrogacy, but some estimates put this market at six billion dollars annually worldwide (Smerdon 2008, quoted in Mohapatra 2014, 147).

Since most of the surrogates in India, for example, are gestational surrogates, meaning that the gametes used in the conception are not theirs, the resulting child can be expected to look like the commissioning couple rather than the surrogate herself. The surrogate's genetic makeup thus becomes irrelevant, since she provides only her womb. This is one of the factors that have allowed the surrogacy market to go global. Affluent consumers from the Global North can "take advantage of the capacity of Indian surrogates to reproduce white children at a discount" (Cooper and Waldby 2014, 65).[8] While most of the surrogates in India never received any medical care or prenatal check-ups during the pregnancy or the delivery of their own children, their surrogate pregnancies are highly monitored, disciplined, and medicalized processes.[9]

Most feminist theorists share the view that something is ethically and politically amiss with this global fertility industry, but there are differing accounts as to why and as to the remedy for the perceived problems. At one extreme are the liberal feminists, who view surrogacy potentially as a free choice and an empowering economic opportunity.[10] Feminists at the other extreme see surrogates as victims of cruel and immoral neocolonial exploitation and underscore the serious physiological and psychological risks involved in surrogacy—risks of which the surrogates themselves are often unaware.[11] In socialist-feminist assessments of gestational surrogacy, the central idea has been that it should be considered as a form of value-producing labor.[12] The implicit, or sometimes explicit, claim behind this idea is that such a concept would not only be theoretically more accurate, but also ethically and politically more progressive.

Melinda Cooper and Catherine Waldby (2014) advance the labor paradigm in opposition to bioethical accounts that advocate viewing surrogates as altruistic donors. Cooper and Waldby understand bioethics essentially as an ideological discourse, which functions as an indispensable disciplinary instrument in the service of biotechnological capitalism (2014, 8, 14). Although the bioethical framework of donation, voluntarism, and informed consent is supposed to protect research subjects and tissue donors from market forces, Cooper and Waldby contend that these key elements of bioethical regulation have proved remarkably adaptable to the task of governing an informal clinical labor market. "In many of the cases we examine, the ethical insistence that *the biological should not be waged* only serves to facilitate atavistic (yet fully functional) forms of labor contract and desultory forms of compensation" (8). They note, for example, how reproductive contracts position the contracting parties in exceptional ways by excluding gestational surrogates and oocyte vendors from negotiations over price.

> Women who attempt to bargain on their own behalf are considered not psychologically appropriate for the task and may be excluded on those grounds. This paradox is generated by the marketing rhetoric used by brokerage companies, saturated with references to "the gift of life" and the maternal generosity of potential surrogates and oocyte providers. By imagining the transaction as a gift relation, the parties can experience the exchange in less starkly commercial and adversarial terms than those stated in the contract. Without this softening language, the spectacle of the oocyte vendor as an efficient negotiator of her reproductive capital threatens to contaminate the maternal generosity that has formed part of her market appeal. (Cooper and Waldby 2014, 56)

Cooper and Waldby's broad feminist claim would thus be that conceptualizing surrogacy as a new form of value-producing labor makes it easier to expose the new mechanism of exploitation it introduces and makes it easier to advance progressive political claims. Rather than fighting the commodification of intimate biological processes by framing them as bioethical questions, it would be politically more effective to unmask these processes for what they really are: commercial exchanges of labor power for money.

However, while advocating the labor paradigm for theorizing surrogacy, Cooper and Walby also recognize that surrogacy is not quite like other forms of productive labor in traditional Marxist accounts. They contend that the proliferation of biomedical production "throws into question the established categories of economic analysis" and challenges "the founding assumptions of classical, Marxist, and post-Fordist theories of labor" (2014, 3–4). Their central claim is that when capitalism intrudes into the terrain of life, it seeks to appropriate something more than just surplus labor. It harnesses the generative capacities of biological processes themselves for value production; it puts "life itself to work" (6). Cooper and Waldby introduce the terms "regenerative labor" and "bioproduction" to refer to biological processes that are generative of both value as well as life (10, 107–8). In other words, the key feature of biocapitalism that these thinkers identify as difficult or impossible to capture with traditional Marxist categories is the value-generative capacity of life itself.

Cooper and Waldby thus recognize that the capitalist production of life in the laboratory or in the fertility clinic does not entirely displace the necessity of "external nature"—biological processes that operate according to their own rules and dynamics that are inherently unpredictable. The incredible, awe-inspiring, and potentially humbling capacity of the pregnant body to turn mere genetic material into a unique, sentient human person is still a fundamental prerequisite for the multimillion-dollar baby business. The attempt to account for this life-generative capacity of gestational biology leads Cooper and Waldby to argue that, rather than laborers who produce inanimate objects or services, surrogates should more correctly be conceived as analogous to proprietors of natural resources. They are proprietors of the womb:

> By becoming a surrogate, the woman takes on an entrepreneurial economic role, but in this case, her collateral is her own body. In order to realize its value, she enters into the surrogacy contract as the proprietor of her own reproductive capacity. *In effect, she consents to the constitution of her uterus as an asset class, able to generate monopoly rent.* . . . The surrogate, by signing the contract, agrees to rent her excess reproductive capacity, which has little monopoly value at home in the village, into a global market where the comparatively prohibitive regulation of commercial surrogacy in most jurisdictions gives such capacity considerable scarcity value. (Cooper and Waldby 2014, 84)

Cooper and Waldby thus end up suggesting that the womb, or the pregnant body more generally, functions analogously to such biological assets as land and other natural resources, which in capitalist societies are privately owned, have scarcity value, and generate rents. These authors'

Marxist appropriation thus vacillates between two alternatives: the surrogates are clinical laborers entitled to wages and labor protections, or they are capitalist rentiers contracting out their (re)productive biology in the global fertility market. Next, I will attempt to show why both of these alternatives are theoretically and politically problematic from a Marxist-feminist perspective.

Theoretical Trouble with the Labor Paradigm

Commercial gestational surrogacy clearly differs from the reproductive labor that women usually perform in the private realm. Unlike most women, surrogates get paid for pregnancy and the birthing of children. In other words, their "work" is waged or productive labor that takes place in the cash nexus. It is nevertheless difficult to fit surrogacy into the format of a service industry, which is characterized by care or assistance, but does not require the manufacturing of a material product. The whole point of surrogacy is to produce a baby, for which the "worker" is essentially rewarded. The surrogates who miscarry usually receive some small compensation, but it is only a fraction of what they would receive for the successful delivery of a baby.[13] This is why, according to some critics, surrogacy is a form of baby-selling: the structure of compensation does not correspond to the selling of the surrogate's services, but of the child itself.[14] So when Amrita Pande (2009a, 145) argues that gestational surrogates, similar to nannies and domestic workers, should be recognized as waged care workers because they are essentially nurturing someone else's baby in exchange for money, she leaves out a significant difference. Surrogates are not in a similar position to nannies and other waged care workers because they are not paid for their time, but for the "product" that they are expected to deliver. While there are clearly aspects of the surrogates' "occupation" that are consistent with the idea that they are care workers—they could be understood as being paid for the time they spend in the hostels gestating the fetus and undergoing various medical procedures—in contrast to clinical trial subjects, for example, this is not all they have to do. They also have to give birth to a baby and then give it away.

However, surrogacy does not quite fit the format of a productive industry either. One significant difference is that the labor productivity of this sector cannot be increased by any reasonable method—at least not with our current medical technology. In other words, the labor process cannot be speeded up or made significantly more efficient with existing technology. The fact that the surrogates are usually implanted with more than one embryo could be viewed as an attempt to increase "output" by increasing the chances of a successful pregnancy. However, if more than one or two embryos develop beyond a certain point, the "extras" are usually aborted.[15] While labor productivity has become the most important measure of economic development in capitalist societies, this schema thus arguably collapses in the case of surrogacy. Attempts to measure value based on working time and output become void (e.g., Morini and Fumagalli 2010).

Viewing surrogates as rentiers whose bodies function as natural assets is also problematic, however. If the reproductive capacity of the surrogate's body is understood as a biological resource, the surrogates themselves are not the proprietors of this asset. Although it seems intuitively obvious that they own their bodies, it is important to recognize that from a purely economic perspective their reproductive capacities themselves are worthless. Their economic value can only be realized with the help of a number of supporting processes and institutions. In vitro fertilization and the implantation of an embryo require advanced medical knowledge, skills, and instruments, and the surrogate's body has to be prepared for this procedure with a complex administration of hormones.[16] In other words, a surrogate cannot just take her body to the global fertility market, rent it out, and realize its value. She is dependent on the bioscientific knowledge of doctors, the biotechnological facilities of clinics, and surrogate brokers, as well as the legal and political institutions regulating surrogacy.

While Cooper and Waldby importantly draw attention to the assetlike qualities of surrogacy, they mistake the surrogates for rentier capitalists because of their problematic understanding of the value-producing capacities of biological processes in capitalism. Kevin Floyd (2015, 71) formulates the problem by contending that Cooper and Waldby attribute the capacities of labor to biological substances isolated and fabricated by biotechnology. This means attributing "value-producing agency to sheer biological substances: a form of agency they call the 'open-ended performativity of the biological itself'" (71). In the Marxist framework, value is always constituted by some form of labor, not by some capacity latent within biological matter. The development of biotechnological capitalism thus does not imply that there is now some new source of value in biological processes as such. Turning biological processes into commercial and profitable products and services still requires significant amounts of both fixed capital and knowledge labor. Birch and Tyfield (2012, 316) argue that the most important property rights in the global bioeconomy today are those pertaining to the ownership of knowledge assets. The realization of value from IPRs (immaterial property rights) through market exchange has marked a major transformation in capital relations in the recent decades.[17]

A rigorous Marxist-feminist analysis of surrogacy must therefore contend that economic value in the surrogacy business is not produced by the "regenerative labor" of the surrogates' reproductive biology; instead, it is produced both by the "dead labor" that has gone into forming the fixed capital of the biotechnology industry, including the biotechnological facilities of the surrogacy clinics and the relevant immaterial property rights, and by the living knowledge labor of the scientists and medical personnel who work in them.[18] In the next section, I argue that rather than being rentier capitalists or clinical laborers, surrogates occupy the position of raw material or a biological resource in the value circuits of biocapitalism. The rentiers are the owners of the clinics who control this raw material and have exclusive access to it through surrogacy contracts.

The Capitalist Expropriation of Life

It is important to recognize that the majority of the poorest and most oppressed people in the world today are not wage laborers. They are people who are often forced to eke out a precarious existence in the informal economy because capitalism appears to have no use for them at all. In other words, while some subjects in contemporary global capitalism have access to labor markets—they possess the right to sell their labor and have the ability to compete within markets—others are simply expropriated of their resources, land, and even life. As I already argued in connection with primitive accumulation, racialization has functioned and continues to function as a key instrument for drawing the boundary between these two groups.

Michael Dawson (2016) poses a crucial question about the relationship between the recent attacks on racialized and seemingly disposable populations, and the new stage of neoliberal capitalism in the twenty-first century. He contends that exploitation-centered conceptions of capitalism cannot explain its persistent entanglement with racial oppression because the ravages of the neoliberal capitalist order "continue to be felt most severely among those oppressed by the logic of expropriation and disposability" (Dawson 2016, 146). Dawson thus foregrounds the necessary and complementary processes of expropriation, which, in contrast to exploitation, do not operate through the contractual relation by which capital purchases labor power in exchange for wages. Rather, expropriation works by violently appropriating resources and integrating them in the processes of capitalist accumulation. Dawson argues that the ontological distinction between superior and inferior humans—codified as race—has functioned and continues to function as a necessary justification for expropriation (147). "This racial separation is manifested in the division between full humans who possess the right to sell their labor and compete within markets, and those that are disposable, discriminated against, and ultimately either eliminated or superexploited" (148). At certain historical periods and places this binary was framed as "human/subhuman," in others, as "full citizen/second-class citizen" or as "civilized/uncivilized," but in each case the division marked a racialized group, whose labor, property, and bodies could be subjected to expropriation, exploitation, and violation without recourse to the same political resources that were available to those classified as fully human (149).

The colonial-based logic of racialized expropriation was particularly evident in capitalism's early history as defined by primitive accumulation—for the slavery, colonialism, and the genocides that accompanied it—but as I showed already in chapter 1, many critics of capitalism argue that this process is still ongoing. As Chris Chen contends, the initial moment of contact between the European colonial order and an unwaged, racialized "outside" to capital has been progressively systematized within capitalism itself as a racialized global division of labor and the permanent structural oversupply of racialized labor. "At the periphery of the global capitalist system, capital now renews 'race' by creating vast superfluous urban populations from close to one billion slum-dwelling and desperately impoverished descendants of the enslaved and colonized" (Chen 2013).

Building on Dawson's account, Nancy Fraser too identifies prison labor, transnational sex trafficking, corporate land grabs, and foreclosures on predatory debt as the modern instances of racialized expropriation. Forms of transnational commercial surrogacy could, in my view, be added to the list. "The confiscation may be blatant and violent, as in New World slavery—or it may be veiled by a cloak of commerce, as in the predatory loans and debt foreclosures of the present era. . . . The confiscated assets may be labor, land, animals, tools, mineral or energy deposits—but also human beings, their sexual and reproductive capacities, their children and bodily organs" (Fraser 2016, 166). Hence, rather than being an instance of gendered exploitation, transnational commercial surrogacy should be viewed as gendered and racialized *expropriation*.[19]

It is contestable to what extent such abstract liberal notions as "consent," "freedom," "choice," and "contract" are meaningful in the context of dire economic need. Such difficult philosophical questions are made even more vexing, given that many surrogates in India, for example, are illiterate and have little familiarity with legal contracts. According to Daisy Deomampo's recent ethnographic study of gestational surrogacy in India, contract procedures are often extremely opaque, and the surrogates she spoke with almost invariably reported a lack of power in negotiating them:

> Contracts are typically written in English, so a doctor or a lawyer explains its contents to the surrogate. However, many surrogates reported receiving only cursory explanations of its contents, while others were simply instructed where to sign. In general, the contracts included no stipulations regarding payment; their main goal was to establish the parentage of the commissioning parents and to ensure that the surrogate would not attempt to prevent the parents from collecting the baby. (Deomampo 2016, 52)[20]

Even if we disregard these problems by assuming that the surrogates were well-informed and received adequate guidance on the economic details of the contract from an independent social worker or a financial counselor, my contention is that the surrogacy contracts remain fundamentally problematic. By signing the contract, the surrogates effectively give up autonomy over their bodies in the sense that they no longer have any choice in the medical procedures performed on them. This renders them passive recipients of invasive and risky medical interventions, such as the hyperstimulation of ovaries with hormone shots, the implantation of up to five embryos in the womb, the concomitant selective reduction of fetuses through abortions, and the mandatory cesarean delivery of babies (Rudrappa 2014, 145). This is ultimately the reason why it is erroneous to claim that the surrogates are selling their labor; they are in fact selling control over their bodies. While the gametes and the "intension" are understood to give the commissioning parents ownership of the baby, the surrogate contracts crucially secure the clinics' ownership of the means for gestating the fetus, including the surrogate's body. Surrogacy can thus be viewed as structurally similar to such "nature-based industries" as animal husbandry, for example, in which the emergent and unpredictable character of biological systems typically represents both significant challenges as well as opportunities for capital. As I noted above, surrogacy is dependent on biological growth processes that are difficult to speed up.[21]

By casting surrogates as biological resources and comparing them to female animals, I obviously do not intend to make any derogatory claims about their moral or political agency; my analysis is politico-economic and functional. Clearly, it is important not to see these women as helpless victims devoid of agency in the attempt to situate their lives and decisions within the broader economic imperatives of biocapitalism. Ethnographic studies of gestational surrogacy make very clear that surrogates employ complex strategies for negotiating and responding to the structural constraints they face, as well as defying social norms and securing self-defined needs and desires (e.g., Deomampo 2016, 196). However, it is also important to recognize that feminist theoretical analyses have concrete political consequences: whether we understand surrogates as occupying the position of exploited laborers, rentier capitalists, or biological resources in the functioning of capitalist economy has radically different implications for feminist political projects on surrogacy.

My concern is that the view that surrogates are either rentiers or laborers implies falsely optimistic ideas about their economic opportunities in the surrogacy business. As ethnographic studies of Indian surrogates show, once the surrogate signs the contract, her uterus effectively becomes the property of the clinic. Her possibilities for negotiating monetary compensation are either absent or extremely restricted. The commissioning parents usually negotiate the fee with the clinic, and the clinic directors distribute the pay to the surrogates.[22] Hence, a key political finding of my analysis thus far is that it is counterproductive, or at best merely cosmetic, to insist that surrogates should be understood as laborers when the fact remains that the economic system around them operates according to a logic that makes it impossible for them to occupy such a position. The premises of the whole system would have to change in significant ways in order for such a view to be emancipatory or even to make sense.

It could be objected, however, that the political demand embedded in the labor paradigm is exactly that. In other words, the socialist-feminist demand would be that we should transform the conditions of their work so that the surrogates could *become* laborers. A more generous reading of Cooper and Waldby's account would thus insist that theirs is not a descriptive account, but a normative one. Even if surrogates are currently expropriated as biological resources rather than exploited as laborers, the economic premises of this business could and should be transformed in such a way that the women could occupy the position of clinical laborers. If the surrogates were paid competitive wages for the full time of their pregnancy regardless of its outcome, if they retained their bodily autonomy in the sense that they were given informed and meaningful choices about the medical procedures they must undergo, and if they were insured, compensated, and protected against possible medical complications, then they could be more accurately described as clinical laborers. More importantly, their concrete situation would dramatically improve as a result. The concluding proposition of Cooper and Waldby's book—"It is these terms of exchange that must be redressed if clinical labor is to be undertaken in more equitable ways"—suggests that perhaps this is the political project those authors seek to advance (2014, 228).

As appealing as this may sound, we would still be left with significant ethical and political problems that are imbedded in the labor paradigm. It is necessary to be mindful that, for Marx, the exploitation or even the expropriation of labor are not the only problems with capitalism; he also critiqued the poverty of meaning and the erosion of human dignity in capitalist societies.[23] The intertwinement of advanced biotechnology with global capitalist markets mandates new kinds of political responses and interventions because it forces us to confront thorny and profound ethical problems concerning embodiment, sexuality, kinship, autonomy, and dignity. It forces us to insert new kinds of ethical and experiential issues into our political and economic analyses of capitalism and to question our traditional liberal compartmentalization of ethics and politics as private and public, respectively.

Feminist Politics of Surrogacy

Gestational surrogacy necessarily acquires meaning in a contested discursive space in which multiple understandings of its significance compete for hegemony. This means that discourses, whether medical or Marxist-feminist, that view the fetus and the uterus of the surrogate as technically and legally isolatable components of a production process, are not neutral descriptions. They are constitutive of actual practices that treat the womb of the surrogate as the property of the clinic. They partake in the specific cultural construction of surrogacy, in which pregnancy is detached from the embodied experience of the surrogate. In other words, despite its seemingly emancipatory objective, the theoretical framework that views gestational surrogates as "clinical laborers" is politically problematic because it relies on an economic understanding of the uterus as a productive instrument and inadvertently reduces the surrogate to her womb.[24]

When the process of gestating a child is conceived as being analogous to labor and understood as a process of commodity production, we can understand it as a process of externalization only with serious difficulty. Both the womb that is supposed to be "the means of production" and the fetus that is the "product" are physiologically integral parts of the surrogate's body. During the pregnancy, these parts can only be detached and externalized as abstractions. In other words, what is produced is not an external commodity or a detachable service, with the surrogate's body functioning merely as a means of production. What is in fact produced is a different body—a pregnant body. Post-natally, the baby can obviously be physically detached, but arguably only with significant psychological cost to the surrogate. As Seema Mohapatra (2014, 148) notes, the contested regulatory environment surrounding commercial surrogacy reflects mixed public sentiments about whether it is realistic to expect a surrogate mother to relinquish all rights to a baby that she has carried to term, regardless of the earlier contractual and monetary agreements.[25] While theorists such as Sayantani DasGupta and Shamita Das Dasgupta (2014, 188) have compared the surrogate mother's alienation to "an Indian MNC worker who spends her lifetime making chips, but never gets to see the completed computer, which is manufactured overseas," it seems clear that the surrogate mother is "alienated" from "the product" of her labor in a much more profound and philosophically problematic sense. Surrogacy contracts are thus ultimately different from all other labor contracts, no matter how fair or generous they might be, because the "worker" cannot be separated from the contracted "product," the baby, for at least nine months.

Pande's (2014, 70) pioneering ethnographic study of gestational surrogacy in northern India analyses the processes and narratives through which the surrogates are trained to understand the womb as a distinct body part that is separate from themselves as pregnant persons.[26] The doctors in the clinic are careful to explain the process to the surrogates in terms that emphasize that the baby does not belong to them. A surrogate will only provide a home for a baby in her womb for nine months because the baby does not have a house of its own. It is someone else's baby who just comes to stay in her house for a while. She will take care of it, like a nanny, for nine months, and then she will give it to its mother. In other words, these women are deliberately trained to adopt a new understanding of their bodies that allows them to conceive of the body as containing an empty space that is not being used, and therefore can be hired out.

Pande (2009b, 2014) also demonstrates, however, that the surrogates themselves contest this view. They do not just passively accept the doctor's description of their role as passive and empty vessels or wombs for rent. While the women Pande interviewed recognized, for example, that having no genetic connection to the baby made it easier to justify giving it away, they nevertheless emphasized that, since it was their blood and their milk that nourished the baby, they clearly shared substantial ties with it. As one of the surrogates interviewed by Pande observed, "After all it's my blood even if it's their genes" (Pande 2014, 148).[27]

Pande argues that the idea of the blood tie that the surrogate forms with the baby should not be dismissed simply as illiterate women's ignorance of Western medical science (Pande 2009b, 384). Instead, these women should be understood as advocating and developing alternative views of kinship that are based on the idea that kinship relations are formed in everyday practices through affective labor. In addition to the substantial ties of blood, the surrogates also emphasize the embodied labor of gestation, giving birth, and breast-feeding. According to Pande, the surrogates understand these "blood, sweat and milk ties" as legitimate bases for making claims on the baby, but these kinship ties also allow them to resist the medical discourses of the clinics that portray them as disposable wombs for rent. "Unlike the medical portrayal of surrogates as temporary and disposable wombs, the surrogates are able to assert that their relationship with the baby is real and often stronger than the one between the genetic mother and the baby" (Pande 2014, 150).

The alternative views of kinship advocated by the surrogates should, in my view, be recognized as extremely pertinent in the contemporary world, which is characterized by advanced biotechnology, a broadening range of legal forms of sexual partnership, and new family constellations. By emphasizing the problems inherent in viewing surrogacy as just another form of labor, I am not arguing for romanticized or naturalized notions of a "real family." On the contrary, I want to advocate a feminist politics that denaturalizes kinship ties understood in the strictly genetic sense and emphasizes the everyday affective labor involved in forming and maintaining those ties. Feminists should welcome the fact that surrogacy has the potential for radically destabilizing biological parenting and "queering" traditional nuclear family and kinship structures.[28]

What this fact should imply, however, is the realization that gestational surrogates cannot be viewed as ordinary laborers engaged in care work. Instead, we should recognize and take seriously the new forms of kinship that surrogacy creates: the surrogates become members of a new kind of extended family. The feminist political implication would be that the surrogates should be given more concrete power to define their role in these new forms of kinship introduced by gestational surrogacy. For example, feminists should advocate for the right of surrogates to arrange an open surrogacy/adoption if so desired in order to secure a future connection to the child and to the commissioning family.[29] Attitudes as well as legislation and policy around national and international adoption have shifted in a direction that prioritizes open adoption—a model in which all the parties to the contract retain contact with the child—and adopted children's right to know their birth parents is recognized as important for the child's well-being. Similar issues should be central in connection with gestational surrogacy. Children born through surrogacy, similar to adopted children, should also have the right to know about their background and their birth circumstances, as well as retaining the possibility to have contact with their surrogate mother.[30] Currently, one of the attractions of transnational surrogacy is the relative ease of getting rid of the surrogate mother. However, it is precisely her disposability that should be recognized as the crux of the ethical problems surrounding surrogacy.

The monetary compensation to the surrogate should also reflect the idea of an extended family relationship. Critical analyses of surrogacy in India have found that the monetary compensation the surrogates receive hardly ever changes their lives significantly by lifting them out of the cycle of poverty. In most cases, the money is quickly spent on family medical expenses, dowry costs, or one-time constructions, and in the long run has little effect on the everyday life of the surrogates.[31] However, if we took seriously the idea that the surrogate mothers are members of a new transnational family, then the monetary compensation should not be a one-time windfall, but should instead be similar to the dependable monetary support that we expect family members to extend to each other.

It is, of course, possible that many of the surrogates would not want any kind of continuous affective relationship with the commissioning couple or even with the child; perhaps they just wanted the money without any strings attached. However, currently only the commissioning parents can make a genuine choice regarding their relationship to the surrogate: the cultural and geographic distance provides an opportunity for them to engage in transnational surrogacy without the problems of emotional connection. Based on the available ethnographic studies, it also seems that many of the surrogates expect to be involved in the child's life. Pande, for example, observes that the surrogates often attempt to establish some kind of affective relationship with the intended parents. In interviews, they emphasize the exceptional bond they have with the commissioning couple and mistakenly assume that they will continue to keep in regular contact with them, as well as with the child they are carrying. In the rare cases in which the commissioning couple actually forms familial relationships with the surrogate, these relationships are an important source of pride and value for the surrogate. One of these surrogates, Diksha, described the day the clients came to get the baby: "When Jessy came and took the baby in her arms, she started crying out of happiness. And you won't believe it, but she kept pointing me (out) to the baby and saying, 'See, this is your mom.' I know the baby did not understand what she was saying to her but it meant a lot to me. So many clients say, 'This is your auntie.' But Jessy said, 'This is your mom'" (Pande 2014, 157). Pande contends that by attempting to form affective ties to the commissioning parents, the surrogates manage to resist the commercial nature of exchanging babies for money and challenge their disposability as people and the consequent loss of dignity.

It is important to recognize that ethical problems such as dignity and personal worth cannot be remedied with better wages, because they are essentially caused by the monetized nature of the exchange and therefore challenge philosophically what kinds of things can be given monetary value. In other words, a key problem with the current commercial practices of gestational surrogacy is that the relationship between the surrogates and the intended parents is understood as temporary, monetized, and contractual. Better wages and labor protections are therefore, at best, a limited and partial remedy and, at worst, normalize and make invisible what are perhaps the most troubling ethical issues at stake. Feminists should therefore demand, not the institutionalization of surrogates' status as care workers, but rather the institutionalized recognition that their status is significantly different from that of other care workers due to the specificity of their kinship tie to the child.

A feminist understanding of gestational surrogacy as constitutive of new forms of kinship thus also requires new transnational feminist projects and alliances. My functionalist analysis has hopefully made clear that the micro-politics of forming new kinds of relationships between surrogate mothers and intended parents only becomes possible in the macropolitical context of transnational, anticapitalism feminism. While transnational feminism and its relationship to global capitalism remains a contested topic in feminist theory, my contention is that transnational feminism is necessary for foregrounding feminist activist practices as forms of resistance against global capitalism. The critical feminist study of gestational surrogacy should make clear that feminists must continue to challenge ideas about "global sisterhood" while nevertheless collaborating across cultural contexts. It would be naive to insist that the Indian surrogate mother and the Western intended mother should simply become sisters. Yet recognizing the power asymmetries in their relationship should not preclude attempts to level those asymmetries or work towards more equitable relationships between women across national borders and cultural contexts. As several feminist theorists have insisted, transnational feminism must be grounded on both the ideal of global solidarity among women across nation-state borders and the acute recognition of profound differences in their circumstances.[32] In contemporary global biocapitalism, women from very different geographic locations and socioeconomic situations are directly linked to each other by capitalist markets even if they experience these links in asymmetrical ways. Conversely, these links also make possible a transnational feminist resistance against global capitalism, even if the forms it takes might be at times heterogeneous, compromised, or internally conflicted.[33]

4

Can Gender Subordination Be Eliminated in Capitalism?

Up to this point, my ecofeminist critique of capitalism has mainly focused on forms of expropriation—on the fact that, despite appearances, "free" wage labor does not form the only indispensable and stable source from which capitalism can draw its profits. Like icebergs, capitalist economies fundamentally rely on the large, invisible part below the surface—on the expropriation of nature, as well as on forms of "unfree" racialized and gendered labor such as unwaged reproductive labor. I will now, in chapters 4 and 5, turn to investigate the more limited feminist question of contemporary wage labor and the significance of gender for it; in other words, the question of women's labor market parity and economic opportunities in contemporary neoliberal biocapitalism. In the sixth and final chapter, I will then bring together these two strands of my critique—the one focusing on expropriation operating below the surface of the official economy, and the other directed at waged work—through the question of domestic labor and the Left's debate on universal basic income.

The persistent question in Marxist-feminist theory since 1970s has been the nature of the link between gender subordination and capitalism: does capitalism, and liberalism as its moral justification and political legitimization, structurally require gender subordination, or could the forms of oppression and discrimination based on gender be eliminated within some future capitalist life form? In her seminal book *Edgework*, Wendy Brown surmised that feminists had finally been forced to accept a conclusive answer to this question:

> It is clear enough that women and men can be rendered interchangeable cogs in a contemporary and future capitalist machinery, where physical strength is rarely an issue, where continuity on the job matters little, where reproductive work has been almost completely commodified and reproduction itself is nearly separable from sexed bodies and is in any event separable from a sexual division of labor. Notwithstanding the protracted Marxist-feminist analyses of the indispensability of unpaid housework to the production of surplus value, the home as a necessary if stricken haven in a heartless world, and the need for a malleable surplus

army of labor (all of which were straining to prove both the materiality of gender subordination and its necessity to capitalism), it is evident
today that the equal participation and remuneration of women in the
economic and civic order can be achieved, even if unevenly and with
difficulty. (Brown 2005, 106)

According to Brown, Marxist feminism thus came to a dead-end
because "the feminist ambition to eliminate gender as a site of subordination could technically be met within a capitalist life-form" (Brown 2005,
105). She concludes decisively: "there is nothing in sexed bodies or even
in gender subordination that capitalism cannot live without" (105).

My aim in this chapter is to challenge such a conclusion, and to
demonstrate that we still need to engage with the "protracted Marxist-
feminist analyses" of social reproduction. While neoliberalism and the
rapid development of biotechnology have reconfigured the context for
investigating the question of gender subordination in capitalism, the centrality of this question for feminist theory has not been eradicated. On
the contrary, it is vital that we pose it in renewed forms today.

My argument moves from empirical facts to theoretical thought
experiments. I begin by explicating the liberal position that, rather than
being oppressive, capitalism is in fact emancipatory for women. It is important to understand the force of this argument because, in many ways,
it is the commonsense view today. I will therefore outline its theoretical
underpinnings before subjecting it to a Marxist-feminist critique in the
second section. There, I will distinguish between two different ways that
the liberal position has been rebutted in Marxist-feminist theory: Marxist
feminists have argued that the link between capitalism and women's subordination is historically contingent and opportunistic, or it is necessary
in the sense that it is inherent to the systemic logic of capitalism. I will
follow those Marxist feminists, such as Lise Vogel, who have attempted to
show that gender oppression stems necessarily from the economic logic of
the capitalist mode of production due to the indispensability of women's
reproductive labor for capitalist accumulation. My claim is that only this
latter, theoretical form of the Marxist-feminist argument on social reproduction provides an effective refutation of the liberal-feminist apologies
for capitalism.

I will conclude by considering the consequences that my investigation has for the future of feminist politics. Whereas both forms of Marxist-
feminist critique, what I term the historicist and the functionalist, imply a
negative answer to the question of whether capitalism is good for women,
they have radically different consequences for feminist politics. If the link
between capitalism and gender oppression is understood to be merely

historically contingent and opportunistic, then capitalism could be re-fashioned in the future in such a way that it becomes gender-egalitarian. However, if the link is systemic in the sense that it is hard-wired into the economic logic of capitalism, then such a political project becomes more difficult, if not completely futile. My aim is to show that the latter is closer to the truth.

I also want to emphasize, however, that once we begin to dig deeper into the relationship between capitalism and gender subordination, the stark for-or-against framework turns out to be simplistic. If we adopt a complex and theoretically differentiated approach to capitalism, it becomes apparent that capitalism has both emancipatory and oppressive effects, at least for those who are incorporated within it as workers. Stating this outright should be recognized as being in line with Marx's own highly ambivalent appraisal of capitalism: while it is unquestionably a bloody, exploitative, and oppressive economic system, it has nevertheless also enabled a massive expansion of forces of production and has under-girded emancipatory political transformations, even if they have been partial and exclusive.

The Possibility of Enlightened Capitalism

In their book *Capitalism, For and Against: A Feminist Debate* (2011), Ann E. Cudd and Nancy Holmström take up opposing sides of the debate on whether capitalism is good for women. They each present a number of empirical arguments and statistical data in support of their positions. In her defense of capitalism, Cudd presents a mass of data showing how the advent of capitalism started humanity on a path of improvement to length and quality of life. Her key contention is that it brought about a significant improvement in the lives of women and girls measured in terms of various indexes, such as longer life expectancy and lower fertility and child mortality rates, as well as better schooling rates by gender, and increased women's political and economic participation (Cudd and Holmstrom 2011, 33).

Cudd is aware, however, that it is difficult to demonstrate empirically a robust causal connection between capitalism and some of these developments, which could equally be attributed to technological development, industrialization, or more democratic forms of governance. She also recognizes that statistics clearly show that, in all existing capitalist societies, women are significantly poorer than men, as well as subject to much higher levels of violence and discrimination. Hence, in order to prove something conclusive about the relationship between capitalism and gender equality, it is necessary to advance theoretical, not merely empirical arguments that show systemic connections or structural relations, as well as to make a distinction between capitalism as an actually existing economic system and capitalism as a theoretical model.

The theoretical or systemic argument in favor of capitalism that Cudd puts forward relies on a strong theoretical separation between patriarchy and capitalism: the harms and inequalities that women experience in capitalist societies today are due to patriarchy—both the ideology of institutionalized sexism and the patriarchal social system itself—not capitalism. While capitalism in some instances clearly benefits from patriarchy, for example, by paying women less, "capitalism does not entail patriarchy, or more to the point . . . capitalism provides no better home for patriarchy than does socialism" (Cudd and Holmstrom 2011, 28). According to Cudd, patriarchy must therefore be understood as a parallel social system that can exist in more than one economic order (27). The rampant sexism in the former socialist states is a clear indication of this. The reasons why patriarchy is currently coupled with capitalism in our societies are thus merely historical and opportunistic. Theoretically, capitalism does not need patriarchy, but "offers women a way out of patriarchal, traditional culture" (28).

Cudd then reiterates the central liberal political idea that capitalism is a great equalizer because it relies on individualism and abstract labor power, not on traditional status hierarchies and the rigid divisions of labor based on them. In other words, because capitalism has no intrinsic ties to particular identities, inequalities, or extra-economic, political, or juridical differences, it has helped women to "free themselves from the bonds of tradition, home, and clan" (Cudd and Holmstrom, 2011, 28). Capitalist accumulation essentially depends on there being free individuals who are able to sell their labor power in the market, and from the perspective of capital, the gender and age of these individuals are irrelevant. Similar to Brown, Cudd concludes that women and men can ultimately be rendered interchangeable cogs in the capitalist machinery.

The feminist defense of capitalism thus relies on the theoretical premise that the relationship between capitalism and women's subordination is merely opportunistic and historically contingent and that there is nothing in the economic logic of capitalism as such that produces or requires it. In political terms, this means that capitalism could, in principle, be reformed to achieve gender equality and abolish sexist practices and attitudes. The fact that no capitalist societies anywhere at the moment are even close to gender equality should not be attributed to the systemic logic inherent to capitalism, but to historically contingent social attitudes and

institutions, which could be eliminated by political means, such as legislative measures against gender discrimination, positive discrimination in
some sectors of employment, redistribution of wealth through taxation,
and so on. In Cudd's view, the development of such "enlightened capitalism" would guarantee "women's best opportunity for liberation from
both poverty and domination by men" (Cudd and Holmstrom 2011, 5).

   In her reply, Nancy Holmstrom accepts the historically contingent
as opposed to the theoretically necessary connection between capitalism
and gender oppression, which underlies Cudd's argument. She deliberately leaves open the question of "whether progress can continue to the
point of complete gender equality within capitalism or whether some
gender inequalities are inevitable in the system" (Cudd and Holmstrom
2011, 219). For her, the attempt to engage in such theoretical speculation
and to establish this kind of systemic connection is itself misguided. It is
an instance of "ideal theory," meaning theory that abstracts from "the
actual oppressive social world, conceptualizing that reality in ways that
reflect the status quo" (290). Instead, Holmstrom professes to formulate
"nonideal theory," which is "full of messy, unsavory, and decidedly non-
philosophical facts about our current world that would be quite inappropriate in mainstream political philosophy" (291). In other words, Holmstrom grants that one could coherently and rationally imagine a version
of capitalism that was not sexist, and notes that in principle, "capitalism
is 'gender-neutral'" (217), but this is not relevant for our critical analyses
of the real world.[1] According to her, supposing that the logical possibility
of a nonsexist capitalism implies that real-world capitalism is not sexist,
is an instance of ideal theory. Ultimately, "the question of whether capitalism is good for women must rest on capitalism *as an actually existing,
historically evolving political, economic system, not just as a logically possible system. To focus on capitalism as an idea—without powerful arguments showing that
it is also feasible—would be to make an apologia for capitalism*" (138; italics in
the original).

   Holmstrom then makes a strong appeal to the actual social reality
we are faced with as the grounds for her feminist critique of capitalism.
She notes, for example, how one-third of female-headed households of all
races in the United States live in poverty and how globally the feminization of poverty is arguably even starker. The trafficking of women for sex
work has become a growing market globally, and despite women's massive
entry into the global labor market in the last few decades, women are still
predominantly responsible for all caregiving (Cudd and Holmstrom 2011,
236–42). The problem with such empirical arguments, however, is that no
matter how many dismal facts we pile up against capitalism, they do not
refute the possibility that it could and should be reformed in the future.

They are irrelevant in the face of Cudd's philosophical argument about the eliminability of gender insubordination in enlightened capitalism.

Holmstrom also reiterates the theoretical argument against dual system theories, in other words, those theoretical attempts to make a distinction between capitalism and patriarchy. The problem faced by the early Marxist-feminist projects was economic reductionism. The motivation behind developing so-called dual systems theories was the realization that gender oppression was not merely an economic phenomenon but traversed all aspects of social life. It was not only capitalists who were benefiting from gender oppression, but all men. As Heidi Hartman (1979, 24) noted sharply in her definitive essay: "Men have more to lose than their chains." In other words, if feminists were going to analyze women's subordination through the theoretical framework of capitalism and if they were to avoid economic reductionism, they had to either complement the existing economic analyses of capitalism with their own analyses of other complementary or intersecting forms of oppression, or they needed to adopt a broader, "non-economic" conception of capitalism.

The unitary theory that Holmstrom defends opts for the latter alternative. She contends that if we posit a parallel system of patriarchy to account for women's subordination within capitalism, this requires also positing a system of racism and a system of heterosexism and so on. For her, such a theoretical move would inevitably lead to the question of how many systems are enough and what constitutes a system. She believes that "it is clearer to describe the system in which we live as one integrated system of capitalism which is sexist and racist" (Cudd and Holmstrom 2011, 298). This means understanding capitalism not merely as an economic system or a distinct mode of production definable with distinct economic features and imperatives. Instead, capitalism must be understood as a complex social order that consists of varied power relations connected to gender, sexual orientation, race, nationality, and religion. Such an enlarged conception of capitalism makes it possible for feminists to then incorporate gender, race, and sexual oppression in the total framework of capitalism, rather than treating them as separate forms of domination.[2]

My key contention is that such a broad conception of capitalism, combined with Holmstrom's refusal to engage with philosophical or functionalist analyses—analyses that seek to expose the systemic features that are necessary for capitalism to function satisfactorily—is a deeply problematic strategy for feminist critiques of capitalism. As I argued already in connection with Nancy Fraser's structurally similar position in the introduction, such an integrated approach suffers from several serious theoretical and political problems. First, once we understand capitalism as a diffuse totality of intersecting oppressions, there is not much else that can be significantly stated about its connection to gender subordination other than that the two are intertwined. The proposition becomes non-falsifiable. Stating that something in a total social formation is connected to something else in it is obviously true in a trivial sense. To explain anything more specific at all about their connection, we must retrieve a more precise understanding of capitalism, identify its systemic imperatives or economic logic, and then study the specific ways in which they determine, intersect, or shape historically specific, gendered social practices. In other words, once we insist that capitalism is a total social formation that includes all forms of oppression, we seem to be rapidly emptying the notion of its explanatory force.

Second, such an integrated account has political limitations. Appraising capitalism politically with the help of a broad conception of it means losing the ability to differentiate between its contradictory demands and effects on gender equality. As I already noted, and will further show, capitalism not only harbors fundamentally contradictory compulsions regarding social reproduction, but it also has, at times, both emancipatory and oppressive effects on women. These effects are furthermore distinctive from other forms of oppression such as racial or sexual oppression. Today we can identify at least two different and opposing ways that the capitalist logic of accumulation—the imperative of economic growth—intersects with gender oppression. On the one hand, the rapid neoliberalization and globalization of capitalist economies in recent decades has resulted in a constant drive to extend the reach of the market. This is consistent with attempts to commodify the private realm and to turn women into wage laborers.[3] On the other hand, it is also clearly beneficial for capitalism in the current historical conjuncture to rely on women's unpaid reproductive labor in the private sphere. This must be counted as at least part of the explanation for why the feminist movement, despite decades of political struggle by now, has had very little success in socializing and ungendering reproductive labor. Women are still expected to take the main responsibility for the early provision of child care, as well as for most of the housework.

A similar contradiction characterizes the gendered consequences of recent economic crises. The instability of capitalist economies has been negotiated in recent decades through neoliberal forms of governmentality—new political technologies of power and social regulation that emphasize individual responsibility in risk management. While a stable nuclear family was previously understood to provide the necessary counterweight to competitive and individualistic capitalist societies, today social volatility and economic risks have become increasingly central for profit-making. It is especially the poor and the most vulnerable segments of the population who have been pushed into unprecedented levels of debt in recent decades and whose indebtedness has partly made possible the growth of lucrative credit markets and the rapid financialization of Western economies. In other words, the breaking up of the stable nuclear family and the collapse of the traditional gender order based on the family wage can be understood as both useful and harmful for capitalist accumulation: on the one hand, the dissolution of social cohesion and the growing number of poor, single-parent households has provided lucrative new opportunities for capitalist accumulation in the form of subprime lending, for example; on the other hand, the intensification of the traditional gender order has resulted in an intensified crisis of care in Western societies and made the political issues around social reproduction appear as acute problems for capitalist accumulation.

In sum, it seems to me that few feminist theorists would deny the central claim of the integrated approach: gender oppression has become an integral part of capitalist society through a long historical process that has dissolved preceding forms of life (Arruzza 2014b). The crucial question that remains is what we can legitimately conclude from this fact in terms of our feminist future. Why does capitalism continue to reproduce gender oppression? What kind of social transformation would be required to eliminate it? Could it be achieved by an "enlightened capitalism" as Cudd suggests? Would it be enough to improve capitalism by legal reform and economic redistribution? Answering central political questions such as these requires feminist investigation that is able to engage in theoretical philosophical arguments. Only by understanding the systemic constraints that capitalist economies place on the achievement of gender equality is it possible to imagine realistic possibilities for politically transforming or subverting those constraints.

The Necessity of Generational Reproduction

The second route for Marxist feminists to argue against a beneficial alliance of feminism and capitalism is to focus on systemic gender inequality in capitalism based on the necessity of women's generational reproductive labor. There are clear advantages to taking this route. It undercuts the key theoretical premise of Cudd's argument: capitalism and women's subordination cannot be so easily separated in some future version of "enlightened capitalism" because gender inequality is built into the systemic logic of capitalist accumulation. It is understandable why many Marxist feminists are reluctant to take this route, however. It means courting biological essentialism by drawing a strong connection between gender oppression and women's biological capacity to bear children, and it seems to mistakenly treat women as a homogenous category. Many cis women choose not to, or cannot have children, while trans men, transmasculine individuals, and nonbinary people also get pregnant, give birth, chest feed, and do parenting. Trans and nonbinary experiences of pregnancy, childbirth, and parenting thus clearly call into question any simple reliance on binary gender in discussions of reproductive labor. I nevertheless believe that following this route merits consideration, and that this line of reasoning can be developed without assuming a binary gender difference rooted in biology. Toward this end, I will attempt to use, for the most part, the inclusive language of "childbearing people" instead of "childbearing women." However, when we investigate such large-scale and structural economic issues as capitalism's effects on gender equality, gendered poverty, or women's labor-market parity, analyses often use the category "women" in a relatively unproblematized sense for the simple reason that, on this scale, the overwhelming majority of childbearing people are cis women. It should be kept in mind, however, that when I use the term "childbearing women" in such contexts, childbearing men and nonbinary people should be understood to be included in my assertions.

Lise Vogel develops a sophisticated version of such a functionalist argument in her classic book *Marxism and the Oppression of Women* (1983), in which she analyzes women's oppression through the necessity for social reproduction.[4] Like Holmstrom, Vogel too aims to develop a single integrated account that links together the oppression of women and the capitalist mode of production, but her argument is unapologetically theoretical: "No attempt is made to develop detailed analyses of women's oppression in, for example, contemporary society" (Vogel 1983, 142). Rather, her aim is to expose the deep systemic conditions through which the capitalist mode of production reproduces itself and to show how these conditions are inherently tied to gender subordination in capitalist economies.

Vogel's starting point is the Marxist feminist critique which maintains that Marx and his socialist followers never sufficiently confronted the theoretical problem of the reproduction of labor power. Marx famously shows in *Capital* how every social process of production is at the same time a process of reproduction: continuing production requires the simultaneous reproduction of its own operating conditions (Marx [1867] 1990, 531). This reproduction must also include the labor force: it too must be replenished, biologically and socially, daily and generationally. Rather than theorizing the gendered social relations and practices through which this reproduction of labor power happens, however, Marx reverts to naive naturalism, writing that when it comes to "the maintenance and reproduction of the working class, capitalists may safely leave this to the workers' drives for self-preservation and propagation" (718).

Marxist feminists were acutely aware, however, that "these drives for self-preservation and propagation" could only be organized and reproduced within sociocultural forms of life (Ferguson and McNally 2013, xxvii). Someone had to bear children, care for them, and teach them various skills so that they could then be usefully employed by capitalists when they grew up. Unpaid reproductive labor in the home thus had to be understood as indispensable for capitalism: it constituted a significant amount of socially necessary production, even though it was not considered "real work" because it fell outside of the money economy. In her groundbreaking article "The Political Economy of Women's Liberation" ([1969] 1997), Margaret Benston showed already in 1969 that there was a material basis to gender oppression: the patriarchal nuclear family effectively functioned as a production unit for housework and child-rearing in capitalism. Over the following decade, Marxist feminists produced a significant corpus of work on domestic labor, showing how it formed an integral aspect of the capitalist mode of production.

Vogel's theorization of social reproduction extends beyond considering merely domestic labor and the daily processes of reproduction, however. She identifies the different aspects of social reproduction—the maintenance of direct producers, the maintenance of non-laboring members of the subordinate class, and generational replacement processes—and notes that only the last requires a gender division of labor of at least a minimal kind. If children are to be born, it is women who must carry and deliver them (Vogel 1983, 150). In a crucial passage, she writes: "What raises the question of gender is, of course, the phenomenon of generational replacement of bearers of labor power. . . . If generational replacement is to happen, biological reproduction must intervene. And here, it must be admitted, human beings do not reproduce themselves by parthenogenesis. Women and men are different" (146).

Vogel refers to "women" and "childbearing women" throughout her book, but it is important to recognize that the core of her argument does not change even if we update her terminology to "childbearing people." As I already noted, today there are an increasing number of men as well as transmasculine and nonbinary individuals who get pregnant, give birth, chest feed, and parent children.[5] The theoretical core of Vogel's functionalist argument, holds, however: competitive, capitalist labor markets discriminate against those people whose reproductive biology makes them primarily responsible for childbearing, and currently the overwhelming

majority of these are cis women, even though gestation is not solely undertaken by them. Capitalism, at least in its current forms, structurally depends
on biological reproductive processes—pregnancy, childbirth, lactation—
to secure the reproduction of the labor force. And in an economic system
based on wage labor, in which resources are primarily distributed to individuals according to their ability to compete for them as opposed to their
need or their right to these resources, the people who carry the burden
of generational reproduction cannot participate in this game on equal
terms. Instead, capitalism structurally exploits and economically disadvantages them by placing them in a contradictory position in which they
are expected to compete in labor markets for the economic resources necessary for survival, while at the same time also carrying the extra burden
of generational reproduction outside of markets.

It is important to acknowledge that Vogel does not hold the view
that women's distinctive role in generational reproduction would imply
that their oppression has been an ahistorical or transhistorical phenomenon determined by their biology. Vogel identifies a biological difference
grounding the gender division of labor, but she makes clear that it is not
biology per se that dictates women's oppression. The biological fact that
women and men are often differently involved in the generational reproduction of labor power during pregnancy and lactation is not sufficient by
itself to constitute a source of oppression. All kinds of divisions of labor
have always existed in societies and do not by themselves determine social
hierarchies. The problem is rather that in capitalist societies, which are
based almost exclusively on wage labor, women's childbearing capacity
creates a significant hindrance to the appropriation of surplus value. As
Vogel puts it: "Child-bearing threatens to diminish the contribution a
woman can make as a direct producer and as a participant in necessary
labor. Pregnancy and lactation involve, at the minimum, several months
of somewhat reduced capacity to work" (Vogel 1983, 151).

In sum, as long as the fact remains that only some people's bodies
have to go through the extra burden of pregnancy and childbirth—and
currently they are predominantly the bodies of cis women—these people
have to take at least some time off from paid employment in order to do
this, which means that during this time they are not productive workers
from the point of view of capital. This places them in a contradictory
and unequal position in capitalist economies. On the one hand, they are
caught up in capitalism's constant drive to turn everybody, regardless of
age or gender, into wage laborers. On the other hand, capitalism's long-
term need to reproduce a workforce means that it must rely on non-waged
reproductive labor in the private sphere (Vogel 1983, 151). Vogel's key
argument is that this contradiction is most effectively negotiated by taking

advantage of the existing patriarchal relationships between women and men that are based on sexuality and kinship. This is the explanation for the historical division of labor according to sex, which assigns women and men different roles. Even though in principle women's and men's different roles in the reproduction of labor power are of finite duration, these roles take specific historical forms in the variety of social structures known as the family. The social organization of the biological difference thus takes on a specific shape in capitalism. "It is the responsibility for the domestic labor necessary to capitalist social reproduction—and not the sex division of labor or the family per se—that materially underpins the perpetuation of women's oppression and inequality in capitalist society" (170).

Vogel's argument thus starts from the premise that capital essentially depends upon the biological processes specific to women—pregnancy, childbirth, lactation—to secure the reproduction of the labor force. This is not a historically contingent state of affairs in capitalism, but a structurally necessary fact. Capitalism necessarily needs reproductive labor because it needs a labor force. Without such reproductive labor, workers cannot reproduce themselves, and without workers, capital cannot be reproduced. Social reproduction in the form of producing and socializing the next generation of workers is thus a necessary condition for the existence of wage laborers and, ultimately, for the functioning of the capitalist economy. However, women's distinctive role in social reproduction does not imply that their oppression has been understood as an ahistorical or transhistorical phenomenon determined by their biology. Vogel's argument hinges instead on the relationship of childbearing to the appropriation of surplus labor in capitalist societies (Vogel 1983, 151). The historically specific family forms and gender orders that preexisted capitalism were adopted and reinforced in order to deal with capitalism's contradictory need to both exploit and renew labor power. Hence, while she advances a functionalist or theoretical argument, it is not a deterministic argument in the sense that capitalism would have deliberately created the heterosexual nuclear family in order to regulate social reproduction or that the patriarchal gender order would form the only imaginable option for reproducing the labor force.[6]

Vogel's account thus importantly leaves open the possibility of imagining different ways of organizing social reproduction in capitalism. Her major contribution is to show how the need for the generational reproduction of the labor force places significant structural constraints on gender equality in capitalism, but she acknowledges that the contradictory pressures on women workers which follow from these constraints can and have been negotiated in different ways, depending on the needs of capital in specific historical situations. As an extreme alternative, it is possible to forego the need for generational reproduction all together: "In principle, at least, the present set of laborers can be worked to death, and then replaced by an entirely new set" (Vogel 1983, 145–46). This is not a purely imaginary scenario; in certain phases of slavery capitalism, it was the dominant strategy.

Slavery or a constant influx of migrant labor has never provided a sustainable, long-term solution for capitalists' need to reproduce labor power, however. Hence, in order to answer the question about the eliminability of gender subordination in capitalism, we need to push this line of questioning further. Is it possible, in principle, to organize social reproduction in capitalism in such a way that gender subordination would be eliminated? What would social reproduction look like in truly gender-egalitarian, "enlightened" capitalism? Is it possible to sever the connection between capitalism and gender oppression once we take into consideration capitalism's reliance on generational reproductive labor?

Enlightened Capitalism and the "Scandinavian Model"

In her defense of capitalism, Ann Cudd recognizes that the most serious objection to gender-egalitarian capitalism is connected with women's role in social reproduction. She acknowledges that there are systemic difficulties in organizing social reproduction in capitalism in a gender-equal way because caregiving has many positive externalities. Since those who are paid for providing care cannot internalize these externalities, economic theory dictates that the service will not be adequately provided in the market, either in terms of quantity or quality. However, Cudd argues that the problems created by the underprovision of care could be remedied in enlightened capitalism by two measures. First, men would have to take up the slack and provide more of the care work; second, governments would have to step in to correct for market failure in this sector (Cudd and Holmstrom 2011, 129).

The problem is that neither of these options is particularly viable. Cudd herself admits that it is possible that "men will not choose to participate in this gift economy" (Cudd and Holmstrom 2011, 129). It is indeed difficult to see what would prompt them to do so in a capitalist economy built on monetary incentives. The second idea, that government will compensate for the market failure in this sector, is problematic too. Many feminist theorists, both those who are critical of capitalism and those who defend it, recognize the importance of women's care work, and insist on the need for some kind of redistributive measures on the part of the state in compensation. According to advocates of the "Scandinavian model," for example, gender equality would require generous caregiver allowances for the parents of young children, the free or subsidized state provision of early childhood education and care, limits on the number of hours in the working week, the availability of partial employment, and generous family leave policies that would provide incentives for equal use by both fathers and mothers. In other words, the contention is that such arrangements would neutralize the harms that women's childbearing capacity bestows upon them in capitalism and thereby bring about their labor market parity with men.

Given that such models are not only a theoretical thought experiment, but in fact have been operating in the social-democratic welfare systems of the Nordic countries for decades, we have a number of empirical studies on the effects of these models on gender equality. While it remains unchallenged that these regimes promote labor market equality for women better than any other type of system that currently exists, they also have serious drawbacks. Generous maternity leaves function as strong disincentives for companies to hire women because of the inconvenience and expense involved. Moreover, the Nordic experience clearly shows that generous caregiver allowances, long parental leaves, and the availability of part-time employment tend to entrench gender disparities in income. They institute what Nancy Fraser (1996, 61) has called "a mommy track" in employment—a market in flexible, noncontinuous full- or part-time jobs. "As such jobs pay considerably less even at the full-time rate than comparable breadwinner-track jobs, two-partner families would have a clear economic incentive to keep one parent on the breadwinner track rather than to share spells of care-work between them" (61). When we add to this economic incentive the biological fact that, in the overwhelming majority of cases, it is the woman who is forced to take at least some time off work in order to give birth, then for heterosexual couples, making the breadwinner the man will usually be the economically most advantageous option by far, irrespective of the couple's feminist beliefs. In other words, the family organization itself and the division of labor in it tend to remain unchanged in this model. Instead of promoting gender equality, the model merely reinforces in many ways the existing sexual division of labor by giving women an even greater economic incentive to undertake more unpaid care work in the household. While obviously not all women bear children, statistical discrimination against even those women who prioritize their careers means that it is more difficult for them too to get hired and promoted.[7]

The systemic problem underlying these empirical findings must be traced back to the economic logic of capitalism: in an economic system based on wage labor, in which resources are primarily distributed to individuals according to their ability to compete for them in the economic game as opposed to their need or their right to these resources, generational reproductive labor can only ever be a handicap in this competitive game. Capitalist societies can be made to compensate the people who undertake this reproductive labor with various political and social measures external to the market, but at least with the current level of biotechnology, it cannot remove this handicap.

A valid objection to my account at this point might be that the systemic gender subordination that affects childbearing women in capitalism is a relatively minor problem. Feminist defenders of capitalism such as Cudd might concede that, if childbearing women received compensation by various means external to the market, their labor-market disparity and diminished earning power would constitute a relatively small sacrifice for them to make in comparison to the huge benefits that capitalism has otherwise bestowed on them as consumers. However, if this is the real argument in the feminist defense of capitalism, then we should at least clearly spell out what capitalism entails for childbearing women: they are required to make this economic sacrifice. Feminists should not fool themselves into believing that full gender equality will be realized anytime soon in enlightened capitalism.

Trans Parenting and Universal Commodification

Since my investigation is decidedly theoretical or philosophical, we can also engage in thought experiments on how we might be able to level the playing field for childbearing women, without abolishing capitalism. The development of artificial wombs or other biotechnological means of producing babies outside of the human body would be one solution. Shulamith Firestone's *Dialectic of Sex*, published in 1970, was a pioneering attempt to argue for precisely this. Firestone acutely recognized the central role that generational reproduction played in capitalism and saw the ultimate source of women's oppression to reside in their reproductive capacity. She presented a radical vision of a future in which women would be freed from childbirth through technological means, and sex distinction would become irrelevant. Artificial reproduction would mean that "children would be born to both sexes equally, or independent of either, however one chooses to look at it" (Firestone [1970] 1972, 19). Firestone's ideas were marginalized or dismissed, however, as second wave feminism developed; liberal feminism came to dominate the movement.[8] Despite some developments in uterine transplants, the technological developments that Firestone imagined have also not been realized. It seems unlikely that the connection between capitalism and gender subordination will be dissolved through technological means any time soon.

Another possibility would be the eventual dissolution of our current gender and family order to the point of completely uncoupling childbearing from the gender binary. This is not only theoretically possible, or a mere thought experiment, but an increasingly visible reality today through the development of trans-affirming spaces and practices of parenting. As Loren Cannon writes (2016, 242), the future that Firestone envisioned has begun to be actualized within many trans-affirming communities: "Although Firestone envisioned artificial wombs rather than pregnant men, the result is the same. That is, through the use of technology . . . essentialistic ideas regarding both men and women become untenable." Trans communities include pregnant dads and sperm-providing moms, and "wombs, penises, sperm, and ovaries have been disconnected from the role and functions of motherhood and fatherhood" (237).[9] As I contended already in the last chapter in connection with surrogacy, we are experiencing radical changes in biological parenting which can potentially help us queer or unsex traditional nuclear family and kinship structures. Trans parenting must be recognized as an important aspect of this political project. We must challenge cisgenderism, recognize trans parenting, and advocate for pregnant men's and trans individuals' reproductive freedoms and rights in law. We must address issues such as forcible sterilization as a condition of transition, trans parents' inability to have their status as mother/father/parent accurately recorded on state-issued documentation, and the denial of certain benefits from insurers and employers, for example.[10] However, we must also recognize that law reform by itself is not enough to eradicate oppression; it must be connected to a critique of capitalism and the role of generational reproduction in it. Otherwise, even if we succeeded in completely unsexing pregnancy and parenting, we would have merely arrived at a situation in which we were not just exploiting and discriminating against childbearing women in capitalism, we would be also exploiting and discriminating against childbearing men, and nonbinary people. Hence, my argument here cannot be read as a claim that Marxist-feminist theory on social reproduction is irrelevant to, or even exclusive of trans issues. On the contrary, my argument should demonstrate the importance of anticapitalist critique for trans activism, and vice versa, and bring out the important affinities between them.

It is also necessary to recognize that, sadly, we are currently not anywhere close to witnessing the *complete* collapsing of the gender binary. As feminist and trans philosophers have critically argued, the gender binary runs deep in our thought, language, conceptual schemas, and ways of perceiving the world. In the overwhelming majority of cases, it is still cis women who gestate, give birth, and care for children, and we have to acknowledge that currently this has significant structural effects on gender discrimination and gender subordination in capitalist economies.

The third possible way to dissolve the connection between capitalism and gender subordination would be to completely commodify gestation and open up literal markets for children. If we were able to completely commodify generational reproduction, then the theoretical argument through which I have constructed a systemic connection between capitalism and women's subordination would dissolve. For childbearing women to be able to participate in the economic game on equal terms would in fact require the very opposite of the Scandinavian model: their reproductive labor should be completely commodified, down to its most intimate aspects, and its price freely determined in the market the same way as the price of other commodities. As disturbing as this might sound, it would constitute equality of opportunity for childbearing people in capitalist economy. In such a scenario, childbearing people would be able to bring their special talents and productive capacities to the market, compete freely for the monetizable gains that these could generate, and reap the benefits. A free market for babies would, through the price mechanism, recognize the opportunity costs of the person's time during the period of pregnancy when they are precluded from working, as well as "any pain or other disutility of the pregnancy and delivery" (Landes and Posner 1978, 337). We might not want to live in a world in which reproductive labor had been completely commodified, but in that world, we would no longer have grounds for arguing that capitalism necessarily exploits and economically disadvantages childbearing women by placing them in a contradictory position in which they are expected to compete for economic resources in free labor markets, while also carrying the extra burden of generational reproduction outside of them.

Few feminists, no matter how strongly they believe in capitalism, can stomach such a position, however. That is why Cudd, for example, chooses to submerge capitalism's systemic problems by advocating "enlightened capitalism," which covers over the economic sacrifice childbearing women are expected to make. In other words, she is forced to acknowledge, at least implicitly, that capitalism's economic rationality is incommensurable with some of our deeply held values and commitments about human relationships and what we believe should be for sale. Many readers might also be ready by now to regard my argument as a form of reductio ad absurdum: the argument that capitalism can be made gender-equal leads to a ridiculous, absurd, or impractical conclusion.

The reasons why most of us consider a market for babies abhorrent are, for the most part, moral: despite living in capitalist societies, in our current life form love and children are understood as something that should not be for sale. But our moral beliefs can change, and arguably it is precisely the historical development of capitalism that has significantly extended the realm of those activities and products that we believe are salable. The market rationality organizing capitalism as an economic system has encroached upon other competing and incommensurable sets of norms organizing our societies. As my discussion of commercial gestational surrogacy in the previous chapter showed, irrespective of our prominent moral beliefs, there is a fast-growing market for it—a market many critics equate essentially with baby selling. The moral resistance against the commodification of women's reproductive labor could thus be viewed merely as an example of what some theorists call "commodification anxiety," a culturally reinforced conception that it is wrong or impossible to commodify women's reproductive labor, since it is an expression of their love.

In order to assess the extent to which women's reproductive labor could be completely commodified *in principle*, it is useful to follow Margaret Radin (1996) and make a distinction between a broad or metaphorical commodification and a narrow or literal one.[11] In metaphorical commodification, social interactions do not necessarily involve actually handing over money for goods. Rather, these interactions are made intelligible through economic rationality. One might approach one's dating life, for example, in the mode of an entrepreneur or an investor. The narrow or literal meaning of universal commodification, on the other hand, refers to a claim about actual markets. Now the question of whether everything can be commodified becomes a strictly economic question and falls within the economics of externalities. The only reason for leaving something outside of markets would be the practical control of externalities, which would prevent the market from achieving an efficient result. The economics of externalities deals with problematic cases in which the attempted sale of certain commodities results in market failures: free-riders, holdouts, and information costs.

As Cudd already noted, care work creates important externalities that cannot always be captured in individual market transactions. She does not explicitly discuss the externalities involved in organizing a free market for children, but if we accept the premise that the functioning of capitalism requires not only care work, but also the actual children who have to be gestated and birthed, then these activities should also be included in our assessments of the possibility of gender equality in capitalism. Perhaps understandably, this is a topic that has not been extensively researched by economists, but there are some famous attempts to develop strictly economic approaches to family. In discussing the possibility of a market for children in his seminal work *A Treatise on the Family*, Gary Becker (1981, 98–99), for example, predicts market failure. According to him, the scope of a "child market" would be limited "because parents would be more likely to put their inferior rather than superior children up for sale or adoption if buyers were not readily able to determine quality." Parents might thus try to unload their "lemon" children on buyers, keeping the superior children to themselves. Elisabeth Landes and Richard Posner (1978), on the other hand, argue that in a legal and competitive market for newborn infants, market failures could be eliminated to a large extent through legally enforceable contracts and by establishing some procedure for the prescreening of prospective baby buyers. They recommend "taking some tentative and reversible steps toward a free baby market in order to determine experimentally the social benefits of using the market in this area" (Landes and Posner, 347). Hence, if we side with Becker in this theoretical debate, there might be economic reasons connected with externalities for arguing that women's reproductive labor cannot, even in principle, be completely commodified. If we side with Landes and Posner, however, we could argue that such problems could be relatively easily eliminated and there are no grounds for dismissing the viability of complete commodification.

I will not take sides in such an economic argument here. Rather, I hope to have shown that my thought experiment has now brought us to a point where feminist critiques of capitalism are forced onto a moral terrain. Instead of accepting the purely economic framework which reduces all questions of value, including our assessments of gender equality, to monetizable economic questions and to the optimal functioning of markets, our next move can only be to refuse this framework itself. We must be able to make visible the limitations of an argument, such as Cudd's or Becker's, which ultimately relies on market failure as the only justification for restricting the extent of capitalist markets. Feminists, including Marxist feminists, have to enter into a different conceptual framework and utilize an alternative set of values if they want to raise effective objections against those apologists for capitalism who are prepared to defend its emancipatory potential even to the point of accepting universal commodification and the commensurability of values it entails. Radin (1996, 122), for example, suggests that while there is no knockdown philosophical argument that would compel someone advocating universal commodification to recognize the incommensurability of values, an effective philosophical strategy might be to expose the inconsistency of such a position. If we constantly and consistently viewed social reality only through market rationality—if we truly lived in a world where literally everything had a price—the human "texture" of that world would become unrecognizable to us, and personhood, as we know it, would disappear.

Hence, feminists have to be able to pose critical questions, not only about women's economic opportunities in capitalism, but also about the potential threats to their personhood if the buying and selling of their sexual and reproductive activities, for example, is normalized and becomes widespread. In other words, they have to engage in philosophical and moral critiques of commodification—the meanings it constitutes, the values it reinforces, and the conceptual schemas it installs. I hope that my philosophical investigation in this chapter has set the stage for such critiques and made clear the fundamental, theoretical incompatibility of capitalism and the kind of feminist politics that most of us can believe in.

To sum up my argument so far, in a capitalist economy—built on the principle that individuals must compete for economic resources in free, nondiscriminatory markets—governmental interference can, at best, only ever provide a partial remedy to the problem that generational reproduction presents for gender equality. At worst, it constitutes a discriminatory mechanism against childbearing people that legitimizes their exclusion from the supposedly free labor markets. The entwinement of capitalism and gender oppression thus appears less and less like a contingent historical configuration that could be dissolved in the future. Instead, it appears structurally indispensable for capitalism for reasons related specifically to generational reproduction. This implies that if we do not want to settle for an approximation of gender equality, feminist politics will have to engage in a much more profound critique of capitalism than merely demanding affordable nurseries and longer maternity leaves. If we really wanted gender equality, even in purely economic terms, resources would not be primarily distributed through markets according to the principle of competition, but rather according to some other principle, such as the need for or the right to those resources. In order to seriously address the problem of generational reproduction in capitalism, feminist politics would have to return to some of the most extreme strands of radical feminism and demand a complete reorganization of our current modes of social reproduction, as well as our current modes of economic production.

I will return to the question of what such politics might look like in more detail in chapter 6. I want to make clear already, however, that such politics cannot take the form of identity politics—an exclusive project built on essentialist identity and including only childbearing cis women. On the contrary, I hope to have shown that the Marxist feminist position which foregrounds the importance of social reproduction for capitalism clearly shows that the social organization of reproductive labor is an issue that cannot be limited to the specific interests of any particular gender or group.[12] Rather, it has to be understood as a political issue that directly concerns the future and the economic productivity of society as a whole. Although the liberal political framework effectively portrays generational reproduction as a consumer choice—the decision to have a child is another costly preference—from a Marxist-feminist perspective, children have to be recognized as a necessary condition for any form of continuing social life as well as economic production. Feminist politics must acknowledge this and pose questions about our collective responsibility for it, as well as for its consequences for all of us, irrespective of our gender. Neither does my position entail that I would view sexual or racial oppressions as somehow secondary to gender oppression. My argument here concerns merely the explanatory strategies of feminist critiques of capitalism. Feminists need to engage in critical analyses of capitalism's systemic need for social reproduction, in order to explain what the structural constraints on gender equality are in capitalism, and what is therefore possible in terms of a more equal future.

I began this chapter with Wendy Brown's pessimistic assessment of the future of Marxist-feminist theory: it was largely based on the observation that, at the time, the Euro-Atlantic Left was in mourning for "two particular revolutionary dreams that died in the last quarter of the twentieth century" (Brown 2005, 103). One was the socialist, the other the feminist revolutionary dream. Furthermore, she contended that the collapses of these two revolutionary dreams were intertwined: after the collapse of the socialist revolutionary dream, there were limits to the realizability of the feminist one. Today, more than a decade later, it seems that the political climate in which we dream about revolutionary socialism and feminism is markedly different. There is an ongoing mobilization of the socialist Left as well as a new wave of militant feminist activism, exemplified by women's strikes, for example, that build on the recognition of the growth of economic and social inequality among women.[13] However, as political theorists, it is not enough for us to observe and identify shifts in the political climate. The decisive question must be whether the theoretical issues that brought capitalism and feminism to an irresolvable conflict have somehow been resolved or transformed. I hope to have shown that they have not, and that our revolutionary dreams are therefore more solid and timely than ever.

5

The Commodification of Affects

Neoliberalism, along with economic globalization and the rapid development of biotechnology over the last thirty or forty years, has put women and feminist thought in a new political situation. One of the key issues that it forces us to reassess is contemporary working practices, and their role in feminist politics. Many of the premises about work on which Marxist-feminist theory was built in the 1970s appear outdated. Women's role in the labor market has changed dramatically; for example, *the feminization of labor* has become a sociological catchphrase. This widely used but ambiguous notion not only denotes the quantitative increase of women in the labor market globally—the growth of service industries and the way women have been progressively transformed into a strategic pool of labor. It also denotes a qualitative change in the nature of labor: the characteristics historically present in female work—precariousness, flexibility, mobility, fragmentary nature, low status, and low pay—have increasingly come to characterize most work in global capitalism.[1] The classic figures of the male proletarian and the housewife do not adequately represent the gendered spheres of advanced capitalist production and reproduction any longer.

Kathi Weeks's seminal book *The Problem with Work: Feminism, Marxism, Antiwork Politics, and Postwork Imaginaries* (2011) analyzes the changes in advanced capitalist production, laboring processes, and contemporary forms of the subject. The book is an important feminist appropriation of Michael Hardt and Antonio Negri's conceptual framework. In their influential trilogy, *Empire* (2000), *Multitude* (2004), and *Commonwealth* (2009), Hardt and Negri bring together post-structuralist and Marxist frameworks in order to chart the profound changes that capitalist production has undergone in recent decades. Weeks draws the consequences of these changes for feminist theory and particularly for our conception of work. She wants to add to the Marxist critique of the exploitative and alienating dimensions of work a Foucauldian "focus on its political relations of power" (Weeks 2011, 21).

I fully agree with Weeks and other Marxist feminists who contend that a critical analysis of work is a pressing task for feminist theory today. Feminist theoretical attempts to analyze the changes in contemporary working practices and their implications for feminist politics by turning to Hardt and Negri's thought are highly problematic, however. My critical analysis here focuses, in particular, on the political potential of their influential notion of affective labor, which plays a crucial role in their analysis of contemporary capitalism. While I acknowledge the strengths of the notion in characterizing some contemporary laboring practices, I nonetheless want to expose its shortcomings in advancing feminist politics, particularly in connection with feminist critiques of commodification. I will highlight the need for such critiques and study the philosophical presuppositions that they must build on. I contend that effective feminist critiques of the commodification of affects must appropriate both post-structuralist accounts of subjectivation, as well as Marxist-feminist analyses of socially reproductive labor. In sum, my aim in this chapter is to demonstrate that a critical assessment of the notion of affective labor can bring to the fore some of the key issues that are at stake in feminist critiques of contemporary capitalism.

Affective Labor

Hardt and Negri's seminal claim is that there has been a shift from an industrial paradigm in which industry and the manufacture of durable goods formed the dominant sector of the economy to a paradigm prevailing today in which the production of services and the manipulation of information dominates. This passage to an "informational economy" has necessarily brought about a radical change in the quality of labor and in the nature of laboring processes (Hardt and Negri 2000, 289). Information, communication, knowledge, affects, and relationships have come to play a foundational role in the production process. Since the production of services results in no material and durable goods, Hardt and Negri define the labor involved in this production as "immaterial labor" (290). The labor involved in all immaterial production remains material in the trivial sense that it involves bodies and brains, but its products are immaterial (Hardt and Negri 2004, 109).

Hardt and Negri's key argument is that immaterial labor is the paradigmatic form of labor today—not quantitatively the most common, but a hegemonic model toward which all forms of work are tending. In other words, they are not claiming that most of the workers in the world are producing primarily immaterial goods. They recognize that such a claim would be clearly false: immaterial labor constitutes a minority of global labor, and it is concentrated in some of the dominant regions of the globe. Their claim is rather that immaterial labor has become hegemonic in qualitative terms and has imposed a tendency on other forms of labor and society itself. Hence, immaterial labor is today in the same position that industrial labor was 150 years ago, when it accounted for only a small fraction of global production and was concentrated in a small part of the world, but nonetheless exerted hegemony over all other forms of production. Just as in that phase all forms of labor and society itself had to industrialize, today labor and society have to become intelligent, communicative, and affective (Hardt and Negri 2004, 109).

Affective labor is theorized as an important subcategory of immaterial labor. Hardt and Negri (2000, 293) distinguish three types of immaterial labor that drive the service sector. The first is involved in industrial production, which has incorporated communication technologies in a way that transforms the production process itself. Manufacturing can be regarded as a service, and the material labor of the production of durable goods mixes with and tends toward immaterial labor. The second is the immaterial labor of analytical and symbolic tasks, which divides into creative and intelligent manipulation on the one hand and routine symbolic tasks on the other. Finally, a third type of immaterial labor, affective labor, involves the production and manipulation of affects. It is the labor of human contact and interaction and its "products" are relationships and emotional responses: "a feeling of ease, well-being, satisfaction, excitement or passion" (Hardt and Negri 2009, 108). Affective labor is thus immaterial in the sense that its products are intangible, even though it is usually corporeal and mixes with material forms of labor. Hardt and Negri (2009, 109) note how health care workers, for example, perform affective, cognitive, and linguistic tasks together with material ones, such as cleaning bedpans and changing bandages.

The idea of affective labor appears to have at least three crucial advantages in terms of feminist theory and politics. First, it identifies and recognizes an important contemporary form of labor. The affective labor of human contact and interaction forms an essential component of almost all work today. Characteristics such as emotional resources and communicative skills have become increasingly important. Workers are expected to mobilize them for professional goals, resulting in the blending of the private and the public, the informal and the formal, skills and resources.[2] The potential domains of affective labor are also rapidly expanding beyond what anyone could imagine a couple of decades ago, creating businesses such as breast-feeding consultants and wedding planners. As the marketization and commodification of everyday life expand, people have increasingly come to rely on the affective services that they buy and which they used to receive from their families and communities—whether in health care, child care, entertainment, dating, and so on. Affective labor is increasingly outsourced, and the domestic, private realm is marketized.[3]

While most feminist critiques of Hardt and Negri's thought have focused on their omission of gender analysis, Hardt and Negri explicitly recognize the pioneering feminist work done on affective labor.[4] They write that it is best understood "by beginning from what feminist analyses of 'women's work' have called 'labor in the bodily mode'" (Hardt and Negri 2000, 293). Domestic labor is a paradigmatic example of affective labor for them: it requires repetitive material tasks such as cleaning and cooking, but it also involves producing affects, relationships, and forms of communication and cooperation among children, in the family, and in the community (Hardt and Negri 2004, 110). In the third volume of their trilogy, *Commonwealth*, they also acknowledge that affective labor is disproportionately required of women, both at work and at home.

> In fact, any woman who is not willing to do affective labor on call—smile appropriately, tend to hurt feelings, knit social relationships, and gener- ally perform care and nurturing—is viewed as a kind of monster. Despite their massive entry into the wage labor force, furthermore, women are still primarily responsible in countries throughout the world for un- paid domestic and reproductive labor. . . . Women's double workday is a powerful obstacle to greater education and access to better and better- paid work. (Hardt and Negri 2009, 134)

While highlighting women's care work and emotional labor, the second benefit of the notion of affective labor is that it does not rely on naturalized gender dualism or reified gender identities. Affective labor is gendered—it is in an important sense feminized labor—but it is im- portant to acknowledge that is not performed exclusively by women. As Weeks (2007, 238–39) writes, "the practice of affective labor and presum- ably the potential political subjects that can be constituted on its basis cuts across the older binary divisions of both space and gender. Women and men are indeed still often engaged in different laboring practices, but these differences cannot be mapped onto a binary schema secured by recourse to a model of separate spheres." To assume the persistence of a gender division of work in our contemporary context when the binary of men's and women's work has become increasingly unstable would be both theoretically and politically debilitating.

Third, the notion of affective labor is an important intervention in the Marxist debates on the role of reproductive labor in capitalism. The so-called domestic labor debates were a prolonged controversy in socialist feminism in the 1970s over the value and role of domestic work in capitalist production.[5] This debate mainly centered on the question of whether domestic labor was productive or unproductive labor and consequently, whether it was integral to capitalist production or not. Productive, as opposed to unproductive labor, as Marx argues in *Capital*, is labor that creates surplus value directly, and is therefore usually understood to comprise only certain forms of waged labor.[6] The traditional Marxist position, including that of most Marxist feminists, was that domestic labor was unproductive labor. This view has been expounded by various Marxist thinkers, from Friedrich Engels to Juliet Mitchell.[7] Although women at home performed services and produced things—cooked food, cleaned the house, cared for children, and so on—the products and services that resulted from their work were consumed directly and were not exchanged in the market. In Marxist terms, these products and services had use value but no exchange value.[8]

Hardt and Negri's radical intervention in this debate was to deny the theoretical distinctions between unproductive and productive labor, as well as between material production and social reproduction. According to them, productive labor "cannot be limited to waged labor, but must refer to human creative capacities in all their generality" (Hardt and Negri 2009, 105). In the period of industrial capitalism, it seemed as if only the labor of waged workers was productive and all other types of labor, such as domestic labor performed by women at home, appeared as merely reproductive and unproductive. Hardt and Negri's claim is that in the context of contemporary capitalism, however, in which the production of capital converges with the production and reproduction of social life itself, it becomes impossible to maintain the distinctions among productive, reproductive, and unproductive labor. All forms of labor today must be recognized as socially productive and understood as part of "biopolitical production." In other words, all labor produces and reproduces social life, and in the process is exploited by capital.

Kathi Weeks follows Hardt and Negri in arguing that in today's advanced capitalism, material production and social reproduction are thoroughly integrated, and, according to her, this situation forces feminist politics onto a new footing. The traditional Marxist-feminist category of reproductive labor used to include only the forms of unwaged work through which individuals meet their daily needs for food, shelter, and care, and raised a new generation to take their place. Today social reproduction must be understood in a much broader sense than reproductive or domestic labor. It denotes the production of all the forms of social cooperation on which capitalist accumulation depends, since capital continually seeks to harness all of life to "its times, spaces, rhythms, purposes, and values" (Weeks 2011, 29).

Weeks argues that the most compelling contributions to the domestic labor debate, therefore, were those unorthodox arguments that
disregarded the division between productive and unproductive labor in
arguing that women's domestic labor had to be understood as productive
labor too (Weeks 2011, 140). She refers to the Marxist feminists influ-
enced by the Italian *operaista* movement, such as Silvia Federici and Mariarosa Dalla Costa.[9] According to Weeks (2007), the failure of these early
Marxist-feminist accounts nevertheless consisted of ultimately settling for
a too-narrow conception of affective labor: in their accounts, affective labor was still equated strictly with unwaged housework and domestic labor
and was confined to the space of the household. A contemporary analysis
of affective labor makes clear that such a narrow conception no longer
suffices. Commodities are increasingly replacing domestically produced
goods and services, and forms of caring and household work are being
transformed into feminized, racialized, and globalized forms of labor in
the service sector (Weeks 2007, 235–36). Weeks argues that feminist politics today must proceed from a theoretical recognition of this situation.
She urges feminists to adopt a broader conception of social reproduction
that includes all these different forms of affective labor.

When social reproduction is understood in this broad sense, the
unemployed and housewives are no longer excluded from production,
or, consequently, from the proletariat or the multitude. Because all the
different segments of society produce in common, they also share a common potential to resist the domination of capital (Hardt and Negri 2004,
106–7). "This wide landscape of biopolitical production allows us finally
to recognize the full generality of the concept of proletariat and to eradicate the boundary between material production and social reproduction"
(Hardt and Negri 2000, 402). The upshot for feminist politics appears
to be that women's affective labor is finally recognized as being directly
productive of social reality, and all women, not only working women, are
recognized as important agents in the struggle against capitalism since
they too belong to the proletariat or the multitude.

In sum, the notion of affective labor appears to offer several benefits for feminist theory and politics. It is a much broader concept than
the notion of domestic labor, and is therefore able to elucidate in a novel
way contemporary laboring practices. It is inclusive of women's labor and
gives feminist concerns a central role in critical Marxist theory, while at
the same time troubling any stable distinction between two radically distinct gendered spheres of labor, women's unproductive and reproductive
labor in the domestic realm and men's productive and material labor in
the public sphere. It cuts across such dualisms as mind/body, public/

private, and economy/culture and thereby bridges the gap between a purely economic understanding and a broader sociopolitical understanding of capitalism.

While all this sounds promising, I nevertheless have serious reservations about feminists embracing this notion. I want to show that by treating very different kinds of experiences, activities, and services as the same, the notion ends up obscuring the forms of oppression and exploitation at stake and leaves feminists unable to formulate concrete proposals for forms of resistance against them.

Feminist Politics of Affects

Affective labor includes at least four different kinds of labor that traditional Marxist-feminist analyses have sharply distinguished with the help of the distinctions between productive and unproductive labor, and between material production and social reproduction. Let me first briefly clarify these different types before I proceed with the argument.

First, affective labor denotes care work that is not commodified, such as child rearing at home or looking after sick or elderly members of the family. In other words, it is what traditional Marxist-feminist analysis understands as unproductive labor as opposed to productive labor. Second, affective labor can also be care work or reproductive labor that is commodified and as such productive labor. Examples of such affective labor would include, for example, day care providers and workers in nursing homes. Third and fourth, affective labor denotes waged and unwaged labor that does not directly reproduce labor power but instead aims at producing affects. When it is waged labor, its principal objective is usually to realize a profit for a specific company, not to reproduce workers. Such affective labor normally requires face-to-face or voice-to-voice contact with the public. A paradigmatic example is flight attendants: their work requires inducing or suppressing emotions in order to produce in others the feelings of safety, confidence, and well-being.[10] In addition, Hardt and Negri also include in affective labor waged work that aims at producing affects but does not require personal contact. Their example would be people working in the entertainment industry (Hardt and Negri 2000, 293).

Hence, the notion of affective labor inadvertently eradicates the differences between such varied laborers as childbearers, child rearers, hospitality industry workers, wedding planners, and Walmart greeters.

Because these forms of affective labor are so varied, it seems clear that the political consequences, power relations, and forms of exploitation associated with them are also vastly different in the different cases. An effective feminist politics can only be built on the theoretical recognition of these differences and not on their eradication.

I will raise three different sets of political issues that I claim are at stake in our analyses of affective labor and outline three·corresponding feminist political projects: the demand for a recognition of women's reproductive labor in capitalism, the demand for better work, and the demand for the moral limits of the market. All these feminist political projects build in different ways on affective labor. However, they require that we make both theoretical and normative distinctions between different forms of affective labor and that we recognize the theoretical and political specificity of each of these forms. While my first set of political issues challenges the eradication of the distinction between material production and social reproduction, the second and third challenge the viability of eradicating the distinction between productive and unproductive labor, understood in the sense of commodified and uncommodified care work/emotional labor. I will sketch the first two political projects relatively briefly and focus in more detail on the third one.

Affective Labor as Generational Reproduction

My first political issue reiterates the argument I made in the previous chapter, and so I will only go over it briefly here. From the perspective of feminist politics, it is important not to lose sight of the fact that affective labor, when it is understood as reproductive labor, not only produces positive externalities such as socialization, education, and interpersonal values of belonging, but it produces, essentially, human beings. To put it bluntly, babies are not positive externalities of biopolitical production that add value to commodities; from an economic perspective, they have to be recognized as a necessary condition for any form of continuing production. As I have already shown, the reproduction of labor power is an essential condition undergirding the dynamic of the capitalist system. Social reproduction in the form of producing and socializing the next generation of workers is a necessary condition for the existence of wage laborers and the functioning of capitalist economies.

Weeks criticizes traditional Marxist-feminist accounts for relying on the gendered distinction between reproduction and production and thereby settling for a too-narrow conception of affective labor. But as I already argued, feminist critique has to be able to identify and theorize the indispensable role of affective labor in capitalism in the narrow sense of women's generational reproductive labor. Weeks is clearly concerned that if contemporary feminist politics focuses on issues that are seen to be affecting only certain women, such as childbearing, this inevitably means falling back on exclusionary forms of identity politics. She advocates a political demand for an unconditional basic income, for example, on the grounds that it is precisely the gender neutrality of the demand for basic income that should be counted as its feminist strength because this means that its benefits are not exclusive to any particular group. The demand can speak to the concerns of a number of differently situated subjects, including a much broader constituency of women than those who are directly involved in social reproduction (Weeks 2011, 149).

I will assess the feminist demand for a basic income in more detail in the next chapter. I, too, will advocate for it, but in contrast to Weeks, only on the condition that we challenge precisely its gender neutrality.[11] As I already argued in the previous chapter, to see reproduction as an issue that concerns only a particular group of women means to accept the liberal framework, which views it as a consumer choice: the decision to have a child is another costly preference. Weeks herself convincingly exposes and criticizes such an individualizing framework by writing, for example, that "the family and its ideology help to obscure the cost of productive labor by privatizing, feminizing, and naturalizing much of the work involved in its reproduction" (Weeks 2011, 143). Feminist politics must not only expose and criticize the structural relationship between capitalism and the heterosexual nuclear family. We must also proceed from this theoretical insight to the radical political acknowledgment that the social organization of reproductive labor is not an issue that can be limited to the interests of any particular group. It must be understood as a political issue that directly concerns the future and the economic productivity of society as a whole.

Hence, the first feminist political project stemming from the centrality of affective labor must seriously address the role of generational reproduction in capitalism and demand a complete reorganization not only of our current modes of social reproduction but also of our current modes of economic production. While the feminist movement has had some limited success in socializing and ungendering reproduction, the biggest change by far in the conditions under which we reproduce ourselves has been the commodification and globalization of care work. The gendered nature of reproductive labor has therefore hardly changed at all. Reproductive labor has only been redistributed to different women—largely to poor and immigrant women from the Global South.[12]

The Commodification of Emotions

My second political issue and corresponding feminist project can be understood as a variant of traditional labor struggles. When Hardt and Negri discuss affective labor in *Empire*, they note in passing: "when affective production becomes part of waged labor it can be experienced as extremely alienating: I am selling my ability to make human relationships, something extremely intimate, at the command of the client and the boss" (Hardt and Negri 2004, 111). From the perspective of feminist politics, this is a key aspect of emotional labor, however. When the work requires the worker to supply not only intellectual and manual skills but also emotional capacities, something very different is drawn into the labor process.

Arlie Hochschild's groundbreaking sociological study of flight attendants, *The Managed Heart* ([1983] 2012), introduced the concept of emotional labor into feminist theoretical debates and made the powerful argument that emotional laborers in the service sector do not just sell their ability to create human relationships. They are selling emotions that require drawing resources from a source of the self that we usually honor as deep and integral to our individuality. She asks what happens to the worker and to the way she relates to her feelings when the rules about how to feel, and how to express feelings, are set by the management and when private capacities for empathy and warmth are put to corporate use (Hochschild [1983] 2012, 89). In the flight attendant's work, smiling, for example, is separated from its usual function, which is to express a personal feeling, and attached to another one—expressing a company feeling (127). Hochschild documents the problems that flight attendants experience when what is usually a private management of feeling is transformed into emotional labor for a wage. Their work experience includes the difficult task of managing the estrangement between the private self and the public feeling, or between self and display (131).

Hochschild thus exposes an unseen and undervalued aspect of waged work most often performed by women and strongly associated with femininity. The upshot of her analysis for feminist politics is fairly obvious but, nevertheless, significant. Feminist political projects attempting to reconfigure the role of work must make emotional labor visible and demand political recognition and respect for it. Care work, mostly done by women, continues to be very badly paid compared to industrial blue-collar labor most often performed by men, for example, yet care workers do much more than just perform menial tasks. By understanding the psychological costs of different forms of emotional labor, we can try to mitigate or remove them by adequate compensation and by increasing the workers' control over the conditions of their work (Hochschild [1983] 2012, 187).

Hardt and Negri contend, optimistically, that rather than subsuming and organizing all labor in an attempt to exploit it, in the new informational economy capital increasingly seeks to capture and expropriate autonomously produced "commonwealth" such as knowledges, languages, codes, information, social relationships, and affects. This is possible because immaterial labor always involves social interaction and cooperation, but this cooperative aspect is no longer imposed or organized from the outside by capital, as it was in the case of industrial labor, for example. Instead, such cooperation is completely immanent to the immaterial laboring activity itself, providing "the potential for a kind of spontaneous and elementary communism" (Hardt and Negri 2000, 294). In other words, affective labor produces spontaneously positive externalities such as social networks, attachments, and passions that capital needs and wants to appropriate. These positive externalities could, however, also form the bases for alternative modes of production and forms of life.

Hardt and Negri are undoubtedly right in insisting that the exploitation of immaterial labor assumes new forms today, such as the buying of patents and intellectual property rights. In the case of affective labor, however, the principal way that capital still attempts to expropriate it is by organizing it from the outside and transforming it into low-wage, productive labor. The increasing marketization of care work is a paradigmatic example of this trend. Care workers are predominantly performing affective services today as low-waged laborers, not as innovators and cognitive capitalists. Their work is poorly paid and of low status, and it is disproportionately performed by women from subordinated racial-ethnic minorities in most Western countries. The current "crisis of care," the lack of sufficient numbers of qualified care workers who actually care, and the failed attempts to introduce nursing robots in elder-care facilities, for example, must be understood as symptomatic of this drive to commodify emotional labor and the serious difficulties in doing so.

For a critical, feminist analysis of this development, it is crucial that we make a theoretical distinction between unproductive and productive labor, not in any evaluative or moral sense, but in the Marxist sense of whether the labor in question produces surplus value that capitalism can extract—in other words, whether it is uncommodified or commodified emotional labor. This distinction is necessary in order to pose the question of what the political consequences are of the former increasingly becoming the latter. In other words, what is politically relevant for feminist struggles against capitalism, and particularly for effective feminist critiques of commodification, is not the distinction between productive and unproductive labor in the sense of whether a form of labor contributes to social production or not. What is essential is whether a service is brought within the domain of the markets, or whether its appropriate place is considered to be outside of that domain.

This brings me to my third set of political issues. We must not only ask the economic question of how certain affective services can be appropriately compensated; we must also ask the more fundamental ethical question of whether they should be for sale in the first place.

Feminist Critiques of Commodification

While labor struggles aiming to achieve political recognition and better compensation for emotional labor are undoubtedly important, the more fundamental problem concerns the question of how certain affective services can be properly compensated at all. How do we monetize emotional labor? The positive emotions that emotional labor produces are curious products in the sense that their sale radically alters their meaning and value. If I pay for friendship or love, it seems legitimate to question whether it really is friendship or love any longer. We must consider the argument that many affective services cannot be compensated with money at all, not just for the economic reason that they are externalities, and their value cannot therefore be easily monetized, but for the philosophical reason that we believe their value to be fundamentally incommensurable with money.

Markets allocate good and services, but they also importantly express and promote certain meanings, values, and attitudes toward the goods and services that are exchanged. Flight attendants suffer from problems of estrangement, but when commodified emotional labor is also commodified reproductive labor, the issue becomes much more troubling. As my discussion of gestational surrogacy in the third chapter hopefully made clear, the feminist problems surrounding it are not reducible to economic issues. They point toward a dimension of critique that is not just concerned with exploitation and economic equity, but with the moral harms of commodification: how it transforms our deeply held beliefs about personhood and the meaning of different laboring practices. Thus, feminist critiques of capitalism must also attempt to resist our affects from becoming yet another thing to be bought and sold. As Kristen Ghodsee (2018, xiii) writes, this is one meaning of the phrase "the personal is political": "If we can better understand how the current capitalist system has co-opted and commercialized basic human emotions, we have taken the first step toward rejecting market valuations that purport to quantify our fundamental worth as human beings."

But what does such feminist critique of the commodification of affects entail philosophically? My contention is that here we crucially need to combine Marxist theory with post-structuralist insights on subjectivation. Feminist critiques of commodification need to build theoretically on a sophisticated account of subjectivation—understood here broadly as the social formation of the subject. We need to analyze the techniques of governing through which we are constituted as subjects in order to be able to identify the potential ways to alter or overthrow them. In other words, once we make critiques of commodification central to feminist anticapitalist struggles, the upshot is that not only political economy and political institutions need to change radically, but also the political subjects themselves.

A central idea in many strands of Marxist theory is that commodification not only expresses, but also creates alienation by bringing about an impoverished form of human life where people begin to view themselves, their central attributes, and each other as commodities. Weeks's appropriation of autonomist Marxist theory means refusing any recourse to such a traditional critique of alienation. She criticizes Marxist theorists of alienation for "a tendency toward nostalgia for an earlier time" in which small-scale production dominated, and deems their critique as "a romanticization of craft production" (Weeks 2007, 87). But irrespective of our moral beliefs, we need to recognize that it is a significantly different moral claim to argue that we should all build our own furniture in our garden sheds than it is to argue that we should "make" our own babies instead of outsourcing pregnancy to India. Whether we want to use the concept of alienation or not, there nevertheless seems to be a range of human activity, specifically activity associated with the production and management of emotions, that for ethical reasons lends itself poorly to commodification.

Weeks also attacks the conception of the subject that feminist resistance to the commodification of affective labor seemingly presupposes. She criticizes Hochschild's work on emotional labor for being outdated to the extent that Hochschild still relies on the notions of "authenticity" and "an essential self." According to Weeks, Hochshild's argument is animated by an ideal of a separate world of emotional contact with one's "true" self—the possibility of which it simultaneously disavows in acknowledging the social construction of emotions (Weeks 2007, 244). Instead, Weeks (2011, 90) notes approvingly how Negri, for example, expresses no interest in the problematic of alienation as a discourse of interiority concerned with the loss and restoration of an essential human nature.[13]

Weeks's critique of an essentialist and authentic conception of the subject clearly builds on Foucault's work, but because she interprets it through Hardt and Negri's distinctive account of subjectivation, in my view, she misconstrues its political consequences. Perhaps Foucault's most significant contribution to critical social and political theory was his account of productive power: the insight that any analysis of power relations must recognize how these relations are constitutive of the subjects involved in them. The Foucauldian feminist critique that became dominant in the 1980s and 1990s targeted earlier socialist and Marxist-feminist theory precisely for the latter's inability to account for the different ways in which female and feminine subjects are constituted in diffuse and intersecting networks of power. While effectively exposing forms of exploitation and alienation, Marxist feminist theory had tended to theorize men and women as more or less given identities, with more or less authentic desires and interests. Foucault's productive and capillary conception of power made it possible to destabilize and politicize such identities and to bring into theoretical focus a whole spectrum of intersecting dominations that had been relatively invisible before: sexual minorities, transgender individuals, prisoners, and the "abnormal," for example.[14]

Hardt and Negri appropriate Foucault's idea of productive power for their own distinctive account of subjectivation. They borrow his concept of biopolitics, but this notion becomes radically transformed into the notion of biopolitical production in their thought. Instead of designating distinct governmental technologies centered on the optimization and regulation of life, the term "biopolitics" comes to designate the total process by which social reality is materially produced. Biopolitical production is thus not limited to economic phenomena, but involves all aspects of social life, including networks of communication and information, linguistic forms, the production of knowledge, collaborative social relationships, affects, and the producers themselves (Hardt and Negri 2000, 32).

Hardt and Negri argue that Marx already introduced in *Capital* the idea that power relations are constitutive of the subjects, in the significant passages that describe the transition from formal subsumption to real subsumption of labor (e.g., Hardt and Negri 2000, 25). Marx's key claim there is that capitalist production only truly begins when the subjection of labor to capital becomes real rather than simply formal—when the labor process itself is transformed and consequently transforms the laborers themselves (Marx [1867] 1990, 645, 1019–38). In other words, capital not only takes over and manages an already existing labor process, but completely alters its nature and, by extension, the laborers themselves.

Hardt and Negri's idea of biopolitical production radically transforms this account, however, by eradicating Marx's distinctions between production and reproduction, as well as productive and unproductive labor. Although a key tenet of Marx's theory is the idea that in capitalism labor power is a commodity that is exchanged in the market, it is understood as a special kind of commodity, not only because it is capable of producing surplus value, but also because it is produced in an essentially different way than other commodities. With the idea of biopolitical production these insights are lost because capitalism is understood not as a distinctive form of economic production, but as a comprehensive social formation. The relations of production and the relations constitutive of the producers themselves become superimposed. Hardt and Negri sum up the idea in the following way: "The great industrial and financial powers thus produce not only commodities but also subjectivities. They produce agentic subjectivities within the biopolitical context: they produce needs, social relations, bodies and minds—which is to say, they produce producers" (Hardt and Negri 2000, 32).[15]

The way Hardt and Negri understand subjectivation thus differs radically from Foucault. They understand it according to an economic model of production: in the quotation above, the way power produces subjects appears essentially no different from the causal process in which commodities are produced. In contrast, Foucault argues against "economism" in analyses of power, against the idea that we can analyze power relations according to economic models of commodity production and exchange.[16] His idea of disciplinary power, for example, should not be understood as a simple empirical claim about disciplinary practices and institutions causally producing the people involved in them. Rather, power relations in disciplinary institutions formed the historical conditions of possibility for the production of true discourses in the human sciences, which then formed the matrix of intelligibility for identities and normalized subjectivities. Normalization is therefore a complex process of subjectivation that produces numerous other, intersecting forms of the subject besides "docile laborers" or "the producers." It involves large-scale techniques of governing that are always linked with games of truth and forms of scientific knowledge. My contention is that such a complex understanding of subjectivation can better help us identify both the difficulties of mounting feminist political resistance against the commodification of affects, and the germane nodes for such resistance. We need to understand the often conflicting and dispersed techniques of governing through which we are constituted as subjects in contemporary capitalist societies in order to be able to identify the potential ways to alter or overthrow them.

Capitalist modernity must be understood as a historical process that has resulted in the idea of the subject as a possessor of unique, irreducible, and essentially private emotions.[17] Modern capitalist subjects are thus formed through the recognition that their "true" emotions are expressions of their inner and authentic selves. At the same time, these emotions are now increasingly detached from the subjects, reified, and constructed as interchangeable and measurable things that can be commodified—exchanged in the market and sold as skills. The "alienation" experienced by people selling emotional labor must be understood to lie precisely in this contradiction. It should not be conceptualized as a contradiction between naturalness and artificiality, or authenticity and inauthenticity, but rather as a contradiction between two different and conflicting forms of experience that are both socially constituted and form an essential aspect of what it means to be a subject in contemporary capitalist society.

This insight then implies that we should not seek resources for resistance against commodification in romantic ideas of authenticity and naturalness, but neither should we conclude that the forms of social constitution and management of affects are fundamentally the same in all spheres of society. The corporate management of workers' emotions has specific and problematic aspects when compared to the way that all people sometimes hide their "true" feelings in social contexts for various reasons. The disconnection between the lived emotions and their outward display must be sustained for significant periods of time, for example, and takes the form of a double disconnection in the sense that the form that the "false" outward display takes is determined by the employer. In other words, feminist resistance to the commodification of certain forms of affective labor is not a matter of defending private authenticity against social reification, but rather an attempt to mediate, shape, and manage our affects through freer and less exploitative social relations. In contrast to what Weeks claims, such a political project does not have to rely on the idea of a "true self" or "true love." Nor does it imply that we cannot challenge those contemporary discourses that naturalize and idealize certain forms of the family. Rather, the feminism critique of capitalism should be viewed as a political project, which demands restrictions on the commodification of our everyday life precisely in order to create new, different, and freer forms of the subject, love, and relationships.

It could be objected that while it might be unethical or absurd to monetize affective labor, this does not mean that it is not actually happening. Feminist politics can only be rooted in a conceptual grasp of contemporary reality, not in its disavowal and sanctimonious moral condemnation. However, neither can feminist politics amount to merely watching on the sidelines as the processes of commodification unfold. Rather than suggesting that feminists should simply condemn the morality of capitalist markets in toto, I believe that feminism should form a bold and vocal strand in the public, political, and moral debate on the desirable limits of the market—for example in the ongoing debates on sex work and commercial surrogate pregnancy—debates that our societies acutely need today. Rather than engaging in such a debate here, however, my aim has been to expose the philosophical or theoretical requisites for such a debate: we must retain the ability to draw theoretically nuanced distinctions between commodified and non-commodified affective services, as well as different forms of socially reproductive labor.

6

Is It Wrong for Feminists to Pay for Housework?

Gabrielle Meagher's article "Is It Wrong to Pay for Housework?" (2002), published in the leading journal of feminist philosophy, *Hypatia*, left me pondering this question for a long time. The article is essentially a philosophical apology for paid housework, since Meagher finds no adequate moral justification for rejecting it. Her philosophical reasoning is impeccable, and despite defending paid housework, her position could be characterized as "socialist-feminist." It is not a conservative or a right-wing libertarian position; rather, it represents a recognizable and dominant view among many left-leaning, progressive feminists. Nevertheless, her position seemed profoundly flawed to me, as well as being suspiciously convenient—it requires neither engaging in radical feminist politics nor having to make uncomfortable personal changes.

In keeping with the tradition of Marxist feminism, her question itself appears to be incorrectly formulated: paid housework cannot be assessed as an abstract philosophical question about individual moral responsibility; rather, it has to be placed in the specific historical and socioeconomic context in which it is encountered today and given a rigorously structural, socioeconomic analysis. Yet, the Marxist tendency to completely dismiss questions about individual responsibility and practices of living as politically irrelevant also seems problematic to me. My critical concern is that Marxist socioeconomic analyses would provide an answer identical to Meagher's. Marxist critics of paid housework could also conclude that paying other women for housework is morally sound, only they would reach this conclusion from different premises. They would argue that because the socioeconomic injustices embedded in paid housework are essentially caused by structural problems inherent in capitalism, no individual can be expected to take moral responsibility for them. Instead, we would have to assign collective moral responsibility for them to the capitalist class. This idea would then get us mired in divisive debates concerning which women belong to which class and what kinds of individual moral responsibilities such a collective understanding of responsibility might nevertheless entail. If the structural inequalities between "mistresses" and "maids" could ultimately be combatted only by overthrowing the whole capitalist system, it would obviously make little sense to expect individual women to refuse to hire cleaning ladies. The only political action they could consistently be expected to engage in would perhaps be to incite a proletarian revolution. Identifying the structural character of a political problem can thus also function as a convenient strategy for avoiding having to make uncomfortable personal changes.

I want to therefore try to sketch a middle path here between the two extremes of moral individualism and Marxist structural analysis. The argument proceeds in three stages. In the first section, I will provide a functionalist analysis of paid housework that exposes its conditions of possibility in the economic logic of capitalist economy. Such a politico-economic analysis of paid housework should open our eyes to the fact that feminists need to make political demands that are not merely ameliorative but embody a radically emancipatory future for all women. In the second section, I will critically assess one such demand, namely the idea of universal basic income (UBI)—a monthly income paid by the government to each member of society regardless of income from other sources and without any conditions attached. My contention is that a feminist demand for UBI could contribute to the attempts to tackle the deep causes of the growing socioeconomic disparities between women, while also promoting decentralized and individual experiments in alternative ways of living. However, UBI can function as an effective means of profound political transformation only in the context of a feminist revolution of everyday life. In the concluding section, I will ask what such a revolution might entail. While I insist that scapegoating women who pay other women for housework misses the real problem, I will nevertheless conclude by giving compelling political reasons for feminists to boldly answer the question in my title in the affirmative.

Servant Economies

Meagher summarizes and then refutes what she sees as the most compelling arguments advanced in feminist and socialist critiques of paid housework by distilling them into three distinct propositions. First, domestic service subjects workers to a uniquely exploitative employment relationship because it takes place in domestic isolation. In other words, it leaves workers exceptionally vulnerable to economic abuse because a clear boundary between work and non-work, professional and personal, is difficult to establish (Meagher 2002, 55). Second, paying others to do the work of self-maintenance, which people can do perfectly well themselves, amounts to paying to enhance one's social status and for the pleasure of being served. Paid housework should thus be understood as a set of activities that are servile by virtue of their content, irrespective of the kinds of relationships within which they are performed (58). Third, by paying for housework, people promote the destructive encroachment of the market into private life. When people pay others to do the work of maintaining their bodies and homes, they lose the knowledge and skills to look after themselves, as well as the opportunities for non-instrumental sharing of their labor and themselves (59).

Meagher refutes all three propositions on essentially the same grounds. If we accept that we live in a capitalist, free-market society in which a variety of services are bought and sold, then housework does not provide a distinctive enough case to warrant our moral condemnation. There is nothing morally unique about it. We are paying daily for services that are essentially similar such as the services of flight attendants, waiters, and hairdressers, and it would be impossible, on ethical grounds, to refuse to pay directly or indirectly for these services and still participate in the capitalist economy as a consumer (Meagher 2002, 58). In sum, Meagher argues that the distinction between paid housework and other forms of contemporary service work is not robust enough for feminists to single out housework for moral condemnation.

Meagher acknowledges that there nevertheless remain outstanding "problems of socio-structural justice" with paid housework and that any critical evaluation of it must also take a position on them (Meagher 2002, 53). The growing disparity between different groups of women is clearly problematic: the use of domestic workers frees some socially and economically privileged women from burdens other women must continue to bear while leaving the sexual division of domestic labor more or less intact (61). However, in a liberal society, individuals cannot be assigned responsibility for such socio-structural injustices. Individuals are "responsible for only those aspects of decision-making in transactions over which they have discretion as individual actors" (54).

The political remedies prescribed by Meagher for these socio-structural injustices include the formalization of housework, as well as political support for labor organization and other collective action for improved wages and working conditions (Meagher 2002, 62–63). She thus tacitly accepts the capitalist economic order as desirable, or at least as inevitable, but recognizes the need to push it politically towards a more social democratic variant through the traditional arsenal of redistributive and welfare measures such as living wages for all workers, improved social service provision, and the obliteration of racial-ethnic and gender discrimination in labor markets. Individual moral responsibility is only limited to support for such political measures.

My contention is that feminist critiques of paid housework will have to reach significantly deeper in their analyses of "the problems of socio-structural justice." In order to have real teeth, such critiques will have to expose the systemic conditions on which paid housework as a specific type of economic activity rests. This requires stepping outside of the realm of normative moral philosophy into the contested sphere of political economy and analyzing "the laws of motion" of capitalist economies.

As I have already noted several times, a key feature of capitalist economies is the constant push to increase productivity through inno-vation, competition, and technological development. During the last hundred years, production has roughly doubled every twenty-five years in Western societies, but the number of working hours necessary to achieve the huge increase in wealth has been steadily dropping. This is obviously capitalism's major strength and the number one reason that is usually given for why free markets are the most efficient way to organize eco-nomic activity. As Marx already recognized, this strength is, paradoxi-cally, also a weakness and a source of capitalist crisis. When less and less labor power is required to produce more and more things, the question arises as to what we should do with all the workers who are no longer needed. If the result is mass unemployment, it will quickly begin to slow down economic growth through reduced consumption.

The neoliberal shift from an industrial economy to a service econ-omy has been an attempt to deal with this problem of increasing labor productivity and its evil twin, unemployment. In the last decades, the broadly accepted consensus across the political spectrum has been that the service sector will have to provide a significant portion of future em-ployment growth. Politicians and economists have been hard at work de-vising ways to stimulate service jobs in the private sector with such direct policy instruments as tax incentives for hiring paid housework, as well as with broader neoliberal measures such as weakening unions and making global labor markets more flexible.[1] While more and more industrial jobs in the Global North have become obsolete as a result of increased labor productivity and globalization, and the number of workers in industrial production continues to fall, the number of jobs in the service sector has been steadily rising. In 1969, when the Marxist-feminist writer Margaret Benston published her groundbreaking article on the economic signifi-cance of women's domestic labor, she already recognized a growing trend in the commodification of traditional home production—the emergence of takeout meals, day care services, and cleaning companies. Benston observed at the end of her article that if these "embryonic forms" develop further, the contradiction between the pressure for the commodification of housework, on the one hand, and the need to keep women at home, on the other, would grow (Benston [1969] 1997, 22). She was skeptical, however, as to how far the commodification of housework could extend and doubted that the economy could expand enough, thanks to the growth of such service industries, in a way that would put all women to work as part of the normally employed labor force. In the past, this had happened only in the exceptional circumstances of a war economy. "The present trends in the service industries simply create underemployment in the home; they do not create new jobs for women" (22).

Benston clearly underestimated the innovativeness of capitalism and the growth potential of service industries. We have seen the increasing transformation of activities that people used to perform for themselves into paid services, whether in child care, elder care, or housework. The private realm has been marketized to an unprecedented extent, and personal and intimate activities are increasingly performed in relationships that are commodified. This development is clearly gendered because service sector jobs are traditionally female jobs. The new jobs in the domestic services sector have represented a significant gain for women in terms of overall workforce participation, but they are usually precarious, low-wage and low-status jobs disproportionately performed by women from subordinated racial-ethnic minorities. As Meagher (2002, 61) observes, the proportion of women employed as domestic workers in the United States, for example, is strongly correlated to two factors: household income inequality and the percentage of the labor force that is African American, Latina, or foreign-born.[2]

The precariousness of housework is further underscored by the fact that it is often performed in the informal sector: large numbers of undocumented migrant women and asylum seekers are employed in undeclared jobs in the domestic service industry both in Europe and the United States. These women do not usually have a work permit or speak the language sufficiently to qualify for work in the formal economy.[3] Housework is thus typically the occupation of those who have very few other opportunities in the labor market and are therefore forced to accept low-paid and low-valued domestic work.

While measures such as the formalization of housework and better labor protection seem like effective remedies for these problems, socialist theorists such as André Gorz ([1994] 2012) have forcefully argued that they merely mask the economic logic that necessarily underlies the growth of personal services. Gorz ([1994] 2012, 48) contends that we need to recognize that the professionalization and monetization of personal services no longer obeys the same logic as the economic development of the past, namely the logic of "productive substitution." The idea of productive substitution in economics refers to situations in which the substitution of waged work for an individual's own production for themselves results in efficiency gains. In such cases, the substitution is productive because the working time saved can be, at least in theory, reemployed within the economy to produce more wealth.

> In the past, economic growth did, in effect, have "productive substitu-
> tion" as its engine: tasks which people had for centuries performed in
> their domestic sphere were progressively transferred to industry and
> service industries which possessed machines more efficient than those
> to which a household had access . . . No one spins their own wool any
> longer, or weaves their cloth, . . . since all these activities, which people
> still frequently performed for themselves two or three generations ago,
> are carried out more quickly, and often better, by industries employing
> wage-laborers. (Gorz [1994] 2012, 48)

Hence, Gorz accepts that industrialization and the new division of labor achieved through capitalist labor markets saved working time for everyone throughout society. His problem is that the new jobs created today in personal services are essentially different. They do not usually provide any more efficiency than if the person performed the chore herself. Paying someone else to clean my house or to look after my child is no more efficient that doing these chores myself. It simply frees my time to do something else that I would rather do. In other words, they are not instances of "productive substitution," but of "equivalent substitution" (Gorz [1994] 2012, 49).

Since personal services do not increase the overall productivity of labor, meaning that no extra wealth can be produced in this way, at least two economic conundrums arise. First, the question arises as to where consumers are going to get the extra purchasing power to enable them to buy the increasing quantities of personal services from a growing host of service providers. Gorz notes that most economists reply by pointing out that automation brings down the relative prices of products. This fall in prices increases purchasing power and enables people to afford the new personal services, resulting in a growing service economy. His objection to this is sharp:

> An essential aspect of the question is left out of account: where does the
> fall in relative prices due to automation come from? The answer is that it
> comes from automated enterprises having reduced their "payroll," from

their having reduced the volume of wages they distribute. They have reduced the "payroll" by reducing their workforce. (Gorz [1994] 2012, 49)

In other words, what is left out of these accounts are the people who have lost their jobs due to automation. The people with extra purchasing power include only those workers who have been lucky enough to keep their jobs. They are going to have additional purchasing power due to automation decreasing production costs, but this occurs because fewer workers are required for production. The people who therefore lost their jobs now have to find new jobs in the service sector. The catch for them is that this sector will pay them considerably less.

The second economic conundrum is the following: even if some people now have the extra purchasing power with which they can potentially buy personal services, those services have to be competitively priced, otherwise the buyers are likely to spend their money on something else. The economist Brigitte Young explains this problem with the notion of "Baumol's cost disease": "Baumol has showed that the assumption of price inelasticity of demand for services is not justified in cases where the consumer can switch to substitution. Simple services at home have always competed with 'self-service'" (Young 2001, 321). In other words, economic rationality dictates that if one of the parents earns less money than what it costs to hire a nanny or a cleaning lady, they will probably do the job themselves. The market for domestic services is only economically viable if these services are priced low enough.

In sum, a "servant economy" requires, as its conditions of possibility, that there are people who can afford to buy the services of the new servants and that it makes economic sense for them to do so. These economic requirements imply that significant social and economic inequality is the politically necessary precondition for a market in domestic services. The disparity between different groups of women is thus not a merely contingent problem that can be remedied with the political measures that Meagher supports. Those political measures can be ameliorative at best, and purely cosmetic at worst, because significant social and economic disparity is a structurally necessary precondition for paid housework to be a feasible economic activity in the first place.

Hence, if feminists want to defend paid housework, they need to begin by at least recognizing the economic logic on which this type of employment rests and be clear about its social and political costs. The growth of personal services means that unemployment can be kept low, and some women can compete in the labor market on a par with men, but "an enormous underclass of servants develops to ease the lives and leisure of the better-off classes" (Gorz [1994] 2012, 50). Brigitte Young (2001,

316) describes this new division of labor provocatively by paraphrasing Marx: "On one side is the 'mistress' and on the other stands the 'maid,' separated by different racial, ethnic, class and national belonging and backgrounds."

So far, I have attempted to show that functionalist, politico-economic analyses are indispensable for feminist assessments of paid housework and that they point to an urgent need for a radical economic restructuring of our societies. It is crucial to take seriously the Marxist-feminist insight that tackling the socio-structural injustices that paid housework perpetuates requires moving from an inquiry that focuses on individual moral responsibility to a thorough politico-economic analysis. Such an analysis should open our eyes to the fact that in today's advanced capitalist economies, which are to a large extent characterized by automation, globalization, and extremely high labor productivity, feminists need to make more radical political demands than lending support for the formalization of housework and for the traditional social-democratic goals of full employment, higher minimum wages, and better labor protections. We need to make demands that are not merely ameliorative but embody a radically emancipatory future for all women.

Universal Basic Income

One such radically emancipatory demand that is widely debated today is the idea of universal basic income (UBI): an income paid unconditionally to individuals regardless of their family or household relationships, regardless of other income, and regardless of their past, present, or future employment status (e.g., Van Parijs 1992, 3). UBI is currently studied in several fields, and the growing literature on it includes philosophical theories and economic analyses of implementation proposals and labor market effects, as well as various socioeconomic analyses of social policy and welfare reforms.[4] To provide a comprehensive assessment of UBI, one would obviously have to take into account all the details of the proposal which would be implemented and the particularities of the economic system of the country under consideration. My aim here is merely to assess the key theoretical issues that UBI introduces into feminist debates on paid housework. The amount of the monthly payment is of crucial importance even for any purely theoretical evaluation of UBI, however. I will therefore assume here that the monthly payment would be generous enough to live on without any supplementary income. As several critical analyses of UBI have shown, if the payment is not high enough to allow people to refuse work entirely, UBI will merely push down wages and support precarious employment—in other words, create more "bullshit jobs."[5]

The first key advantage of UBI from the perspective of my questioning is that it promises a concrete alternative to the servant economy discussed above. It can be defended precisely on the functionalist grounds that advanced economies in the Global North no longer need the full-time employment of everybody. These societies produce increasing wealth with a decreasing amount of labor, but they do not redistribute the resulting wealth or the remaining work in a fair manner. Instead, a section of the population works full-time, another section is unemployed, and a third works in precarious jobs for reduced pay. For Gorz, the reason for this is clear: "Work time as the basis for the distribution of socially produced wealth is clung to solely for the reasons of ideology and political domination" ([1994] 2012, 75). Some people benefit tremendously from the current arrangement, namely the elite who are able to hold on to their higher-paying jobs in a growing economy, while also being able to outsource their unpleasant chores to someone else.

A feminist demand for UBI would thus recognize and attempt to tackle the deep causes behind the growing socioeconomic disparity between different groups of women. It would not merely seek to ameliorate the situation of individual domestic workers while leaving intact the structural, socioeconomic conditions for the emergence of this type of employment. Economic independence has traditionally been a key goal of feminism, and many feminists have insisted that women's full-time employment is the only feasible route to it. However, this argument rests on the assumption that there are or could be enough well-paid jobs for everyone to live on. In the current economic situation in the Global North, such feminist politics has arguably become a means of restricting the right to good income only to certain groups of women while penalizing economically those who cannot find full-time employment. It also arguably devalues care work by conveying the message that only paid work is valuable from a feminist standpoint.

UBI also has a second significant advantage. It cuts out the need to debate the abstract moral question about the true nature and intrinsic value of housework. In other words, it makes redundant the type of ontological and moral reasoning upon which Meagher's defense of paid housework relies—whether it differs in significant enough respects from other types of unpleasant service work. Even the people defending paid housework usually agree that it is unpleasant: it is physically strenuous, mind-numbingly repetitive, and dirty, offering no opportunities for promotion or self-actualization (Bowman and Cole 2009, 172). Debating such views would be beside the point, however. UBI would cut out the problem of the black box—the attempts to second-guess whether workers find housework servile and degrading or a source of pride and fulfillment—because it would make possible a real choice between paid and unpaid work and between different types of paid work.

UBI would thus not change the nature of housework itself, but it would alter the background conditions under which people make choices and conduct negotiations about housework. It would provide all workers with a realistic fallback position and thereby give them a real option of refusing housework. Many discussions of UBI predict that it would have the effect of pricing unskilled female labor out of the labor market. Such a disappearance would be a concrete, and perhaps the clearest refutation of the attempts to defend paid housework. It would be difficult for feminists to insist that we have to preserve unwanted, low-paid jobs in a situation where there are alternative and preferred sources of income available.[6]

Many socialist advocates of UBI argue that the strongest *moral* argument in favor of it is precisely that it is a concrete means of freedom. Instead of striving politically for the outdated goal of full-time employment for everybody, we should strive to work less and better. The task of the Left today should consist "in transforming this release of time into a new freedom and new rights" and finding "autonomy and self-fulfillment through a freely chosen activity" (Gorz [1994] 2012, 52, 60).

David Calnitsky (2017), for example, defends UBI on Marxist grounds by noting that it ought to be part of a normative leftist vision because it facilitates an exit from the relations of exploitation and domination.

> The foundational Marxist objection to the structure of capitalist labor markets is that they are superficially free but substantively unfree. Dispossessed of the means of production, and therefore of subsistence, workers can happily choose between capitalists, but are ultimately forced to choose one . . . For those who object to the compulsory nature of the capitalist labor market, basic income is appealing because it ensures that people not only have the abstract right to freedom, but the material resources to make freedom a lived reality. It gives people the power to say no—to abusive employers, unpleasant work, or patriarchal domination. (Calnitsky 2017)

Following Calnitsky, the moral question at the heart of the feminist debates on paid housework should thus not concern the inherent value or nature of this work. Rather, the question should be whether feminists can justifiably defend and uphold the coercive and compulsory quality of capitalist labor markets.

Many analyses of UBI are astonishingly gender-blind, however. They do not recognize the economically distinctive position that childbearing women hold in capitalist society or the gendered division of labor that fundamentally structures it. While Calnitsky (2017), for example, considers UBI's effects on gender equality and makes a convincing argument that it would provide women an exit option from abusive marriages, he only notes briefly that UBI would probably "disproportionately reduce female labor market participation and entrench a gendered division of labor." His rather optimistic response to this concern is that since the gender wage gap is now narrowing, many women would find "the opportunity costs of work withdrawal to be too high, and thus decide, like most men, to continue to work." In other words, he completely fails to raise any questions about childbearing and rearing children, as if the question of whether to work or not could be reduced to a simple calculation of opportunity costs in a gender-neutral context in which children grow up by themselves.

While most feminist assessments of UBI agree that it could significantly improve the situation of the "maid"—the poorly paid domestic worker in precarious employment—the problem lies in its effects on the "mistress"—the woman who has to combine waged work with caring for children or for the elderly, sick, or disabled members of the family. UBI could potentially also increase her freedom by supporting a variety of lifestyles, but only in a world where men and women had equal economic bargaining power and where preferences were formed under structurally just circumstances. The problem is that we do not live in that world.

The neoliberal stimulation of private service-sector growth has been complemented with another economic policy development that has also been central to restructuring most advanced economies in recent decades, namely significant cuts in the state provision of care services. The advocates of neoliberal reform invariably praise the virtues of a leaner state, but usually remain silent on how to reconcile the need for a job with the demands of taking care of children and other dependent family members. As Brigitte Young (2001, 318) notes: "In the Fordist era reproductive work was at least socially recognized, despite its private seclusion. With the flexibilization of the labor market, child-rearing has again become an economic and social externality, and the dialectical relations between market and non-market activities has disappeared from the neoliberal discourse of the global economy." The implication is that often the only option left for working women has been paid housework: they have been pushed into buying marketized household services merely in order to maintain their labor market status. While most feminists readily recognize the moral and political problems in a situation in which some women are pursuing their careers at the cost of others, the political and economic developments of the last decades have left working women with few other options than perpetuating exactly such a development.

Scapegoating women who pay other women for housework thus appears to miss the real problem. Capitalist economies fundamentally rely on the unpaid and gendered work of social reproduction performed in the private sphere. Women are routinely expected to work a double shift combining unpaid housework in the family with waged work in the labor market. Empirical studies on housework repeatedly show that despite the increasing integration of women into the labor force in the last decades, men are not equally sharing the burden of household work.[7] As Barbara Ehrenreich and Arlie Hochshield (2003, 9) contend: "Strictly speaking, the presence of immigrant nannies does not enable affluent women to enter the workforce; it enables affluent men to continue avoiding the second shift."

Given the gendered division of labor, the gender pay gap, and the prevailing gender norms on care, the strong feminist criticism of UBI becomes more readily understandable. Instead of promoting gender equality, a basic income would instead reinforce the existing sexual division of labor by giving women an even greater incentive to undertake more unpaid care work in the household. The key feminist argument against UBI is that, inevitably, more women than men would take advantage of their UBI in order to care for the dependent members of their families. This would reinforce the gendered division of labor and result in statistical discrimination even against those women who remained committed to their careers, making it more difficult for them to get hired and promoted. In other words, when more women drop out of the labor market and care becomes increasingly privatized, then gender discrimination will be even more exacerbated. The result will be an overall drop in female labor-market participation, in women's economic bargaining power within the household, in women's human capital, and in their expected income in the long run.[8]

Even if we insisted that gender equality should not be understood simply in economic terms but also includes more and better lifestyle options and revalued caregiving, most feminists agree that even these goals could not be achieved with UBI alone.[9] Despite promoting the idea that a person's social value should not depend on whether they are in paid employment, many feminists worry that with current gender norms in place, introducing UBI would only lead to further public devaluation of care-based lifestyles. Anca Gheaus (2008), for example, argues that although UBI could, in theory, free more men to do unpaid work at home and thus promote the idea that caregiving should be recognized as a universal duty of citizenship, this is unlikely to happen in current gender-unjust societies. "As long as most men will resent doing care work as demeaning, tedious, and unimportant, or otherwise regard it as a threat to their masculinities, a BI would merely perpetuate the devaluation of care" (Gheaus 2008, 5).

In sum, UBI alone will not guarantee that men would scale back time spent in paid employment, or if they did, that they would thereby increase the time spent in care work. Women's position in the labor market combined with deeply rooted beliefs about the appropriate tasks of men and women make this seem, if not unlikely, at least far from inevitable. The feminist defenses of UBI must thus present it as a complement, not as an alternative to public provisions of care. UBI would also have to be accompanied by carefully planned compensatory mechanisms mitigating its harmful effects for gender equality.[10] These could include measures such as gender quotas and a mandatory 30-hour workweek, for example, to make sure that both the care work at home and the paid work outside of it were shared more equally between men and women. Hence, when we assess the freedom from compulsory capitalist labor markets that UBI promises, we must do so in the context of gender-related preference formation mechanisms and gender-related constraints on choices. Feminist critiques of liberalism have effectively demonstrated that the idea of free and autonomous choice is difficult to uphold in our current gender-structured society.[11] The constraints on choices for men and women are clearly different and heavily dependent on their gender.

I want to nevertheless defend UBI as an important feminist tool primarily for the following reason. The feminist political opposition against servant economies can no longer be grounded only on the problems of income inequality or lack of autonomy, as serious as these problems are. The feminist defense of UBI must be incorporated into a broader vision of social transformation that includes an acute awareness of the ecological limits to growth. As this book has attempted to argue, feminist theory can no longer operate in a political context that does not take seriously the ecological limits of the planet.

Most blueprints for ecologically sustainable degrowth economies foster the pivotal idea that people will be working less while the remaining work will be distributed more equally. UBI should be assessed as an important policy instrument in the necessary transition to such degrowth economies that awaits us. It can pave the way to ecologically more sustainable societies in which people will engage in socially valuable activities other than waged work: they will pursue unwaged social and political projects, undertake care work, or engage in an array of other, non-consumption-related activities that have a low environmental impact. As Kathi Weeks (2020, 581) suggests, this would mean defending UBI not just as a technocratic fix which would substantially improve people's lives; UBI could also provide the material support for the time and effort necessary to fight for further more radical reform and to pry open a conceptual space in which we might think more critically and imaginatively about work. The demand for UBI could thus become part of a political movement which challenges the environmentally unsustainable economics of growth and cultivates desires for new ways of living.[12]

In sum, UBI should be recognized as a radical political strategy, but only in the context of a broad, anticapitalist, feminist, and ecological transformation of society. Rather than UBI being the political goal and feminism the means for mitigating its harmful effects on gender equality, UBI should be understood as one of the means of radical feminist ecopolitics. The political goal should be an ecofeminist revolution, which UBI, along with many other strategies, measures, and policy instruments, would help to facilitate.

My analysis of UBI here has focused on the Global North, where we desperately need to transition to economies that are not based on the constant growth imperative, and this, most profoundly, will require feminists to rethink the role of work. The situation is obviously radically different in the Global South, however. Climate change and the environmental crisis more generally place us at a new political juncture because averting their catastrophic consequences will inevitably require the massive generation and transfer of state-provided public goods: new energy and transportation infrastructure, floodgates, other safety equipment, and so on. In order to be effective on a global scale, this generation and transfer of wealth must be transnational and fundamentally shaped by considerations of global environmental justice. Feminist ecopolitics must be built on solidarity with the Global South, and it must strive for decolonization and reparations, or else it is bound to fail. We must invent concrete ways for wealthy nations not just to recognize their greater responsibility for climate change mitigation, but to pay their climate debt to poorer nations. Environmental theorists such as Ashley Dawson (2016) suggest that a transnational UBI could function as one instrument for the payment of this climate debt.[13] A universal basic income for the inhabitants of important biodiversity hot spots in the Global South, for example, would create a genuine counterweight to the attractions of poaching and land clearing. In short, in the Global North, a UBI could strengthen people's ability to engage in activities they find intrinsically valuable, promote decentralized and individual experiments in alternative ways of living, and aid the expansion of the cooperative and social economy sectors. In the Global South, a transnational UBI could be developed as a mechanism for mitigating the conflict between global environmental concerns and local progressive welfare politics.

Politics as Life / Life as Politics

I want to conclude this chapter with a brief look not into the future, but at the past. I find it salient that the answer to the question in my title—is it wrong for feminists to pay for housework—would have been, at one time, a resounding yes. As Charlotte Shane (2018) characterizes the second-wave feminism of the 1970s, "outsourcing childcare or household chores to less advantaged women would have been apostasy, especially if done in the service of professional gain." It was taken for granted that feminism was about uniting women across class divides and not about them exploiting each other. The fact that it is difficult to find any feminists today, whether on the Right or the Left, who would condemn paid housework suggests that our understanding of feminism has transformed significantly. Many feminists have critically observed how feminism has been shaped into an individualistic and entrepreneurial project in recent decades. Nancy Fraser (2013), for example, points to the dangerous liaison between neoliberal individualism and feminism in recent decades: feminist ideas that once formed part of a radical worldview are increasingly expressed in individualistic terms.

I want to suggest that the key difference between the second-wave feminists of the 1970s and today's feminists does not lie in the latter's lack of appropriate class consciousness, however. Rather, the key difference lies in their conception of politics itself. For the second-wave feminists, feminist politics was understood as a life: it was a practice that essentially included experiments with ways of living. The aim was to politicize the private through various concrete means. In her provocative political memoir *Making Trouble: Life and Politics* (2017), Lynne Segal, for example, describes her personal-political journey in 1970s London and foregrounds the idea that feminism was "a politics touching upon every aspect of life" (68). While social transformation was the goal, "tackling the connection between the personal and political was our method" (70). Despite being a single mother and working full-time as a university lecturer, Segal never paid for a babysitter, "let alone dreamed of a world with 'nanny' back in the nursery" (88). Instead, she lived with a group of women who supported each other by sharing the chores and child care they provided one another. For these feminists, collective living was not just a more practical economic arrangement than living alone or in the traditional nuclear family. Their motives were primarily political: collective living encouraged "more open, supportive and creatively shared forms of companionship, domesticity, childcare, political work and community engagement" (75).

Wanda Vrasti (2016, 264) places second-wave feminism and its refusal to separate the political and the personal in the lineage of New Left politics and tactics stretching from the late 1960s all the way to the recent Occupy and Indignados movements. What unites these diverse political movements is the idea of "prefigurative politics." Living one's politics means embodying a vision of the social relations one hopes to see in a more egalitarian future. Vrasti argues that we must recognize the impact of this kind of politics beyond the transformation of individual lives. People's concrete experiences of an alternative world, no matter how brief, will inevitably contribute to their common political memory and to their ability to imagine what is possible. According to Vrasti, the distinctive and provocative contribution that feminism brings to such prefigurative politics is the importance of daily reproduction. The domestic sphere was important for the feminists of the 1970s not only because it was the sphere of women's work, but because it was where the reproduction of life and social relations took place. "Placing care and reproduction at the center of life, where it belongs, has the power of bringing people together and in contact with a dimension of collective living otherwise banished from life under capitalism" (Vrasti 2016, 264). Whereas many anticapitalist struggles and strategies involve one-off spectacular events, such as demonstrations and strikes, feminism could teach us how greater attention to our everyday needs helps "resistance extend to all moments of life, across the entire fabric of our communities" (252). Feminist politics centering on social reproduction could show us another model for how to confront capitalism collectively (252). As Zhivka Valiavicharska (2019) writes, this might mean care work, material support, jail support, or the work of healing—work which remains invisible and does not register politically, but which nevertheless reproduces and sustains our struggles, as well as giving communities in struggle the strength and resilience to carry on in the long run.

The visionary communal practices that many of the contemporary advocates of UBI hope it would promote, such as time-banks and service exchange cooperatives formed in neighborhoods, were thus already an integral part of second-wave feminism.[14] It is important to recognize that the utopian vision that these feminists struggled for, however, was not some kind of "fully automated luxury communism," a world of boundless leisure and contemplation where robots and self-replicating machines were fulfilling every material need.[15] As Raj Patel and Jason Moore (2018, 211) write, there is currently "a small boom in manifestos for the end of work, premised on the idea of robots managing the tasks that involve drudgery, thus freeing humans to have almost unlimited leisure." In contrast to such visions, the feminist revolution of everyday life was not understood as an attempt to transcend the necessity of reproductive labor, no matter how monotonous and onerous it was, but to collectivize and revalorize it (Vrasti 2016, 259). Feminists foregrounded the necessity of daily reproduction and dreamt of a world in which everybody, regardless of their gender, had time and knew how to look after children and care for the old, sick, and dying. In other words, the goals were not comfort, leisure, and abundance, but mutuality, connectivity, and sustainability.

The structural changes that I analyzed in the first section have admittedly made personal experiments in alternative ways of living increasingly more difficult. It is important to recognize that the political problem today is not just that our conception of feminism has changed, but that the space for feminist action and alternative ways of living has narrowed. It therefore remains an imperative for feminists to insist on the need to create meaningful political spaces in which personal ethical choices and alternative lifestyles become possible. I hope to have shown, nevertheless, that there are compelling political reasons for feminists to continue answering the question in my title with a resolute yes, and to keep foregrounding the idea that the personal is political. The either-or dichotomy between personal ethical action and systemic political transformation was, and continues to be, a false one.

Feminism against Biocapitalism

Based on the available climate science, there is no doubt that climate change presents an existential threat in the sense of threatening the continued existence of human civilization. The safe limit for atmospheric carbon dioxide concentrations established by the UN's Intergovernmental Panel on Climate Change, 450 ppm, will be reached in less than ten years at the current emission rates. Many important climate scientists, such as James Hansen, have contended, however, that the safe limit was closer to 350 ppm, a level we already overshot in 1988, which is why we are experiencing many of the predicted effects of climate change much earlier than anticipated (Hansen et al. 2008, 229). It seems evident that the political transformation needed in response to this situation has to happen so fast and is going to be so difficult that strategically we cannot be too discerning: we must try and push as hard as we can from multiple directions and see what gives. In other words, the necessary political struggle ahead of us must take multiple forms: global trans-boundary struggles, local direct action, and attempts to radically reform the state and to strengthen forms of global democratic governance. I also strongly agree with theorists who contend that alternatives to capitalism should not be thought of as final outcomes or as a utopia, but as "a continuous process of experimentation that must be constantly made, reflected upon and remade" (Rogers 2014, 15). This is the only way we can avoid reproducing the same structures of oppression we hoped to overcome, as well as preventing the new forms of social organization from degenerating into those that came before them.

Numerous ecosocialist and ecofeminist thinkers, economists, and political activists have explored the possibilities of environmentally sustainable and equitable alternatives to capitalism. There is a burgeoning literature that is developing concrete and detailed alternatives to our current capitalist way of life.[1] There are also real-world political experiments as well as historical and cultural models to build on. As Jason Hickel (2020, 243) writes, when we try to imagine overthrowing capitalism, we do not have to assume that the alternative will be "the command-and-control fiasco of the Soviet Union, or some back-to-the-caves, hair-shirted disaster of voluntary impoverishment." It is possible to build an alternative socioeconomic system, based on concrete plans, and organized around human flourishing and ecological stability. Traditional socialist-democratic demands for the regulation of free markets and for a fairer redistribution of resources must be crucial components of this political project, but we also desperately need a whole new arsenal of political tools: we must scale down ecologically destructive industries, cap resource and energy use, shorten the working week, radically reduce income inequality, decommodify basic goods, expand the commons, cancel unjust debts, and change the current money system based on compound interest, among numerous other changes. The feminist ecopolitics that I am envisaging here thus cannot be merely subsumed into traditional socialist class struggle: it cannot be built on the ideology of work, economic emancipation, and productivism.

Feminist philosophy, not only feminist politics, has an indispensable role to play in expanding the political imagination that must necessarily accompany the profound economic and societal transition that lies ahead. We must be able to imagine the radical expansion of activities not governed by the pursuit of economic productivity and profit, and to find categorically different, socio-ecological criteria for guiding our social and economic practices and way of life. At the same time, we must effectively contest the way these activities and criteria have been and continue to be gendered. The deep-rooted crisis of capitalism must thus have important implications for feminist theory. I have unequivocally defended here the idea that feminist theory needs to engage with ecological problems, and conversely, that environmental theory needs to engage with feminism. Furthermore, this engagement must take the form of a structural critique of capitalism: a systemic analysis of the connections between the core logic of capitalism, gender oppression, and environmental destruction. It is essential for feminist and environmental theory to recognize that there are imperatives that issue from the systemic features of capitalism and that only by understanding them, and their compelling character, can we develop a robust explanatory framework for making sense of a number of acute political and environmental problems.

I have also insisted that our feminist critique of capitalism cannot be developed solely with the traditional conceptual tools of Marxist analysis, but must incorporate the important insights of critical race theory, Indigenous studies, queer and trans theory, critical animal studies, and environmental critique. We must also appropriate the key insights of post-structuralism and not discard them as incompatible with Marxist theory.[2] A theoretically sophisticated account of subjectivation must be recognized as a prerequisite for any philosophically coherent and politically effective theorization of resistance against capitalism, not as an alternative theoretical frame to it. Although the rise of neoliberalism must be understood as inseparable from the structural logic of capitalist accumulation, the subjects that contemporary neoliberal capitalism produces are not traditional class subjects, who merely lack the appropriate consciousness of their situation. Rather, they are already constituted as entrepreneurial subjects fully responsible for their choices and failures, or else they have been pushed outside of formal labor markets altogether. Today, there is a growing global market for the services of gestational surrogates, organ vendors, and undocumented sex workers, for example. Rather than harking back to some era of traditional class politics that no longer exists, it is imperative to theorize the new forms of the subject that neoliberal biocapitalism has produced and to investigate the political limitations as well as the potential they might hold for social transformation.

In sum, the environmental crisis has pushed contemporary capitalism into a constellation that is both philosophically and politically unprecedented. The living bodies of certain groups of people, animals, and whole ecosystems form the very material basis on which today's biocapitalism rests, but this basis is becoming increasingly volatile, unsustainable, and prone to serious crises. This places ecofeminism squarely in front of new challenges. The reason for calling capitalism into question today is no longer merely our exploitative social and economic relationships to other human beings, but the immeasurable devastation we are causing to the nonhuman world.

Acknowledgments

Like most academic books, this book took a frustratingly long time to write. Its earliest ideas began to take shape in the Marx reading group that some friends and I organized in Helsinki in 2011–12. The group met diligently for nearly two years in a bar in eastern Helsinki to read through all the three volumes of Marx's *Capital*. While most of the members of the group understandably shuffled in and out during the group's existence, two members remained steady from the beginning to the end. I would like to thank, in particular, Tuomas Nevanlinna and Timo Miettinen for their excellent readings of Marx, their philosophical acumen, and their insightful views on the continuing relevance of Marx's ideas for a critical analysis of contemporary capitalism.

In 2013, I joined the faculty of the departments of philosophy and politics at the New School for Social Research as a visiting professor. I had just finished writing my book *Feminist Experiences*, which developed a Foucauldian-feminist critique of neoliberalism, and it had become clear to me that I had come to an impasse: to push my line of critique further I needed to engage seriously with Marxist-feminist theory. Upon my arrival at the New School, I contacted Cinzia Arruzza to ask for her advice on how to do that and immediately received an e-mail back containing a very long and helpful reading list which I started to plow through. I remain extremely grateful to Cinzia for her continuing guidance, thought-provoking comments, and above all, her irreplaceable philosophical friendship.

At the New School I also had the immense pleasure and honor to cooperate with Nancy Fraser, whose work has been an ideal to try to emulate ever since I was a student. Nancy generously suggested that we teach a graduate course together, and in 2015 we co-taught 'Feminism, Capitalism and Social Transformation.' The first drafts for several of the chapters here were compiled from my lecture notes for that course. Co-teaching with Nancy was a transformative learning experience, to say the least. I benefited immensely not only from her expertise in the field, but also from observing the philosophical power of her mind in the classroom. Her support, friendship, and astute comments have been vital for this project.

I also want to thank all my students and colleagues in the institutions I have worked at while writing this book—University of Helsinki, the New School, Pratt Institute, and most recently, Loyola University Chicago. There are too many of you to mention by name, and all of you have been important collaborators in the research communities that I have been part of. A special thanks should nevertheless go to Dan Boscov-Ellen, Simon Critchley, Alexis Dianda, Lisabeth During, Eyo Ewara, Jennifer Gaffney, Joy Gordon, Johanna Kantola, Sanna Karhu, Jesús Luzardo, Pilvi Toppinen, Zhivka Valiavicharska, and Carl Zimring. The work of my research assistants, Jeanne Landers, Andrew Krema, and Daphne Pons, has been invaluable. I am also extremely grateful for the exemplary work of Faith Wilson Stein, Anne Gendler, and Elena Bellaart at Northwestern University Press. The book is decidedly better because of them.

Finally, I want to thank my son, Sid, for his unwavering support and remarkable strength during the terminal illness and death of my mother—the long, dark, and difficult years that coincided with the writing of this book. Care work takes many forms, traverses generations and genders, and makes possible everything else we do.

Parts of this work draw on previously published articles: J. Oksala, "Affective Labor and Feminist Politics," *Signs: Journal of Women in Culture and Society* 41, no. 2: 281–303; J. Oksala, "Feminism, Capitalism, and Ecology," *Hypatia: A Journal of Feminist Philosophy* 33, no. 2: 216–34; and J. Oksala, "Feminism against Biocapitalism: Gestational Surrogacy and the Limits of the Labor Paradigm," *Signs: Journal of Women in Culture and Society* 44, no. 4: 883–904.

Notes

Introduction

1. Climate change is, however, by no means the only serious environmental problem that we face. The Stockholm Resilience Centre (SRC), a research initiative for resilience and sustainability sciences, established the planetary boundaries framework in 2009 (updated in 2015). The nine planetary boundaries identified in the framework are argued to be fundamental in maintaining a "safe operating space for humanity." To date, we have crossed four of the nine boundaries: climate change, loss of biosphere integrity, biogeochemical flows, and land-system change. See Stockholm Resilience Centre (2015).

2. Geoff Mann and Joel Wainwright (2018, 187) similarly argue that the contemporary climate change discourse has changed: "Until recently, only a few radical political ecologists, in various shades of red and green, contended that planetary environmental change was a logical consequence of capitalism. No longer. Today even some of capital's best-known champions—Paul Krugman, Joseph Stiglitz, Christine Lagarde, and others—have drawn the connection between the relentless logic of accumulation and climate change."

3. As the recent 2022 IPCC report states, vulnerability to climatic hazards "is exacerbated by inequity and marginalization linked to gender, ethnicity, low income or combinations thereof, especially for many Indigenous Peoples and local communities" (B. 2.4). See also Mellor (1992), Gaard and Gruen ([1993] 2005), and Whyte (2014).

4. See Cuomo (2017).

5. For some foundational texts on ecofeminism, see Daly (1978), Griffin (1978), Merchant (1980), Shiva (1989), Plumwood (1993), and Salleh ([1997] 2017).

6. For some foundational texts on Marxist feminism, see Mitchell (1966), Benston ([1969] 1997), Dalla Costa and James (1973), Davis (1972), Hartman (1979), MacKinnon (1982), Vogel (1983), Nicholson (1987), and Federici (2012).

7. On feminist critiques of dual-systems theories, see Young ([1979] 1997) and Joseph ([1981] 1997).

8. See Shoshana Zuboff's (2020) recent book on surveillance capitalism.

9. Although technological development has reduced the raw material intensity of many industrial production processes, the growth of the world economy continues to be coupled with rising absolute quantities of raw material consumption. See Boyd, Prudham, and Schurman (2001) and Jackson ([2009] 2016).

10. See Floyd (2015, 63). Catherine Waldby and Robert Mitchell (2007, 24)

note that since 1980, when, in a landmark decision, the U.S. Supreme Court allowed the granting of a patent for a genetically engineered bacterium, intellectual property rights have been established in multicellular entities such as mice, in immortal cell lines based on adult human tissue, in embryonic stem-cell lines, and in genetic sequences. Biological entities have come to be conceived of as intellectual property, and this has transformed biomedical research into a lucrative area of investment for increasingly mobile forms of finance capital.

11. For a critical analysis of this idea, see Birch, Levidow, and Papaioannou (2010).

12. The term "biocapitalism," similar to biopolitics, is used in varied ways in today's academic discussions, and theorists are debating whether the new technological developments and forms of commodification are changing something definitive in the functioning of capitalism itself that warrants identifying a significant transformation, one that meaningfully attaches the prefix *bio-* to it. While Kaushik Sunder Rajan (2006, 277–78) argues that biotechnological capitalism represents a new phase of capitalism, Kean Birch and David Tyfield (2012) criticize scholars working in science and technology studies for producing obscure new concepts such as "biocapital" and "biovalue." According to them, the scholars developing these new concepts are merely adopting Marxist language without the necessary adoption of Marx's labor theory of value, which underpins key terms such as value, capital, and surplus value (Birch and Tyfield 2012, 301). In their critique, Birch and Tyfield focus on the work of Catherine Waldby (2000), Nikolas Rose (2007), Kaushik Sunder Rajan (2006), and Melinda Cooper (2008). On the distinction between "biocapital" and "biocapitalism," see Franklin (2007).

13. Timothy Mitchell (2013) contends that while the recent boom in "unconventional oil" such as shale oil and gas, particularly in the United State, has been used to dismiss the evidence of peak oil, in fact this boom is its latest symptom. "The era of easily accessible, cheaply produced and ever-increasing supplies of conventional oil that shaped the politics of the twentieth century is passing away" (260).

14. See Merle (2018), DePillis (2017), R. Cooper (2017), and Stewart (2018).

15. See Oxfam International (2018) and (2019). Thomas Piketty's influential book *Capital in the Twenty-First Century* (2014) analyzes the rising inequality created by the financial industry. Piketty's key claim is that the rate of return on financial assets has been higher than that on growth, and we therefore need higher taxes on the resultant wealth and inheritance to stem the growing inequality. On the economic explanations for rising income inequality in most advanced economies in the last four decades, see also Mazzucato (2018).

16. See Beckett (2019).

17. See Rogers (2014, 3), Fraser (2014, 57–59), Cudd and Holmstrom (2011, 6–8), and Gilabert and O'Neill (2019).

18. Liberal economists such as Adam Smith had argued that free trade and industrialization would inevitably bring about prosperity and improve the lives of common people. When observing the life of the working classes in Britain, it became evident to Marx that this had not happened. The working conditions

in the new factories were extremely harsh and hazardous, children formed an integral part of the workforce, and labor laws and regulations were either non-existent or highly exploitative. Marx wanted to expose the fundamental impera-tives that govern the capitalist mode of production in order to explain such a situation. He needed to explain why, for example, in a capitalist system, improved productivity and free trade did not automatically lead to a shorter workday or bet-ter wages for workers. The small improvements in the workers' situation that he witnessed—the legal limitation on the length of the workday to twelve hours for miners and to eight hours for children, or the legislation that set the minimum age for child laborers to nine years, for example—resulted from victories of hard political struggles, not from the advances of free trade. See Marx ([1867] 1990, 389–411).

19. Jaeggi sums up "the pauperization theory" by explaining that capitalism, in the long run, will not produce enough for people's subsistence, leading to the breakdown of the system. The Marxist theorem of "the tendential fall of the rate of profit," on the other hand, holds that the capitalist dynamic undermines itself through changes in the ratio of living labor to machinery, or what Marx called the "organic composition of capital" (Fraser and Jaeggi 2018, 116–17).

20. Simmons (2000).

21. Prominent eco-Marxist thinkers such as John Bellamy Foster (2000), Paul Burkett (1999), and Kohei Saito (2017) have demonstrated that Marx him-self already engaged extensively with ecological questions. They have also built upon his critique of capitalism to theorize the contemporary era of social and ecological disintegration. Ecosocialism began to emerge as a distinct current of Marxist thought in the 1970s. For some definitive accounts, see Gorz ([1980] 1987), O'Connor (1998), and Foster (2009). For seminal accounts on the signifi-cance of eco-Marxist theory for environmental ethics and environmental post-colonial thought, see Boscov-Ellen (2020a) and (2020b).

22. For a clear and commonsensical explanation on the necessity of eco-nomic growth for a stable capitalist economic order, see Jackson ([2009] 2016).

23. We can make a distinction between *resource decoupling* and *impact de-coupling*. Resource decoupling means decoupling the growth of GDP from the growth of global concrete consumption, for example, whereas impact decoupling means decoupling the growth of GDP from the growth of GHG emissions, for example.

24. See Obama (2017) and OECD (2001).

25. See also Jackson and Victor (2019).

26. In a recent study, Tero Vaden et al. (2020) conducted a survey of recent (1990–2019) research on decoupling on the Web of Science by reviewing 179 articles on the topic. They found that the reviewed articles contain evidence of absolute impact decoupling, especially between GDP growth and CO_2 emissions, and evidence on geographically limited (national level) cases of absolute decou-pling of land and blue water use from GDP, but not of economy-wide resource decoupling, either on national or international scales. In other words, empirical evidence of the needed absolute, global, and fast-enough decoupling is missing. For other recent empirical research showing that there is no convincing evidence

of significant decoupling, see Giljum et al. (2014), Shao et al. (2017), Wood et al. (2018), Hickel and Kallis (2019), and Haberl (2020).

27. See Waldby (2011).

28. For an excellent study on the importance of cheap oil for twentieth-century politics, see Mitchell (2011).

29. See Sandel (2012).

30. See Fraser and Jaeggi (2018, 119) and Hägglund (2019, 301).

31. See Katz (2001), Arruzza (2016), and Bhattacharya (2017).

32. Arruzza, Bhattacharya, and Fraser (2019, 25) understand social reproduction struggles as not being limited to the problem of how to share housework in families more evenly but as also encompassing grassroots community movements for housing, health care, food security, and for an unconditional basic income, as well as struggles for the rights of migrants and domestic workers.

33. See also Fraser and Jaeggi (2018, 136–37) and Fraser (2021).

34. See Oksala (2011).

35. As Karl Polanyi ([1944] 2001) famously argued, a competitive capitalist market economy can ultimately only exist if it is embedded in social and political relations.

36. See King (1988).

37. The relationship between capitalism and sexuality was debated already by pioneering Marxist feminist theorists such as Alexandra Kollontai, and prominent queer theorists such as Judith Butler have analyzed the systemic links between capitalism and heteronormativity. See Kollontai (1977) and Butler (1997). See also Fraser (1997), Hennessy (2000), Floyd (2009), and Oksala (2017).

38. Marxist feminism is often mistakenly presented as predominantly a Western or Anglo-European tradition, but this is a very selective reading of it. The Latin American decolonial feminist tradition, in particular, formed an early and strong current in it, emphasizing how colonization, especially of the western hemisphere, made possible the emergence of capitalism. See Wynter ([1982] 2018). For more recent contributions to this research tradition, see Lugones (2007).

39. Mills (1999, 140) refers to Cedric Robinson's influential book *Black Marxism* (1983) to argue that the growth of capitalism was crucially linked to imperialism's role in establishing a worldwide system of racial domination. Robinson developed the term "racial capitalism" to refer to the historical development and the subsequent structure through which racism and capitalism intertwined. Robinson shows how the racial order that emerged in feudal Europe and organized the relations between European and non-European peoples came to also structure and legitimize the organization of labor in capitalism and the social structures that emerged from it. See also Kelley (2020).

40. See Nixon (2011), Parenti (2011), and Zimring (2015).

41. The connection between capitalism and racism has been theorized in different ways in Black Marxism. Robin D. G. Kelley (2020, xxxi, fn. 14) writes that the "race reductionist" versus "class reductionist" debate has been raging under different names for at least a century. While some Black Marxist theorists such as Charles Mills argue that racial oppression should be viewed as primary, theorists such as Vanessa Wills defend the primacy of class exploitation while denying that

it means relegating racism and sexism to mere epiphenomenal status in capitalism. See Mills (1990) and (1999) and Wills (2018). See also Haider (2018) and Proyect (2020). Black feminists have responded to the ways in which both white feminists and scholars of race have erased the particularities of Black women's unique experience. They have developed theories demonstrating how the overlapping oppressions of race and class must also include gender, producing particular challenges for Black women. See King (1988) and Brewer ([1993] 1997).

42. Nichols shows (2020) how the dispossession of land in a settler colonial context has been notoriously difficult to comprehend because it transforms what were originally nonproprietary relations to the land into proprietary ones while, at the same time, systematically transferring control and title of this newly formed property. In other words, settler colonizers did not simply steal a stable, empirical object called "land" from Indigenous people; rather, as they transferred control over the land, they also recoded its meaning, rendering it an abstract legal entity that could be owned. In this way, dispossession in effect merges commodification and theft into one moment: it creates an object in the very act of appropriating it. Nichols names this process "recursive dispossession" because this peculiar process generates property under conditions that in fact require its divestment and alienation: those negatively impacted by this process—the dispossessed—are figured as the "original owners of the land" but only retroactively, after they have already lost their title to the land.

43. Glen Sean Coulthard (2014, 36) argues that challenging capitalism in the context of existing nation-states means overlooking the crucial supports of colonial domination: the legitimacy of the settler state's claim to sovereignty over Indigenous people and their territories, and the normative status of the state form as an appropriate mode of governance.

44. See Brown (2005, 105–6).

45. See also Mies ([1986] 1998, xiv–xviii), Hennessy (2000), and Walby (2011).

Chapter 1

1. On feminist critiques of ecofeminism targeting its ethnocentrism and its tendency to essentialize the woman–nature connection, see Agarwal (1992), Braidotti et al. (1994), Nanda (1997), and Agarwal (2001).

2. See Mellor (1992, 7).

3. The Marxist-feminist critique of intersectionality theory has focused on this issue in particular. Sarah Farris, for example, argues that although intersectionality theory speaks loudly to Marxists because it refuses to treat racial and gendered oppressions as secondary forms of oppression, it falls short of delivering the comprehensive theory it promises (Farris 2015). For seminal texts on intersectionality theory, see Crenshaw (1989) and Collins (1990).

4. See Vogel (1983), Benston ([1969] 1997), and Federici (2012). For an interesting recent attempt to recenter debates on the nature and origin of value in economics, see Mazzucato (2018). Mazzucato argues that it is imperative that

economists today reinvigorate a serious discussion about who the value creators in contemporary economies are and how we define activities as economically productive and unproductive. She questions the standard explanations for why housework, for example, continues to be excluded from the national accounts. She argues that accounting conventions follow "awkward logic" and have been "cherry-picked" because of their convenience for the current system, which attributes an indiscriminate productivity to those grabbing a large income, whilst downplaying the productivity of those less fortunate (Mazzucato 2018, 92–93, 100).

5. See Meiksins Wood ([1999] 2017, 35).

6. Rosa Luxemburg already argued in her seminal book *The Accumulation of Capital* ([1913] 2003) that primitive accumulation had to be understood as a continuous and constitutive aspect of capitalist expansion. For contemporary thinkers, see David Harvey, who renames primitive accumulation "accumulation by dispossession" (Harvey 2004); see also Guha (1998), Federici (2004), and Coulthard (2014).

7. Robinson ([1983] 2020, 4) argues that this also implies that the Marxist interpretation of history in terms of the dialectic of class struggle is inadequate, "a mistake ordained by the preoccupation of Marxism with the industrial and manufacturing centers of capitalism."

8. Glen Sean Coulthard (2014), for example, shows how settler colonial states such as Canada have historically responded to Indigenous political assertiveness and militancy by attempting to contain these outbursts through largely symbolic gestures of political inclusion and recognition, while refusing to implement alternative structures of law and sovereign authority.

9. Ariel Salleh's work was also central in laying the foundations for Marxist ecofeminism. In *Ecofeminism as Politics*, she argues for the common political goals of feminist, socialist, ecological, and Indigenous struggles against transnational capital (Salleh [1997] 2017).

10. On seminal texts theorizing the connection between sexual and racial expropriation in capitalism, see also the Combahee River Collective ([1978] 2014) and Davis (1981).

11. See also Patel and Moore (2018).

12. See Aho (2016). On views contesting the claim that young forests are more effective carbon sinks, see Ilmasto.org (2008).

13. See Hochschild (2000).

14. By the real subsumption of labor, Marx referred to the way in which capital not only takes over and manages an already existing labor process, but completely transforms its nature and, by extension, the laborers themselves. This idea was essential for exposing the historical transition to a form of capitalism in which surplus value is extracted primarily on the basis of increases in labor productivity rather than through an extension of the working day. See Marx ([1867] 1990, 645, 1019–38).

15. Kean Birch and David Tyfield argue that the most important property rights in the bioeconomic sector today are those pertaining to the ownership of knowledge assets. The realization of value from immaterial property rights

through market exchange is the key issue in the profitability of this sector (Birch and Tyfield 2012, 316).

16. See Davis (1972).

17. For feminist accounts on transnational commercial gestational surrogacy, see Pande (2009a) and (2009b), Bailey (2011), and Vora (2013).

18. See Mellor (2006).

Chapter 2

1. The term "Anthropocene" has been widely debated in recent environmental theory. It was originally introduced by the atmospheric chemist Paul Crutzen as a name for a new epoch to be added to the official geological time scale. Crutzen's contention is that the planet has shifted out of the previous epoch, the Holocene, because of climate change. The term is also widely used in the humanities and social sciences today. There it is often used as a name for our time marked by various environment catastrophes, which have forced us to question our traditional ideas and forms of thinking. The notion of the Anthropocene has been heavily criticized in environmental humanities and political theory, however. Critics have pointed out that the term comes from the natural sciences and is therefore depoliticizing and misleading because it suggests that environmental destruction is a natural event, similar to the previous shifts between different geological epochs, such as the arrival of the last ice age. Jason Moore (2015) has argued that "Capitalocene" would be a more appropriate term because the current epochal shift is driven by specific economic practices that could still be altered. For critiques of the term "Anthropocene," see also Crist (2013); for a philosophical defense of it, see Hamilton (2017).

2. For a discussion on the differences between Foucault's and Agamben's understanding of biopolitics, see Oksala (2011).

3. Steven Vogel adopts this thesis from Bill McKibben's seminal book *The End of Nature* and interprets it as a straightforward empirical statement. Contrary to what Vogel claims, however, McKibben is not making an empirical argument about how "nature itself has been literally destroyed" (Vogel 2015, 2). McKibben is making a philosophical argument about the way the empirical event of climate change is profoundly altering the meaning of our world and our place in it: "When I say 'nature' I mean a certain set of human ideas about the world and our place in it" (McKibben 1989, 8).

4. Vogel intends his book to function as a critique of the naturalization of capitalism, not as an apology for it. He argues, for example, that Marx's account of alienation is in fact a critique of "nature": alienation arises when objects and institutions that are the product of social practices come to seem as though their existence was independent of such practices and instead appear to be natural. He urges us to overcome such alienation by explicitly recognizing and asserting "the sociality of labor by the associated human community" (Vogel 2015, 78).

5. Several environmental ethicists have argued that if we insist that human beings are nothing but another species of animal with a technologically more complex environment, there is no footing left from which to push for moral obligations towards the environment and other species, fight political injustices, and imagine alternative, emancipatory futures for the planet. Human beings must distinguish themselves from animals, not as superior to them, but as capable of assuming something akin to moral responsibility or even moral duty, which we do not expect from animals or from the environment. See Diamond (1978, 333) and O'Neill (1997).

6. Aristotle famously connects the specificity of human politics to our ability to speak, arguing in the first book of *Politics* that human society is distinguished from that of "bees or other gregarious animals" in that it is founded on a political community that is capable of speech. Through language it is possible to express not simply what is pleasant and painful, but what is good and evil, as well as just and unjust: "it is the peculiarity of man, in comparison with other animals, that he alone possesses a perception of good and evil, of the just and the unjust, and other similar qualities; and it is association in these things which makes a family and a city" (Aristotle 1995, 11).

7. See Davion (2011) and Cuomo (2017).

8. According to Foucault, the era of biopolitics is marked by the explosion of numerous and diverse techniques for achieving the control of populations: techniques that coordinate medical care, normalize behavior, rationalize mechanisms of insurance, and rethink urban planning, for example. The protection and enhancement of human life, through management and normalization, have become the overriding aims of modern politics. See Foucault ([1976] 1978).

9. See Arsel (2012) and Lalander (2015).

10. Hugo Echeverría (2017) discusses three successful cases ruled by the Constitutional Court of Ecuador, the top authority on constitutional control: the Biodigester case (2009), the Ecological reserve case (2012), and the Artisanal mining case (2012). Many commentators are hopeful that what is happening in Ecuador could be the beginning of the emergence of a new global legal paradigm. See Whittenmore (2011).

11. See Shorter (2016, 444) and Nichols (2020, 157).

12. We could and should also identify and promote other possible instances of such experimental politics, from the conceptual practice of using the term "nonhuman animal" to concrete, large-scale ecological practices such as rewilding that might be able to contribute, piece by piece, to a transformation in the "deep" or metaphysical structures of our thought.

Chapter 3

1. In her pioneering ethnographic study of transnational commercial surrogacy in India, Amrita Pande (2014, 20) notes that all but one of the surrogates she interviewed reported acute financial desperation. Thirty-six out of the fifty-

two interviewees reported a family income that put them below the official poverty line.

2. For reasons of brevity, I will use the term "gestational surrogacy" from now on, but it should be kept in mind that I mean gestational surrogacy that is commercial and transnational, as opposed to altruistic and national.

3. Cooper and Waldby (2014, 8) recognize that the category of clinical labor cannot account for all the circumstances in which patients donate tissue or participate in clinical trials. They contend that such services should be regarded as labor when the activity is intrinsic to the valorization process of a particular bioeconomic sector and when the therapeutic benefits to the participants themselves or to their communities are absent or incidental.

4. See Benston ([1969] 1997) and Vogel (1983).

5. Important recent monographs include Pande (2014), Vora (2015a), and Deomampo (2016). See also Bailey (2011).

6. India is now in the process of banning commercial gestational surrogacy completely. The proposed surrogacy regulation bill would allow surrogacy only for married Indian couples and it stipulates that the surrogate mother has to be a close relative who has been married and has had a child of her own. Undertaking surrogacy for a fee, advertising it or exploiting the surrogate mother would become legally punishable acts. The bill was passed by the lower house of the Indian parliament in August 2019. To become law, it still requires passage by the upper house of the parliament as well as presidential assent. See PRS Legislative Research (2019). Even if commercial gestational surrogacy is banned in India, however, similar markets are already developing elsewhere in countries such as Nepal, Panama, and Ukraine.

7. Sharmila Rudrappa (2014, 137) explains that India became a major destination for infertility tourism because of the ready availability of infertility drugs at relatively low prices and the lower remuneration for doctors, medical technicians, and nurses, as well as the low price of the surrogate mother's labor. She also emphasizes that in addition to the lower financial costs, there are also lower "nonfinancial transaction costs" when dealing with Indian surrogates because they are able to make fewer emotional demands on the intended parents.

8. Daisy Deomampo's (2016) ethnographic study on commercial gestational surrogacy in India, *Transnational Reproduction*, focuses particularly on the question of race. Her seminal study analyzes the different ways in which transnational surrogacy can be considered a technology of race: certain racialized bodies become characterized as eligible egg providers while others are good womb renters, for example. On the racialization of reproductive labor, see also Glenn (1992).

9. The surrogates in India are often either mandated or strongly encouraged to stay in designated hostels connected with the clinic where their behavior can be kept under surveillance—their food, medicines, and daily activities are monitored by the doctors or the employees of the clinic. The surrogacy contract also normally prohibits the surrogates from having sexual relations with their husbands; staying in hostels effectively prevents this. See Pande (2009a, 2009b, 2014) and Vora (2012).

10. See Andrews (1988) and Andrews and Douglass (1991).

11. See DasGupta and Das Dasgupta (2014), Nayak (2014), and Madge (2014).

12. Amrita Pande argues that gestational surrogacy is a new form of labor that has emerged with globalization and traverses the dichotomy between production and reproduction. It is "gendered, exceptionally corporeal, and highly stigmatized, but labor nonetheless" (Pande 2014, 6). See also Vora (2012) and Rudrappa (2014).

13. Sayantani DasGupta and Shamita Das Dasgupta (2014, 188) write that at least in one clinic in Mumbai which they studied, the surrogate was rewarded with a bonus for producing a high-quality product—a baby weighing at least four kilograms. A surrogate interviewed for an ethnographic study by Kalindi Vora (2012, 682) had signed a contract stating that she would not receive any money other than a maintenance stipend if she did not successfully complete her pregnancy. The draft bill for the regulation of commercial surrogacy released by the Indian Council for Medical Research in 2010 also reflects this idea: payment to the surrogate is to be distributed in five installments and 75 percent of the payment is to be paid at the fifth installment following the delivery of the child (Deomampo 2016, 46).

14. See Satz (1992, 126).

15. This is called "selective reduction procedure." See Madge (2014, 60).

16. Amrita Pande (2009a, 147) explains that preparing the surrogate's body for the embryo transfer first requires birth-control pills and hormone shots to control and suppress the surrogate's own ovulatory cycle. Then she is given injections of estrogen to build her uterine lining. After the transfer, daily injections of progesterone are administered until her body can sustain the pregnancy on its own.

17. Kevin Floyd (2015, 73) argues that in their Marxist critiques Cooper and Waldby mistake the capacities of capital—the form of fixed capital called biotechnology—for living labor, while Birch and Tyfield (2012, 315) emphasize the importance of living knowledge labor.

18. In *Capital*, Marx ([1867] 1990, 342) makes a distinction between "living labor" and "dead labor" to emphasize the idea that capital is always produced by labor. Capital is dead labor because it is constituted by the value-producing power of living laborers.

19. Feminist theorists such as Kalindi Vora (2015b) have argued that the role that India has played this century in providing assisted reproductive technology services globally has historical roots in the international division of labor in British colonial practices, when the colonies were regarded as sites for the plunder of resources for the colonial center. See also Lau (2018). Franz Fanon already noted in his classic study of colonialism, *The Wretched of the Earth*, that the taming of hostile nature and the rebellious population in the colonies formed part of the same process of colonial domination. See Fanon ([1961] 2001, 201).

20. See also Vora (2012) and DasGupta and Das Dasgupta (2014).

21. As I showed in the first chapter, Marxist ecofeminist have made the important argument that the expropriation of women's reproductive labor has

been structurally analogous to and historically contemporaneous with the extraction of natural resources. Women's reproductive capacities and natural resources have a similar, indispensable function in the mechanism of expropriation: they occupy analogous positions in the logic of capitalist accumulation, in which the mechanisms of exploitation are dependent on the invisible base of expropriation. See Salleh ([1997] 2017) and Mies ([1986] 1998). Cooper and Waldby recognize this idea implicitly when they note critically how the scientist's inventive step in isolating DNA or creating a cell line from *ex vivo* tissues, for example, is treated in innovation economics and patent law as the moment that creates both property rights and appreciable commercial value from dumb biological materials. "In this account, the bodily contribution of tissue providers and human research subjects appears as an already available biological resource, as *res nullius*, matter in the public domain" (Cooper and Waldby 2014, 9).

22. See Madge (2014, 65) and Nayak (2014, 7).

23. On the ethical dimensions of Marxist theory, see West (2008).

24. Feminist philosophers have long argued that the experience of pregnancy has been absent from most of our culture's discourse about human existence and that the dominance of medical approaches to pregnancy has devalued women's own experiences. See Young (1990).

25. Ethnographic studies of gestational surrogacy show that surrogates express diverse views about their relationship with the child born through surrogacy, ranging from deep emotional distress when separated from the child to acceptance that they have no relationship to the child they bear. Elly Seman (2008) argues against the commonly accepted view that surrogates would suffer emotionally when relinquishing the child they have carried to term. Her contention is that research on surrogacy has been framed by Western cultural assumptions that "normal" women do not voluntarily become pregnant with the premeditated intention of relinquishing the child for money, together with the assumption that "normal" women "naturally" bond with the children they bear.

26. Pande (2009a, 145) too advocates viewing gestational surrogacy as a new form of care work, but in light of her data, she is forced to contend that the surrogates themselves do not view themselves as laborers. Instead, they usually insist on making sense of their experience in an ethical or religious framework and firmly resist conceptualizing it in the commercial terms of selling a service. Pande writes, "Ironically, while the focus of this study has been on surrogacy as labor, most surrogates and their families do not recognize surrogacy as paid labor performed by women" (168).

27. See also Vora (2013, S100). Vora notes that the surrogates she spoke to first described surrogacy in the way they assumed she wanted to hear and as the clinical staff had counseled them to understand and accept: the uterus is a space in a woman's body that is empty when she is not expecting a child, and surrogacy is simply the renting out of that space for someone else's child. However, the surrogates also insisted on the common-sense notion that it is their body, its blood, and the food that they eat and use that is growing the infant (S101).

28. The famous court cases on surrogacy have reinforced the idea that

motherhood is defined in terms of genetic material. The surrogate mother Mary Beth Whitehead won back her parental rights to Baby M in 1985 in the United States on the basis of being the genetic mother. On the other hand, Anna Johnson, a gestational surrogate, lost such a right, because she bore no genetic relationship to the baby (Satz 1992, 127).

29. See also Vora (2013, S105) and Pande (2014, 179–80).

30. For an analysis of gestational surrogacy from the perspective of the child and its well-being, see Tyson Darling (2014).

31. See Pande (2014, 190–94).

32. See Grewal and Kaplan (1994), Mohanty (2003), and Briggs (2016).

33. Cinzia Arruzza (2017a) has similarly argued that feminism needs to retrieve a form of universalism. She grounds such a political project on Etienne Balibar's idea of capitalism as a "real universality." Such a universality is not based on any definition of human essence or women's nature but is rooted in the universality historically created by the reality of capitalism: capitalism has de facto generated a world in which people are interdependent and in which capitalist accumulation poses objective universal constraints on social production. These totalizing aspects of contemporary capitalism demand the adoption of some form of universalism for a political strategy aiming at overcoming capitalism.

Chapter 4

1. See also Cudd and Holmstrom (2011, 214–15).

2. Cinzia Arruzza adopts a historicized approach similar to Holmstrom's in her theorization of the relationship between capitalism and gender oppression. She too makes a distinction between theoretical and historical arguments and admits that it is "perhaps difficult to show at a high level of abstraction that gender oppression is essential to the inner workings of capitalism" (Arruzza 2014b, 19). As Arruzza explains, an integrated account of gender oppression in capitalism does not mean that every aspect of gender oppression can be understood as a direct consequence of capitalism; rather, arguing for an integrated analysis means denying that gender oppression functions as a separate system, such as patriarchy. The analysis is conducted on the level of lived reality where capitalism denotes a totality—a historically specific social formation consisting of all the myriad social practices in which we are involved daily. It is on this level that capitalism and patriarchy become indistinguishable. See my response to Arruzza in Oksala (2015).

3. The term "global care chain" was first used by Arlie Hochschild to describe the links between people across the globe based on their roles in the transnational division of care work. See Hochschild (2000). On the effects of the neoliberalization and globalization of capitalism on women's role in labor markets, see also Sassen (2000) and Bair (2010).

4. In their introduction to the second edition of Vogel's book, Susan Fer-

guson and David McNally (2013, xvii) write that the book is "arguably the most sophisticated Marxist intervention in the theoretical debates thrown up by socialist feminism."

5. In 2008, Thomas Beatie was the first legally defined male to become pregnant in North America. He stopped his testosterone hormone injections, underwent artificial insemination, and gave birth to his three children, Susan, Austin, and Jensen. See Karaian (2013, 212).

6. Susan Ferguson and David McNally (2013) formulate this by writing that Vogel identifies a historical tendency, not an iron law.

7. By "statistical discrimination," economists refer to the idea that employers make employment decisions based on imperfect information on the applicants' productivity, and therefore use statistical information on the group they belong to in order to infer productivity. In other words, if a group such as "women" is less productive statistically due to the overall time they spend out of waged labor, each individual in this group will be assumed to be less productive.

8. See Firestone ([1970] 1972). On the contemporary relevance of Firestone's ideas, see Cannon (2016) and Merck and Sandford (2010).

9. Jack Halberstam (2016, 373) notes how the television show *Transparent* (2014) marked a shift in mainstream representations of trans kinship. In the show, trans identity is situated firmly within familial networks.

10. See Karaian (2013). Health care providers are also not always aware of the unique challenges faced by trans parents, making it another important arena for reform. See MacDonald et al. (2016) and Riggs et al. (2021).

11. There is a link between metaphorical and literal commodification. The reason why people are troubled by "mere" market rhetoric, when applied in ways they think inappropriate, is that they think it is contagious and will lead to literal commodification. If enough people conceive of children in market rhetoric, for example, and advocate that we exchange children for money, then the literal buying and selling of children will result. In other words, our conceptual schemas shape reality: they open up and close down possibilities for action.

12. The pitfalls of feminist identity politics have been forcefully demonstrated by Judith Butler (1990) and Wendy Brown (1995), for example. Asad Haider (2018, 50) builds on Brown's work in his seminal book *Mistaken Identity*, which argues persuasively that a common interest cannot be built on a given identity but can only be constituted in a political process. See also Butler (2015, 66).

13. See Arruzza (2017b).

Chapter 5

1. For different definitions of the concept of feminization of labor, see Morini (2007, 41–44).

2. See Honneth and Hartmann (2006, 50).

3. See Hochschild (2013).

4. See Quinby (2004).

5. For an account of the domestic labor debates, see Vogel (1983, 13–28).

6. See Marx ([1867] 1990, 644, 1039–49).

7. See Engels ([1884] 1972) and Mitchell (1971).

8. Marxist-feminist thinkers also problematized the question of how the contribution made by domestic labor was determinate of the exchange value of labor power. In Marx's theory, the value of labor power is determined by the value of the commodities necessary for its reproduction. However, it is not clear in Marx's work whether this value covers the individual worker, or the entire household supported by the worker. If it covers the entire household, then the value of the domestic work must factor directly into the value of labor power. See Vogel (1983, 23).

9. The "wages for housework" campaign in the 1970s was an international feminist mobilization that attempted to force the state to recognize that domestic work is work, an activity that should be remunerated because it contributed to the production of the labor force and produced capital. As Silvia Federici (2012, 8–9) describes the movement, it was revolutionary at the time because it recognized that capitalism required unwaged reproductive labor in order to contain the cost of labor power. The idea was that a successful campaign draining the source of this unpaid labor would break the process of capitalist accumulation. See Dalla Costa and James (1973).

10. See Hochschild ([1983] 2012, 7).

11. In her more recent defense of UBI, Weeks acknowledges that UBI might perpetuate the traditional gender division of labor in a heteropatriarchal family, but even if this was the case, she would support it. "The feminist politics that I support . . . approaches feminism as a revolutionary project to transform the intersecting hierarchies of heteropatriarchal racial capitalism, not just the relative positions of men and women within it. Consequently, the future of the domestic gender division of labor is not my only metric of feminist judgement" (Weeks 2020, 587). It is difficult for me to see, however, what "transforming the hierarchies of heteropatriarchal racial capitalism" could mean if this transformation does not result in a change in the relative positions of men and women in it.

12. See Ehrenreich and Hochschild (2002).

13. According to Weeks, it is important to recognize that there is, by Negri's reading of the *Grundrisse*, no concept of work to restore or to liberate. See Negri (1991, 10).

14. See Foucault ([1976] 1978), ([1978] 1980), ([1975] 1991), ([1999] 2003).

15. In the autonomist Marxist tradition, the notion of the "social factory" refers to the idea that capitalist relations cannot be confined within the factory walls but permeate the whole society. See Tronti ([1966] 2019).

16. See Foucault ([1997] 2003, 13).

17. See Arruzza (2014a).

Chapter 6

1. See Bowman and Cole (2009).
2. See Milkman, Reese, and Roth (1998, 500–501).
3. See Young (2001, 316).
4. UBI has ardent defenders on both the Left and the Right. David Calnitsky (2017) notes how many on the Left object to UBI because it is supported by the Right. Their worry is that given the constellation of forces and the political commitments of its right-wing proponents, basic income would be implemented "in a neoliberal guise, dishing out meager payments and accompanied by severe austerity measures." Calnitsky argues that while such a version of UBI should clearly be resisted, this does not preclude the possibility of working towards a better version of it. See also Weeks (2020). Kathi Weeks notably argues for UBI from the tradition of Marxist feminist thought, particularly from the "wages for housework" literature presented in the writings of theorists such as Mariarosa Dalla Costa, Selma James, Silvia Federici, and Nicole Cox. See Weeks (2011) and (2020).
5. See Pateman (2004), Gorz ([1997] 1999), McKay (2001), Weeks (2011), and Zamora (2017).
6. See Elgarte (2006).
7. See Steil (1997).
8. See Robeyns (2001), Pateman (2004), and Zelleke (2011).
9. Jacqueline O'Reilly (2008) argues that it is not empirically clear what type of gender equality BI would result in and suggests that its advocates expect too much from what is essentially just one policy tool.
10. See Robeyns (2001) and Gheaus (2008).
11. See Brown (1995).
12. As Srnicek and Williams (2015, 160–61) contend, the demand for basic income could become a focal point for red-green coalition politics.
13. Dawson envisions a carbon- and biodiversity-based guaranteed income program, which would function as a concrete model for mitigating the environmental crisis we are facing. He notes that of the twenty-five terrestrial biodiversity hot spots around the world, fifteen are covered primarily by tropical rainforests, and consequently are also key sites for the absorption of carbon pollution. All these areas are under heavy assault from the forces of enclosure and ecocide (Dawson 2016, 88–89).
14. See Calnitsky (2017).
15. See Srnicek and Williams (2015) and Mason (2016).

Concluding Remarks

1. For ecosocialist political visions, see Williams (2010), Löwy (2015), Angus (2016), and Magdoff and Williams (2017); on the idea of democratic control of the economy, see Hahnel (2012); on the project of degrowth, see Hickel (2020) and Jackson ([2009] 2016); on social ecology, see Bookchin (1996).

2. While his Marxist critics generally acknowledge that Foucault's work has been important in drawing attention to such neglected issues as gender and sexuality in traditional Marxist theory, the common charge is that Foucault's influence has also resulted in the fracturing of the social realm and a retreat from class analysis. See Amselle (2016, 167) and Zamora (2016, 63–64). On attempts to appropriate Foucault's thought for a critical analysis of the connections between heteronormativity and capitalism, see Floyd (2009).

Works Cited

Agamben, Giorgio. (1995) 1998. *Homo Sacer: Sovereign Power and Bare Life.* Translated by Daniel Heller-Roazen. Stanford, CA: Stanford University Press.

Agarwal, Bina. 1992. "The Gender and Environment Debate: Lessons from India." *Feminist Studies* 18, no. 1: 119–59.

———. 2001. "A Challenge for Ecofeminism: Gender, Greening and Community Forestry in India." *Women & Environments International* 52/53: 12–15.

Aho, Hanna. 2016. "Lyhyt oppimäärä metsien rooliin ilmastopolitiikassa." *Suomen luonnonsuojeluliitto.* https://www.sll.fi/ajankohtaista/blogi/lyhyt -oppimaara-metsien-rooliin-ilmastopolitiikassa.

Amselle, J. L. 2016. "Michel Foucault and the Spiritualization of Philosophy." In *Foucault and Neoliberalism.* Edited by D. Zamora and M. C. Behrent, 159–69. Cambridge: Polity Press.

Andrews, Lori B. 1988. "Surrogate Motherhood: The Challenge for Feminists." *Journal of Law, Medicine, and Ethics* 16, no. 1–2: 72–80.

Andrews, Lori B., and Lisa Douglass. 1991. "Alternative Reproduction." *Southern California Law Review* 65: 623–82.

Angus, Ian. 2016. *Facing the Anthropocene: Fossil Capitalism and the Crisis of the Earth System.* New York: Monthly Review.

Aristotle. 1995. *Politics.* Oxford: Oxford University Press.

Arruzza, Cinzia. 2014a. "The Capitalism of Affects." *Public Seminar,* August 25, 2014. http://www.publicseminar.org/2014/08/the-capitalism-of-affects.

———. 2014b. "Remarks on Gender." *Viewpoint Magazine,* September 2, 2014. https://www.viewpointmag.com/2014/09/02/remarks-on-gender/.

———. 2016. "Functionalist, Determinist, Reductionist: Social Reproduction Feminism and Its Critics." *Science & Society* 80, no. 1: 9–30.

———. 2017a. "Capitalism and the Conflict over Universality: A Feminist Perspective." *Philosophy Today* 61, no. 4: 847–61.

———. 2017b. "From Social Reproduction Feminism to the Women's Strike." In *Social Reproduction Theory: Remapping Class, Recentering Oppression,* edited by Tithi Bhattacharya, 192–96. London: Pluto.

Arruzza, Cinzia, Tithi Bhattacharya, and Nancy Fraser. 2019. *Feminism for the 99%.* London: Verso.

Arsel, Murat. 2012. "Between 'Marx and Markets'? The State, the 'Left Turn' and Nature in Ecuador." *Tijdschrift voor Economische en Sociale Geografie* 103, no. 2: 150–63.

Bailey, Alison. 2011. "Reconceiving Surrogacy: Toward a Reproductive Justice Account of Indian Surrogacy." *Hypatia: Journal of Feminist Philosophy*, 26, no. 4: 716–41.

Bair, Jennifer. 2010. "On Difference and Capital: Gender and the Globalization of Production." *Signs: Journal of Women in Culture and Society* 36, no. 1: 203–26.

Becker, Gary. 1981. *A Treatise on the Family*. Cambridge, MA: Harvard University Press.

Beckett, Andy. 2019. "The New Left Economics: How a Network of Thinkers Is Transforming Capitalism." *The Guardian*, June 25, 2019. https://www.theguardian.com/news/2019/jun/25/the-new-left-economics-how-a-network-of-thinkers-is-transforming-capitalism.

Benston, Margaret. (1969) 1997. "The Political Economy of Women's Liberation." In *Materialist Feminism: Reader in Class, Difference, and Women's Lives*, edited by Rosemary Hennessey and Chrys Ingraham, 159–69. London: Routledge.

Bhattacharya, Tithi, ed. 2017. *Social Reproduction Theory: Remapping Class, Recentering Oppression*. London: Pluto.

Birch, Kean, Les Levidow, and Theo Papaioannou. 2010. "Sustainable Capital? The Neoliberalization of Nature and Knowledge in the European 'Knowledge-based Bio-economy.'" *Sustainability* 2, no. 9: 2898–2918.

Birch, Kean, and David Tyfield. 2012. "Theorizing the Bioeconomy: Biovalue, Biocapital, Bioeconomics or . . . What?" *Science, Technology & Human Values* 38, no. 3: 299–327.

Bookchin, Murray. 1996. *The Philosophy of Social Ecology: Essays on Dialectical Naturalism*. Montreal: Black Rose Books.

Boscov-Ellen, Dan. 2020a. "A Responsibility to Revolt? Climate Ethics in the Real World." *Environmental Values* 29, no. 2: 153–74.

———. 2020b. "Whose Universalism? Dipesh Chakrabarthy and the Anthropocene." *Capitalism, Nature, Socialism* 31, no. 1: 70–83.

Bowman, John R., and Alyson M. Cole. 2009. "Do Working Mothers Oppress Other Women? The Swedish 'Maid Debate' and the Welfare State Politics of Gender Equality." *Signs: Journal of Women in Culture* 35, no. 1: 157–84.

Boyd, William, W. Scott Prudham, and Rachel A. Schurman. 2001. "Industrial Dynamics and the Problem of Nature." *Society and Natural Resources* 14, no. 7: 555–70.

Braidotti, Rosi, Ewa Charkiewicz, Sabine Hausler, and Saskia Wieringa. 1994. *Women, the Environment and Sustainable Development: Towards a Theoretical Synthesis*. London: Zed Books and INSTRAW.

Brewer, Rose. (1993) 1997. "Theorizing Race, Class, and Gender: The New Scholarship of Black Feminist Intellectuals and Black Women's Labor." In *Materialist Feminism: A Reader in Class, Difference, and Women's Lives*, ed. Rosemary Hennessey and Chris Ingraham, 236–47. New York: Routledge.

Briggs, Laura. 2016. "Transnational." In *The Oxford Handbook of Feminist Theory*, edited by Lisa Disch and Mary E. Hawkesworth, 991–1009. Oxford: Oxford University Press.

Brown, Wendy. 1995. *States of Injury: Power and Freedom in Late Modernity*. Princeton, NJ: Princeton University Press.

————. 2005. *Edgework. Critical Essays on Knowledge and Politics*. Princeton, NJ: Princeton University Press.

Burkett, Paul. 1999. *Marx and Nature*. New York: St. Martin's Press.

Butler, Judith. 1990. *Gender Trouble*. London: Routledge.

————. 1997. "Merely Cultural," *Social Text*, no. 52/53, "Queer Transexions of Race, Nation, and Gender," 265–77.

————. 2015. *Notes toward a Performative Theory of Assembly*. Cambridge, MA: Harvard University Press.

Calnitsky, David. 2017. "Debating Basic Income." *Catalyst* 1, no. 3. https://catalyst-journal.com/vol1/no3/debating-basic-income.

Cannon, Loren. 2016. "Firestonian Futures and Trans-Affirming Presents." *Hypatia: Journal of Feminist Philosophy* 31, no. 2: 229–44.

Carlassare, Elizabeth. 2000. "Socialist and Cultural Ecofeminism: Allies in Resistance." *Ethics and the Environment* 5, no. 1: 89–106.

Chen, Chris. 2013. "The Limit Point of Capitalist Equality: Notes toward an Abolitionist Antiracism." *Endnotes* 3, no. 2. https://endnotes.org.uk/issues/3/en/chris-chen-the-limit-point-of-capitalist-equality.

Collins, Patricia Hill. 1990. *Black Feminist Thought: Knowledge, Consciousness, and the Politics of Empowerment*. Boston: Unwin Hyman.

Combahee River Collective. (1978) 2014. "A Black Feminist Statement." *Women's Studies Quarterly* 42, no. 3/4: 271–80.

Cooper, Melinda. 2008. *Life as Surplus: Biotechnology and Capitalism in the Neoliberal Era*. Washington: University of Washington Press.

Cooper, Melinda, and Catherine Waldby. 2014. *Clinical Labor: Tissue Donors and Research Subjects in the Global Bioeconomy*. Durham, NC: Duke University Press.

Cooper, Ryan. 2017. "The Great Recession Never Ended." *The Week*, July 27, 2017. https://theweek.com/articles/714423/great-recession-never-ended.

Coulthard, Glen Sean. 2014. *Red Skin, White Masks: Rejecting the Colonial Politics of Recognition*. Minneapolis: University of Minnesota Press.

Crenshaw, Kimberlé. 1989. "Demarginalizing the Intersection of Race and Sex: A Black Feminist Critique of Antidiscrimination Doctrine, Feminist Theory and Antiracist Politics." *University of Chicago Legal Forum* 1: 139–67.

Crist, Eileen. 2013. "On the Poverty of Our Nomenclature." *Environmental Humanities* 2: 129–47.

Cudd, Ann E., and Nancy Holmstrom. 2011. *Capitalism, For and Against: A Feminist Debate*. Cambridge: Cambridge University Press.

Cuomo, Chris. 2017. "Sexual Politics in Environmental Ethics: Impacts, Causes, Alternatives." In *The Oxford Handbook of Environmental Ethics*, edited by Stephen M. Gardiner and Allen Thompson. Oxford: Oxford University Press.

Dalla Costa, Mariarosa, and Selma James. 1973. *The Power of Women and the Subversion of the Community*. Bristol, UK: Falling Wall.

Daly, Mary. 1978. *Gyn/Ecology: The Metaethics of Radical Feminism*. Boston: Beacon.

DasGupta, Sayantani, and Shamita Das Dasgupta. 2014. "Business as Usual? The Violence of Reproductive Trafficking in the Indian Context." In *Globalization and Transnational Surrogacy in India: Outsourcing Life*, edited by Sayantani DasGupta and Shamita Das Dasgupta, 179–96. Lanham, MD: Lexington Books.

Davion, Victoria. 2011. "Ecofeminism." In *A Companion to Environmental Philosophy*, edited by D. Jamieson. Malden, MA: Blackwell.

Davis, Angela. 1972. "Reflections on the Black Woman's Role in the Community of Slaves." *Massachusetts Review* 13, no. 2: 81–100.

———. 1981. *Women, Race and Class*. London: Penguin.

Dawson, Ashley. 2016. *Extinction: A Radical History*. New York: OR Books.

Dawson, Michael C. 2016. "Hidden in Plain Sight: A Note on Legitimation Crises and the Racial Order. *Critical Historical Studies* 3, no. 1: 143–61.

Deomampo, Daisy. 2016. *Transnational Reproduction: Race, Kinship, and Commercial Surrogacy in India*. New York: New York University Press.

DePillis, Lydia. 2017. "10 Years after the Recession Began, Have Americans Recovered?" CNN Business, December 1, 2017. https://money.cnn.com/2017/12/01/news/economy/recession-anniversary/index.html.

Diamond, Cora. 1978. "Eating Meat and Eating People." *Philosophy* 53, no. 206: 465–79.

Echeverría, Hugo. 2017. "Rights of Nature: The Ecuadorian Case." *Revista ESMAT* 9, no. 13: 77–86.

Eckersley, Robyn. 1995. "Liberal Democracy and the Rights of Nature: The Struggle for Inclusion." *Environmental Politics* 4, no. 4: 169–98.

Ehrenreich, Barbara, and Arlie Hochshild, eds. 2002. *Global Woman: Nannies, Maids, and Sex Workers in the New Economy*. New York: Henry Holt.

Eisenstein, Hester. 2009. *Feminism Seduced: How Global Elites Use Women's Labor and Ideas to Exploit the World*. Boulder, CO: Paradigm.

Elgarte, Julieta Magdalena. 2006. "Good for Women? Advantages and Risks of a Basic Income from a Gender Perspective." Paper presented at the XI BIEN Congress, University of Cape Town, November 2–4, 2006.

Engels, Friedrich. (1884) 1972. *The Origin of the Family, Private Property and the State*. Edited by Eleanor Burke Leacock, translated by Alec West. New York: International.

Fanon, Frantz. (1961) 2001. *The Wretched of the Earth*. Translated by Constance Farrington. London: Penguin.

Farris, Sara. 2015. "The Intersectional Conundrum and the Nation-State." *Viewpoint Magazine*, May 4, 2015. https://viewpointmag.com/2015/05/04/the-intersectional-conundrum-and-the-nation-state/.

Federici, Silvia. 2004. *Caliban and the Witch: Women, the Body, and Primitive Accumulation*. New York: Automedia.

———. 2012. *Revolution at Point Zero: Housework, Reproduction, and Feminist Struggle*. Brooklyn, NY: Autonomedia.

Ferguson, Susan, and David McNally. 2013. "Capital, Labour-Power, and Gender Relations." In *Marxism and the Oppression of Women: Toward a Unitary Theory*, edited by Lise Vogel, xvii–xl. Leiden: Brill.

Firestone, Shulamith. (1970) 1972. *The Dialectic of Sex: The Case for Feminist Revolution*. London: Paladin.

Floyd, Kevin. 2009. *The Reification of Desire*. Minneapolis: University of Minnesota Press.

———. 2015. "Automatic Subjects: Gendered Labour and Abstract Life." *Historical Materialism* 21, no. 2: 61–86.

Folbre, Nancy, and Julie A. Nelson. 2000. "For Love or Money—or Both?" *Journal of Economic Perspectives* 14, no. 4: 123–40.

Foster, John Bellamy. 2000. *Marx's Ecology*. New York: Monthly Review.

———. 2002. *Ecology against Capitalism*. New York: Monthly Review.

———. 2009. *The Ecological Revolution: Making Peace with the Planet*. New York: Monthly Review.

Foucault, Michel. (1975) 1991. *Discipline and Punish. The Birth of the Prison*. Translated by Alan Sheridan. London: Penguin Books.

———. (1976) 1978. *The History of Sexuality, Vol. 1*. Translated by Robert Hurley. New York: Pantheon Books.

———. (1978) 1980. *Herculine Barbin. Being the Recently Discovered Memoirs of a Nineteenth-Century French Hermaphrodite*. Translated by Richard McDougall. New York: Pantheon Books.

———. (1997) 2003. *Society Must Be Defended: Lectures at the Collège de France 1975–1976*. Edited by Mauro Bertani and Alessandro Fontana, translated by David Macey. New York: Picador.

———. (1999) 2003. *Abnormal. Lectures at the College de France*. Edited by Valerio Marchetti and Antonella Salomoni, translated by Graham Burchell. New York: Picador.

Franklin, Sarah. 2007. *Dolly Mixtures: The Remaking of Genealogy*. Durham, NC: Duke University Press.

Fraser, Nancy. 1996. "Social Justice in the Age of Identity Politics: Redistribution, Recognition, and Participation." https://www.intelligenceispower.com/Important%20E-mails%20Sent%20attachments/Social%20Justice%20in%20the%20Age%20of%20Identity%20Politics.pdf.

———. 1997. "Heterosexism, Misrecognition and Capitalism: A Response to Judith Butler." *Social Text*, no. 52/53, "Queer Transexions of Race, Nation, and Gender," 279–89.

———. 2013. *Fortunes of Feminism: From State-Managed Capitalism to Neoliberal Crisis*. London: Verso.

———. 2014. "Behind Marx's Hidden Abode." *New Left Review* 86: 1–17.

———. 2016. "Expropriation and Exploitation in Racialized Capitalism: A Reply to Michael Dawson." *Critical Historical Studies* 3, no. 1: 163–78.

———. 2021. "Climates of Capital: For a Trans-Environmental Eco-Socialism." *New Left Review* 127: 94–127.

Fraser, Nancy, and Rahel Jaeggi. 2018. *Capitalism: A Conversation in Critical Theory*. Oxford: Polity.

Gaard, Greta. 2011. "Ecofeminism Revisited: Rejecting Essentialism and Replacing Species in a Material Environment." *Feminist Formations* 23, no. 2: 26–53.

Gaard, Greta, and Lori Gruen. (1993) 2005. "Ecofeminism: Toward Global Justice and Planetary Health." In *Environmental Philosophy: From Animal Rights to Radical Ecology*, 4th edition, edited by Michael E. Zimmerman, J. Baird Callicott, Karen J. Warren, Irene Klaver, and John Clark. Upper Saddle River, NJ: Pearson.

Gheaus, Anca. 2008. "Basic Income, Gender Justice and the Costs of Gender-Symmetrical Lifestyles." *Basic Income Studies: An International Journal of Basic Income Research* 3, no. 3.

Ghodsee, Kristen R. 2018. *Why Women Have Better Sex under Socialism and Other Arguments for Economic Independence*. New York: Nation Books.

Gilabert, Pablo, and Martin O'Neill. 2019. "Socialism." *The Stanford Encyclopedia of Philosophy*. https://plato.stanford.edu/entries/socialism/.

Giljum, Stefan, Monika Dittrich, Mirko Lieber, and Stephan Lutter. 2014. "Global Patterns of Material Flows and Their Socio-Economic and Environmental Implications: An MFA Study on All Countries World-Wide from 1980 to 2009." *Resources* 3, no. 1: 319–39.

Glenn, Evelyn. 1992. "From Servitude to Service Work: Historical Continuities in the Racial Division of Paid Reproductive Labor." *Signs: Journal of Women in Culture and Society* 18, no. 1: 1–43.

Gorz, André. (1980) 1987. *Ecology as Politics*. Translated by Patsy Vigderman and Jonathan Cloud. London: Pluto.

———. (1994) 2012. *Capitalism, Socialism, Ecology*. Translated by Martin Chalmers. London: Verso.

———. (1997) 1999. *Reclaiming Work: Beyond the Wage-Based Society*. Translated by Chris Turner. Cambridge: Polity.

Grewal, Inderpal, and Caren Kaplan. 1994. *Scattered Hegemonies: Postmodernity and Transnational Feminist Practices*. Minneapolis: University of Minnesota Press.

Griffin, Susan. 1978. *Woman and Nature: The Roaring Inside Her*. New York: Harper and Row.

Guha, Ranajit. 1998. *Dominance without Hegemony: History and Power in Colonial India*. Cambridge, MA: Harvard University Press.

Haberl, Helmut, et al. 2020. "A Systematic Review of the Evidence on Decoupling GDP, Resource Use and GHG Emissions: Part II: Synthesizing the Insights." *Environmental Research Letters*, 2020.

Hägglund, Martin. 2019. *This Life*. New York: Random House.

Hahnel, Robin. 2012. *Of the People, By the People: The Case for a Participatory Economy*. Chico, CA: Soapbox.

Haider, Asad. 2018. *Mistaken Identity: Race and Class in the Age of Trump*. London: Verso.

Halberstam, Jack. 2016. "Trans*—Gender Transitivity and New Configurations of Body, History, Memory and Kinship." *Parallax* 22, no. 3: 366–75.

Hamilton, Clive. 2017. *Defiant Earth: The Fate of Humans in the Anthropocene*. Cambridge: Polity.

Hansen, James, Makiko Sato, and Pushker Kharecha. 2008. "Target Atmospheric CO2: Where Should Humanity Aim?" *Open Atmospheric Science Journal* 2: 217–31.

Hardt, Michael, and Antonio Negri. 2000. *Empire*. Cambridge, MA: Harvard University Press.

——. 2004. *Multitude: War and Democracy in the Age of Empire*. London: Penguin.

——. 2009. *Commonwealth*. Cambridge, MA: Belknap Press of Harvard University Press.

Hartman, Heidi. 1979. "The Unhappy Marriage of Marxism and Feminism: Towards a More Progressive Union." *Capital and Class* 3, no. 2: 1–33.

Harvey, David. 2004. "The 'New' Imperialism: Accumulation by Dispossession." *Socialist Register* 40: 63–87.

Hennessy, Rosemary. 2000. *Profit and Pleasure: Sexual Identities in Late Capitalism*. New York: Routledge.

Hettinger, Ned. 2001. "Environmental Disobedience." In *A Companion to Environmental Philosophy*, edited by Dale Jamieson, 498–509. Malden, MA: Blackwell.

Hickel, Jason. 2020. *Less Is More: How Degrowth Will Save the World*. London: Windmill Books.

Hickel, Jason, and Giorgos Kallis. 2019. "Is Green Growth Possible?" *New Political Economy* 25, no. 4: 469–86. https://doi.org/10.1080/13563467.2019.1598964.

Hochschild, Arlie. (1983) 2012. *The Managed Heart: Commercialization of Human Feeling*. Berkeley: University of California Press.

——. 2000. "Global Care Chains and Emotional Surplus Value." In *On the Edge: Living with Global Capitalism*, edited by Will Hutton and Anthony Giddens. 130–46. London: Jonathan Cape.

——. 2013. *The Outsourced Self: What Happens When We Pay Others to Live Our Lives for Us*. London: Picador.

Honneth, Axel, and Martin Hartmann. 2006. "Paradoxes of Capitalism." *Constellations* 13, no. 1: 41–58.

Ilmasto.org. 2008. "Vanhat metsät sittenkin hiilinieluja." http://ilmasto.org/kirjoitukset/vanhat-metsat-sittenkin-hiilinieluja.

IPCC. 2022. *Climate Change 2022: Impacts, Adaptation, and Vulnerability. Contribution of Working Group II to the Sixth Assessment Report of the Intergovernmental Panel on Climate Change*. Edited by H.-O. Pörtner, D. C. Roberts, M. Tignor, E. S. Poloczanska, K. Mintenbeck, A. Alegría, M. Craig, S. Langsdorf, S. Löschke, V. Möller, A. Okem, and B. Rama. Cambridge and New York: Cambridge University Press.

Jackson, Tim. (2009) 2016. *Prosperity without Growth: Economics for a Finite Planet*. London: Routledge.

Jackson, Tim, and Peter A. Victor. 2019. "Unraveling the Claims for (and against) Green Growth." *Science* 366, no. 6468: 950–51.

James, Simon P. 2015. *Environmental Philosophy: An Introduction*. Cambridge: Polity.

Joseph, Gloria. (1981) 1997. "The Incompatible Menage à Trois: Marxism, Feminism, and Racism." In *Materialist Feminism: A Reader in Class, Difference, and Women's Lives*, edited by Rosemary Hennessey and Chris Ingraham, 107–10. London: Routledge.

Karaian, Lara. 2013. "Pregnant Men: Repronormativity, Critical Trans Theory and the Re(conceive)ing of Sex and Pregnancy in Law." *Social & Legal Studies* 22, no. 2: 211–30.

Katz, Cindi. 2001. "Vagabond Capitalism and the Necessity of Social Reproduction," *Antipode* 33, no. 4: 709–28.

Kelley, Robin D. G. 2020. "Why Black Marxism? Why Now?" In *Black Marxism: The Making of the Black Radical Tradition*, by Cedric J. Robinson. Chapel Hill: University of North Carolina Press.

King, Deborah. 1988. "Multiple Jeopardy, Multiple Consciousness." *Signs* 14, no. 1: 42–72.

Kirk, Gwyn. 1997. "Standing on Solid Ground: A Materialist Ecological Feminism." In *Materialist Feminism: A Reader in Class, Difference, and Women's Lives*, edited by Rosemary Hennessy and Chrys Ingraham, 345–63. New York: Routledge.

Klein, Naomi. 2014. *This Changes Everything: Capitalism vs. the Climate*. New York: Simon and Schuster.

Kollontai, Alexandra. 1977. *Selected Writings*. New York: W. W. Norton.

Knauss, Stefan. 2018. "Conceptualizing Human Stewardship in the Anthropocene: The Rights of Nature in Ecuador, New Zealand and India." *Journal of Agricultural and Environmental Ethics* 31, no. 6: 703–22.

Lalander, Rickard. 2014. "Rights of Nature and the Indigenous Peoples in Bolivia and Ecuador: A Straitjacket for Progressive Development Politics?" *Revista Iberoamericana de Estudios de Desarrollo* 3, no. 2: 148–73.

Landes, Elisabeth M., and Richard A. Posner. 1978. "The Economics of the Baby Shortage." *Journal of Legal Studies* 7: 323–48.

Lau, Lisa. 2018. "A Post-Colonial Framing of Indian Commercial Surrogacy: Issues, Representations, and Orientalisms." *Gender, Place & Culture: A Journal of Feminist Geography* 25: 666–685. https://doi.org/10.1080/0966369X.2018.1471047.

Löwy, Michael. 2015. *Ecosocialism: A Radical Alternative to Capitalist Catastrophe*. Chicago: Haymarket Books.

Lugones, Maria. 2007. "Heterosexuality and the Colonial/Modern Gender System." *Hypatia: Journal of Feminist Philosophy* 22, no. 1: 186–209.

Luxemburg, Rosa. (1913) 2003. *The Accumulation of Capital*. New York: Routledge.

MacDonald, Trevor, Joy-Noel Weiss, Diana West, Michelle Walks, MaryLynne Biener, Alanna Kibbe, and Elizabeth Myler. 2016. "Transmasculine Individuals' Experiences with Lactation, Chestfeeding, and Gender Identity: A Qualitative Study." *BMC Pregnancy and Childbirth* 16, no. 106.

MacKinnon, Catharine. 1982. "Feminism, Marxism, Method, and the State: An Agenda for Theory." *Signs* 7, no. 3: 515–44.

Madge, Varada. 2014. "Gestational Surrogacy in India: The Problem of Technology and Poverty." In *Globalization and Transnational Surrogacy in India: Outsourcing Life*, edited by Sayantani DasGupta and Shamita Das Dasgupta, 45–66. Lanham, MD: Lexington Books.

Magdoff, Fred, and Chris Williams. 2017. *Creating an Ecological Society: Towards a Revolutionary Transformation*. New York: Monthly Review.

Mann, Geoff, and Joel Wainwright. 2018. *Climate Leviathan. A Political Theory of Our Planetary Future.* London: Verso.

Marx, Karl. (1867) 1990. *Capital. A Critique of Political Economy, Vol I.* Translated by Ben Fowkes. London: Penguin.

Mason, Paul. 2016. *Postcapitalism: A Guide to Our Future.* London: Allen Lane.

Mazzucato, Mariana. 2018. *The Value of Everything: Making and Taking in the Global Economy.* London: Penguin.

McKay, Ailsa. 2001. "Rethinking Work and Income Maintenance Policy: Promoting Gender Equality through a Citizen's Basic Income." *Feminist Economics* 7, no. 1: 97–118.

McKibben, Bill. 1989. *The End of Nature.* New York: Anchor Books.

Meagher, Gabrielle. 2002. "Is It Wrong to Pay for Housework?" *Hypatia: Journal of Feminist Philosophy* 17, no. 2: 52–66.

Meiksins Wood, Ellen. (1999) 2017. *The Origin of Capitalism: A Longer View.* London: Verso.

Mellor, Mary. 1992. *Breaking the Boundaries: Towards a Feminist Green Socialism.* London: Virago.

———. 2006. "Ecofeminist Political Economy," *International Journal of Green Economics* 1, no. 1/2: 139–50.

Merchant, Carol. 1980. *The Death of Nature: Women, Ecology, and the Scientific Revolution.* New York: Harper and Row.

Merck, Mandy, and Stella Sandford, eds. 2010. *Further Adventures of "The Dialectic of Sex": Critical Essays on Shulamith Firestone.* New York: Palgrave Macmillan.

Merle, Renae. 2018. "A Guide to the Financial Crisis—10 Years Later." *Washington Post,* September 10, 2018. https://www.washingtonpost.com/business/economy/a-guide-to-the-financial-crisis--10-years-later/2018/09/10/114b76ba-af10-11e8-a20b-5f4f84429666_story.html.

Mies, Maria. (1986) 1998. *Patriarchy and Accumulation on a World Scale: Women in the International Division of Labour.* London: Zed Books.

Milkman, Ruth, Ellen Reese, and Benita Roth. 1998. "The Macrosociology of Paid Domestic Labor." *Work and Occupations* 25, no. 4: 483–510.

Mills, Charles. 1990. "Getting Out of the Cave: Tension between Democracy and Elitism in Marx's Theory of Cognitive Liberation." *Social and Economic Studies* 39, no. 1: 1–50.

———. 1999. "European Spectres." *Journal of Ethics* 3, no. 2: 133–55.

Mitchell, Juliet. 1966. "Women: The Longest Revolution," *New Left Review* 40: 11–37.

———. 1971. *Women's Estate.* Baltimore, MD: Penguin.

Mitchell, Timothy. 2011. *Carbon Democracy: Political Power in the Age of Oil.* London: Verso.

Mohandesi, Salar, and Emma Teitelman. 2017. "Without Reserves." In *Social Reproduction Theory: Remapping Class, Recentering Oppression,* edited by Tithi Bhattacharya, 37–67. London: Pluto.

Mohanty, Chandra Talpade. 1988. "Under Western Eyes: Feminist Scholarship and Colonial Discourse." *Feminist Review* 30, no. 3: 61–88.

————. 2003. *Feminism without Borders: Decolonizing Theory, Practicing Solidarity.* Durham, NC: Duke University Press.

Mohapatra, Seema. 2014. "A Race to the Bottom? The Need for International Regulation of the Rapidly Growing Global Surrogacy Market." In *Globalization and Transnational Surrogacy in India: Outsourcing Life,* edited by Sayantani DasGupta and Shamita Das DasGupta, 147–56. Lanham, MD: Lexington Books.

Moore, Jason. 2015. *Capitalism in the Web of Life: Ecology and the Accumulation of Capital.* London: Verso.

Morini, Cristina. 2007. "The Feminization of Labour in Cognitive Capitalism." *Feminist Review* 87: 40–59.

Morini, Cristina, and Andrea Fumagalli. 2010. "Life Put to Work: Towards a Life Theory of Value." *Ephemera* 10, no. 3/4: 234–52.

Morton, Tim. 2010. *The Ecological Thought.* Cambridge, MA: Harvard University Press.

Nanda, Meera. 1997. "'History Is What Hurts': A Materialist Feminist Perspective on the Green Revolution and Its Ecofeminist Critics." In *Materialist Feminism: A Reader in Class, Difference, and Women's Lives,* edited by Rosemary Hennessy and Chrys Ingraham, 364–94. New York: Routledge.

Nayak, Preeti. 2014. "The Three Ms of Commercial Surrogacy in India." In *Globalization and Transnational Surrogacy in India: Outsourcing Life,* edited by Sayantani DasGupta and Shamita Das Dasgupta, 1–22. Lanham, MD: Lexington Books.

Negri, Antonio. 1991. *Marx Beyond Marx: Lessons on the Grundrisse.* Translated by Harry Cleaver, Michael Ryan, and Maurizio Viano. Brooklyn, NY: Autonomedia.

Nichols, Robert. 2020. *Theft Is Property! Dispossession and Critical Theory.* Durham, NC: Duke University Press.

Nicholson, Linda. 1987. "Feminism and Marx: Integrating Kinship with the Economic." In *Feminism as Critique,* edited by Seyla Benhabib and Drucilla Cornell, 16–30. Minneapolis: University of Minnesota Press.

Nixon, Rob. 2011. *Slow Violence and the Environmentalism of the Poor.* Cambridge, MA: Harvard University Press.

Obama, Barack. 2017. "The Irreversible Momentum of Clean Energy." *Science* 355, no. 6321: 126–29.

O'Connor, James. 1998. *Natural Causes: Essays in Ecological Marxism.* New York: Guildford.

OECD. 2001. "OECD Environmental Strategy for the First Decade of the 21st Century." http://www.oecd.org/environment/indicators-modelling -outlooks/1863539.pdf.

Oksala, Johanna. 2011. *Foucault, Politics, and Violence.* Evanston, IL: Northwestern University Press.

————. 2015. "Capitalism and Gender Oppression: Remarks on Cinzia Arruzza's 'Remarks on Gender.'" *Viewpoint Magazine,* May 4, 2015. https://www.view pointmag.com/2015/05/04/capitalism-and-gender-oppression-remarks -on-cinzia-arruzzas-remarks-on-gender/.

————. 2016. *Feminist Experiences: Phenomenological and Foucauldian Investigations.* Evanston, IL: Northwestern University Press.

————. 2017. "Feminism, Capitalism, and the Social Regulation of Sexuality." In *Feminism, Capitalism, and Critique: Essays in Honor of Nancy Fraser,* ed. Banu Bargu and Chiara Bottici, 67–84. New York: Palgrave Macmillan, 2017.

O'Neill, Onora. 1997. "Environmental Values, Anthropocentrism and Speciesism." *Environmental Values* 6, no. 2: 127–42.

O'Reilly, Jacqueline. 2008. "Can a Basic Income Lead to a More Gender Equal Society?" *Basic Income Studies: An International Journal of Basic Income Research* 3, no. 3.

Oxfam International. 2018. "Richest 1 Percent Bagged 82 Percent of Wealth Created Last Year—Poorest Half of Humanity Got Nothing." https://www.oxfam.org/en/pressroom/pressreleases/2018-01-22/richest-1-percent-bagged-82-percent-wealth-created-last-year.

————. 2019. "Billionaire Fortunes Grew by \$2.5 Billion a Day as Poorest Saw Their Wealth Fall." https://www.oxfam.org/en/pressroom/pressreleases/2019-01-18/billionaire-fortunes-grew-25-billion-day-last-year-poorest-saw.

Pande, Amrita. 2009a. "Not an 'Angel,' Not a 'Whore': Surrogates as 'Dirty' Workers in India." *Indian Journal of Gender Studies* 16, no. 2: 141–73.

————. 2009b. "'It May Be Her Eggs but It's My Blood': Surrogates and Everyday Forms of Kinship in India." *Qualitative Sociology* 32: 379–97.

————. 2014. *Wombs in Labor: Transnational Commercial Surrogacy in India.* New York: Columbia University Press.

Parenti, Christian. 2011. *Tropic of Chaos: Climate Change and the New Geography of Violence.* New York: Nation Books.

Patel, Raj, and Jason W. Moore. 2018. *A History of the World in Seven Cheap Things: A Guide to Capitalism, Nature, and the Future of the Planet.* London: Verso.

Pateman, Carole. 2004. "Democratizing Citizenship: Some Advantages of a Basic Income." *Politics & Society* 32, no. 1: 89–105.

Piketty, Thomas. 2014. *Capital in the Twenty-First Century.* Translated by Arthur Goldhammer. Cambridge, MA: Belknap Press of Harvard University Press.

Plumwood, Val. 1993. *Feminism and the Mastery of Nature.* New York: Routledge.

Polanyi, Karl. (1944) 2001. *The Great Transformation: The Political and Economic Origins of Our Time.* Boston: Beacon.

Proyect, Louis. 2020. "Class Reductionism and Environmental Racism." *Counterpunch,* August 18, 2020. http://www.counterpunch.org/2020/08/28/class-reductionism-and-environmental-racism/.

PRS Legislative Research. 2019. "The Surrogacy (Regulation) Bill, 2019." https://www.prsindia.org/billtrack/surrogacy-regulation-bill-2019.

Purdy, Jedediah. 2015. *After Nature: A Politics for the Anthropocene.* Cambridge, MA: Harvard University Press.

Quinby, Lee. 2004. "Taking the Millennialist Pulse of *Empire*'s Multitude: A Genealogical Feminist Diagnosis." In *Empire's New Clothes: Reading Hardt and Negri,* edited by Paul A. Passavant and Jodi Dean, 231–51. London: Routledge.

Radin, Margaret Jane. 1996. *Contested Commodities. The Trouble with Trade in Sex, Children, Body Parts, and Other Things.* Cambridge, MA: Harvard University Press.

Riggs, Damien, Sally Hines, Ruth Pearce, Carla A. Pfeffer, and Francis Ray White. 2021. "Trans Parenting." In *Maternal Theory: Essential Readings,* 2nd edition, edited by Andrea O'Reilly, 823–31. Toronto: Demeter.

Robeyns, Ingrid. 2001. "Will a Basic Income Do Justice to Women?" *Analyse & Kritik* 23: 88–105.

Robinson, Cedric. (1983) 2020. *Black Marxism: The Making of the Black Radical Tradition.* Chapel Hill: University of North Carolina Press.

Rogers, Chris. 2014. *Capitalism and Its Alternatives.* London: Zed Books.

Rose, Nikolas. 2007. *The Politics of Life Itself.* Princeton, NJ: Princeton University Press.

Rowbotham, Sheila. 1973. *Women's Consciousness, Man's World.* Harmondsworth, UK: Penguin.

Rudrappa, Sharmila. 2014. "Mother India: Outsourcing Labor to Indian Surrogate Mothers." In *Globalization and Transnational Surrogacy in India: Outsourcing Life,* edited by Sayantani DasGupta and Shamita Das Dasgupta, 125–46. Lanham, MD: Lexington Books.

Saito, Kohei. 2017. *Karl Marx's Ecosocialism.* New York: Monthly Review.

Salleh, Ariel. (1997) 2017. *Ecofeminism as Politics: Nature, Marx and the Postmodern.* London: Zed Books.

Sandel, Michael. 2012. *What Money Can't Buy: The Moral Limits of Markets.* New York: Farrar, Straus and Giroux.

Sassen, Saskia. 2000. "Women's Burden: Counter-Geographies of Globalization and the Feminization of Survival." *Journal of International Affairs* 53, no. 2: 503–24.

Satz, Debra. 1992. "Markets in Women's Reproductive Labor." *Philosophy and Public Affairs* 21, no. 2: 107–31.

Segal, Lynne. 2017. *Making Trouble: Life and Politics.* London: Verso.

Seman, Elly. 2008. "The Social Construction of Surrogacy Research: An Anthropological Critique of the Psychological Scholarship on Surrogate Motherhood." *Social Science & Medicine* 67: 1104–12.

Shane, Charlotte. 2018. "Feminist Living." https://www.thenation.com/article/feminist-living/.

Shao, Q., A. Schaffartzik, A. Mayer, and F. Krausmann. 2017. "The High Price of Dematerialization: A Dynamic Panel Data Analysis of Material Use and Economic Recession." *Journal of Cleaner Production* 167: 120–32.

Shiva, Vandana. 1989. *Staying Alive: Women, Ecology and Development.* London: Zed Books.

Shorter, David Delago. 2016. "Spirituality." In *Oxford Handbook of American Indian History,* edited by Frederick Hoxie, 433–52. Oxford: Oxford University Press.

Simmons, Matthew. 2000. *Revisiting "The Limits to Growth": Could the Club of Rome Have Been Correct After All?* Eugene, OR: Mud City.

Smith, Neil. 2007. "Nature as Accumulation Strategy." *Socialist Register* 43: 16–36.

Srnicek, Nick, and Alex Williams. 2015. *Inventing the Future: Postcapitalism and a World without Work*. Brooklyn, NY: Verso.

Steil, Janice. 1997. *Marital Equality*. Thousand Oaks, CA: Sage.

Stewart, Emily. 2018. "How Close Are We to Another Financial Crisis? 8 Experts Weigh In." *Vox*, September 18, 2018. https://www.vox.com/2018/9/18/17868074/financial-crisis-dodd-frank-lehman-brothers-recession.

Stockholm Resilience Centre. "Planetary Boundaries Research." https://www.stockholmresilience.org/research/planetary-boundaries.html.

Stone, Christopher. (1974) 2010. *Should Trees Have Standing? Law, Morality, and the Environment*. Oxford: Oxford University Press.

Sunder Rajan, Kaushik. 2006. *Biocapital: The Constitution of Postgenomic Life*. Durham, NC: Duke University Press.

Tronti, Mario. (1966) 2019. *Workers and Capital*. London: Verso.

Tyson Darling, Marsha J. 2014. "A Welfare Principle Applied to Children Born and Adopted in Surrogacy." In *Globalization and Transnational Surrogacy in India: Outsourcing Life*, edited by Sayantani DasGupta and Shamita Das Dasgupta, 157–77. Lanham, MD: Lexington Books.

United Nations Population Fund (UNFPA). 2009. "State of World Population 2009. Facing a Changing World: Women, Population and Climate." https://www.unfpa.org/sites/default/files/pub-pdf/state_of_world_population_2009.pdf.

Vaden, Tero, Ville Lähde, Antti Majava, Tero Toivainen, Jussi T. Eronen, and Paavo Järvensuu. 2019. "Onnistunut irtikytkentä Suomessa?" *Alue ja Ympäristö*, 48, no. 1: 3–13.

———. 2020. "Decoupling for Ecological Sustainability: A Categorisation and Review of the Research Literature." *Environmental Science and Policy* 112: 236–44.

Valiavicharska, Zhivka. 2019. "Introduction." A presentation at *Dispatches from Resistant Mexico: Screening and Discussion with Director Caitlin Manning*, Pratt Institute, February 12, 2019.

Van Parijs, Philippe. 1992. "Competing Justification for Basic Income." In *Arguing for Basic Income: Ethical Foundations of a Radical Reform*, edited by Philippe Van Parijs, 3–43. London: Verso.

Vogel, Lise. 1983. *Marxism and the Oppression of Women: Toward a Unitary Theory*. New Brunswick, NJ: Rutgers University Press.

Vogel, Steven. 2015. *Thinking like a Mall: Environmental Philosophy after the End of Nature*. Cambridge, MA: MIT Press.

Vora, Kalindi. 2012. "Limits of 'Labor': Accounting for Affect and the Biological in Transnational Surrogacy and Service Work." *South Atlantic Quarterly* 111, no. 4: 681–700.

———. 2013. "Potential, Risk, and Return in Transnational Indian Gestational Surrogacy." *Current Anthropology* 54, no. S7: S97–S106.

———. 2015a. *Life Support: Biocapital and the New History of Outsourced Labor*. Minneapolis: University of Minnesota Press.

———. 2015b. "Re-Imagining Reproduction: Unsettling Metaphors in the History of Imperial Science and Commercial Surrogacy in India." *Somatechnics* 5, no. 1: 88–103.

Vrasti, Wanda. 2016. "Self-Reproducing Movements and the Enduring Challenge of Materialist Feminism." In *Scandalous Economics: Gender and the Politics of Financial Crisis*, edited by Aida A. Hozic and Jaqui True, 248–65. New York: Oxford University Press.

Walby, Sylvia. 2011. *The Future of Feminism*. Cambridge: Polity.

Waldby, Catherine. 2000. *The Visible Human Project: Informatic Bodies and Posthuman Medicine*. London: Routledge.

Waldby, Catherine, and Robert Mitchell. 2007. *Tissue Economies*. Durham, NJ: Duke University Press.

Weeks, Kathi. 2007. "Life within and against Work: Affective Labor, Feminist Critique, and Post-Fordist Politics." *Ephemera: Theory & Politics in Organization* 7, no. 1: 233–49.

———. 2011. *The Problem with Work. Feminism, Marxism, Antiwork Politics, and Postwork Imaginaries*. Durham, NC: Duke University Press.

———. 2020. "Anti/Postwork Feminist Politics and a Case for Basic Income." *tripleC* 18, no. 2: 575–94.

West, Cornell. 2008. *The Ethical Dimensions of Marxist Thought*. Delhi: Aakar Books.

Whittenmore, Mary Elizabeth. 2011. "The Problem of Enforcing Nature's Rights under Ecuador's Constitution: Why the 2008 Environmental Amendments Have No Bite." *Pacific Rim Law & Policy Journal* 659 (2011). https://digitalcommons.law.uw.edu/wilj/vol20/iss3/8.

Whyte, Kyle P. 2014. "Indigenous Women, Climate Change Impacts, and Collective Action. *Hypatia: Journal of Feminist Philosophy* 29, no. 3: 599–616.

Williams, Chris. 2010. *Ecology and Socialism: Solutions to Capitalist Ecological Crisis*. Chicago: Haymarket Books.

Wills, Vanessa. 2018. "What Could It Mean to Say, 'Capitalism Causes Sexism and Racism'?" *Philosophical Topics* 46, no. 2: 229–46.

Wood, Richard, Konstantin Stadler, Moana Simas, Tatyana Bulavskaya, Stefan Giljum, Stephan Lutter, and Arnold Tukker. 2018. "Growth in Environmental Footprints and Environmental Impacts Embodied in Trade: Resource Efficiency Indicators from EXIOBASE3." *Journal of Industrial Ecology* 22, no. 3: 553–64.

Wynter, Sylvia. (1982) 2018. "Beyond Liberal and Marxist Leninist Feminisms: Towards an Autonomous Frame of Reference." *The CLR James Journal* 24, no. 1/2: 31–56.

Young, Brigitte. 2001. "The 'Mistress' and the 'Maid' in the Globalized Economy." *Socialist Register* 37, 315–27.

Young, Iris Marion. (1979) 1997. "Socialist Feminism and the Limits of Dual Systems Theory." In *Materialist Feminism: A Reader in Class, Difference, and Women's Lives*. Edited by Rosemary Hennessey and Chris Ingraham, 95–106. London: Routledge.

———. 1990. *Throwing like a Girl and Other Essays in Feminist Philosophy and Social Theory*. Indianapolis: Indiana University Press.

Zamora, Daniel. 2016. "Foucault, the Excluded, and the Neoliberal Erosion of the State." In *Foucault and Neoliberalism*. Edited by D. Zamora and M. C. Behrent, 63–84. Cambridge: Polity Press.

———. 2017. "The Case Against a Basic Income." *Jacobin*, December 18, 2017. https://www.jacobinmag.com/2017/12/universal-basic-income-inequality-work.

Zelleke, Almaz. 2011. "Feminist Political Theory and the Argument for an Unconditional Basic Income." *Policy & Politics* 39, no. 1: 27–42.

Zimring, Carl. 2015. *Clean and White: A History of Environmental Racism in the United States*. New York: New York University Press.

Zuboff, Shoshana. 2020. *The Age of Surveillance Capitalism: The Fight for a Human Future at the New Frontier of Power*. New York: Public Affairs.

Index

affect: and care, 19, 41; commodification of, 27, 111, 113; feminist politics of, 105–10

affective labor, 28, 30, 75, 99–114; as generational reproduction, 106–7

Agamben, Giorgio, 49, 53, 55–56; vs. Foucault on biopolitics, 25, 48–49, 53, 55–56, 145n2

alienation, 143n42; Marxist theories of, 111–14, 145n4; and surrogacy, 74

Anthropocene, the, 47, 145n1

anthropocentrism, 53, 54

Aristotle, 54, 55, 146n6

Arruzza, Cinzia, 19, 85, 137, 142nn30–31, 150n33 (chap. 3), 150n2 (chap. 4), 151n13, 152n17

Assisted Reproductive Technologies (ARTs), 43, 44, 64, 148

"baby-selling." *See* surrogacy, commercial gestational

Becker, Gary, 96

Benston, Margaret, 87, 119–20, 139n6

Bhattacharya, Tithi, 19, 142n32

biocapitalism, 43, 45, 46, 78, 135, 140n12; and industrial capitalism, 3–4; and surrogacy, 26, 62–64, 66, 69, 72

bioethics, 62, 65

biopolitics, 4, 106, 140n12; Foucault and Agamben on, 25, 48–49, 54–56, 145n2, 146n8; Hardt and Negri on, 103–4, 112

biotechnology, 4, 17, 24, 27, 30, 68, 69, 73, 75, 148; development of, 38, 43, 79, 99

body: and mind, 49; and pregnancy, 66, 74, 92, 104; surrogate's, 71, 73, 148, 149

Brown, Wendy, 78–79, 81, 98, 151n12

Calnitsky, David, 125–26, 153n4

capitalism: capitalist economy vs. capitalist society, 21–22; and expropriation of life, 69–73; and gender subordination, 78–98; implications for women, 80–85; logic of; 2, 7–10, 20, 24, 33, 37, 50, 79–81, 84, 92, 134; and settler colonialism, 23–24; transnational, 144n9. *See also* biocapitalism; feminism, feminist critique of capitalism; racial capitalism; resistance

care: caregiving, 82, 90–91; crisis of, 41–42, 85, 109; as feminist ideal, 18, 19, 21, 85, 132. *See also* affect, and care; care work

care work: compared to surrogacy, 26, 63, 67, 75, 77, 149n26; domestic labor, 23, 102–4, 118, 152n8; Hardt and Negri on, 101–3; impact of UBI on, 127–28; market for, 42, 90, 107–9, 150n3; value external to market, 41, 91, 95, 105–6, 124, 131. *See also* affective labor; surrogacy, commercial gestational

childcare: collective model of, 131, 132; paid, 41, 94, 101, 120, 126, 130; "Scandinavian model" of, 91; unpaid, 84, 87, 103, 105. *See also* social reproduction; surrogacy, commercial gestational

colonialism, legacy of. *See* settler colonialism

commercial gestational surrogacy. *See* surrogacy, commercial gestational

critical race theory. *See under* race

Cudd, Ann E., 80–85

Dawson, Michael, 69, 70

decolonization, 60, 129, 142n38

171

rights: critiques of right discourse, 57, 59;
labor, 26; of nature, 56–60; political,
17, 45, 57, 59–60, 93, 125, 142n32;
property, 43, 68, 109, 140n10, 144n15,
149n21; reproductive, 74, 93, 150n48
Robinson, Cedric, 35, 142n39, 144n7

servant economies, 117–23
settler colonialism, 23, 34, 37, 38, 70,
148n19
socialism, 28, 81, 98, 141n21
socialist environmental theory, 25, 48,
133
social reproduction: Arruzza, Bhattacharya, and Fraser on, 19, 142n32; Cudd
on, 90; Hardt and Negri on, 103–4,
107; Marxist-feminist theory of, 18–21,
27, 54, 79, 84–85, 97–98, 127, 131; vs.
material production, 104–6; Meiksins
Wood on, 6; and trans issues, 93; Vogel,
Lise, on, 86–90; Weeks on, 103, 106–7
Stone, Christopher, 58, 60
subjectivation, 4, 28, 100, 111, 112, 113,
134
surplus value, 34, 37, 78, 88, 103, 109,
113, 140n12, 144n14; theory of, 63,
140n12, 152n8
surrogacy, commercial gestational:
"baby-selling," 67, 95, 96, 151n11; as
clinical labor, 64–67; compensation
of, 16, 45, 148nn12; effect on children,
150n30; feminist politics of, 73–77,
110; labor paradigm for, 63, 67–69;
nature of, 25–26, 62–77. See also body,
surrogate's; feminism, feminist debates
on surrogacy; transnational surrogacy

transnational surrogacy: 145n17; and
colonialism, 23; vs. domestic, 147n2;

economics of, 44; in India, 8, 62–77,
146n1, 147n6, 147nn8–9, 148n13,
149nn25–28; as labor, 26
trans parenting, 86, 93, 151n10

unemployment, 10, 119, 122
Universal Basic Income (UBI), 123–31;
and ecofeminism, 29, 129; feminist
demands for, 29, 107, 124–30; grassroots movement for, 142n32; and
housework, 124–25; impact on care
work, 127–28; and Weeks, 129, 152n11,
153n4
universalism, 150n33

value: commodification of nature, 35,
37–40, 144n15, 148n21; core values/
ideals, 18, 21; of domestic labor, 102,
120, 124–27; incommensurability
of, 25, 40, 46, 94, 97; nonmonetary,
25, 40, 45–46, 52, 57–60 passim, 77,
94, 96, 106, 110; production of, 26,
49, 63, 65, 143n4 (chap. 1), 148n18;
reproductive labor as production
of value, 34, 69, 148n21. See also affective labor; monetary value; surplus
value
Vogel, Lise, 86–90
Vogel, Steven, 25, 47, 48, 51, 145nn3–4
(chap. 2)
Vrasti, Wanda, 131, 132

Weeks, Kathi: critique of Marxist feminism, 106–7, 111; Foucauldian focus
of, 99, 112; on Hardt and Negri, 28,
99–100, 103–4, 152n13; and UBI, 129,
152n11, 153n4

Young, Brigitte, 122, 126